BEYOND HISTORY FOR HISTORICAL CONSCIOUSNESS

Students, Narrative, and Memory

As issues of history, memory, and identity collide with increasing frequency and intensity in the classroom and society, the timing is ideal to investigate the impact of these forces on twenty-first-century students. Relying on the theory of historical consciousness, this book presents the results of a comprehensive study conducted with over 600 French Canadian students that examines their narrative views of the collective past. The authors offer new evidence on how young citizens from various regions and ethnocultural groups in Quebec and Ontario think about their national history and what impact education, historical culture, and the "real-life" curriculum of meaningful experiences have on the formation of narration, identity, and historical consciousness.

STÉPHANE LÉVESQUE is professor of history education and director of the Virtual History Lab at the Faculty of Education, University of Ottawa.

JEAN-PHILIPPE CROTEAU is professor of French literature at Sichuan University in Chengdu, China.

Beyond History for Historical Consciousness

Students, Narrative, and Memory

STÉPHANE LÉVESQUE

AND

JEAN-PHILIPPE CROTEAU

Foreword by Jocelyn Létourneau

UNIVERSITY OF TORONTO PRESS
Toronto Buffalo London

© University of Toronto Press 2020
Toronto Buffalo London
utorontopress.com

ISBN 978-1-4875-0675-9 (cloth)
ISBN 978-1-4875-2453-1 (paper)
ISBN 978-1-4875-3479-0 (EPUB)
ISBN 978-1-4875-3478-3 (PDF)

___

Library and Archives Canada Cataloguing in Publication

Title: Beyond history for historical consciousness : students, narrative, and memory / Stéphane Lévesque, Jean-Philippe Croteau ; foreword by Jocelyn Létourneau.
Names: Lévesque, Stéphane, 1971– author. | Croteau, Jean-Philippe, 1975– author.
Description: Includes bibliographical references and index.
Identifiers: Canadiana (print) 20200156292 | Canadiana (ebook) 20200156403 | ISBN 9781487506759 (cloth) | ISBN 9781487524531 (paper) | ISBN 9781487534790 (EPUB) | ISBN 9781487534783 (PDF)
Subjects: LCSH: Canada – History – Public opinion. | LCSH: Public opinion – Ontario. | LCSH: Public opinion – Québec (Province) | LCSH: Canadian students – Ontario – Attitudes. | LCSH: Canadian students – Québec (Province) – Attitudes. | LCSH: French-Canadians – Ontario – Attitudes. | LCSH: French-Canadians – Québec (Province) – Attitudes. | LCSH: Collective memory.
Classification: LCC FC165 .L48 2020 | DDC 971 – dc23

___

This book has been published with the help of a grant from the Federation for the Humanities and Social Sciences, through the Awards to Scholarly Publications Programme, using funds provided by the Social Sciences and Humanities Research Council of Canada.

We are grateful for the Government of Quebec's financial support, received through its Canadian Francophonie Support Program. This program is administered by the Secrétariat du Québec aux relations canadiennes.

University of Toronto Press acknowledges the financial assistance to its publishing programme of the Canada Council for the Arts and the Ontario Arts Council, an agency of the Government of Ontario.

 Canada Council for the Arts Conseil des Arts du Canada

 ONTARIO ARTS COUNCIL
CONSEIL DES ARTS DE L'ONTARIO
an Ontario government agency
un organisme du gouvernement de l'Ontario

Funded by the Government of Canada   Financé par le gouvernement du Canada

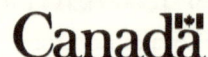

Contents

List of Figures and Tables vii
Foreword ix
Acknowledgments xiii

Introduction 3
1 Narrative Orientations 31
2 History, Territory, and the Nation 61
3 Gender and Language 83
4 Collective Identity 112
5 Narrative Competence 135
Conclusion 155

Notes 167
Bibliography 179
Index 193

Figures and Tables

Figures

I.1   Seixas's history/memory matrix 15
I.2   Lévesque's historical culture matrix 17
1.1   Narrative orientations for Ontario students 41
1.2   Narrative orientations for Quebec students 42
1.3   Narrative orientations of Ontario students by region 54
1.4   Narrative orientations of Quebec students by region 56
2.1   Territorial orientations of Quebec students' narratives 63
2.2   Territorial orientations of Ontario students' narratives 64
2.3   Territorial orientation of Ontario students' narratives by region 67
2.4   Territorial orientation of Quebec students' narratives by region 69
3.1   Narrative orientations for female students in Ontario 85
3.2   Narrative orientations for male students in Ontario 86
3.3   Narrative orientations for female students in Quebec 88
3.4   Narrative orientations for male students in Quebec 89
3.5   Narrative orientations by language group in Ontario 100
3.6   Narrative orientations by language group in Quebec 104
4.1   Narrative orientation and identification with Canada for Ontario students 115
4.2   Narrative orientation and identification with Canada for Quebec students 120
4.3   Narrative orientation and identification with French Ontario for Ontario students 124
4.4   Narrative orientation and identification with Quebec for Quebec students 127
5.1   Munslow's act of narration 141

Tables

I.1 Location of participants in Quebec 23
I.2 Location of participants in Ontario 23
I.3 Demographic data for each student population 23
I.4 Categories and descriptors of narrative orientations 27
2.1 Key terms most frequently mentioned in Quebec and Ontario students' narratives 72
2.2 Key terms associated with New France cited in Quebec and Ontario students' narratives 72
2.3 Key international terms cited in Quebec and Ontario students' narratives 74
2.4 Key terms associated with Regulation 17 cited in Quebec and Ontario students' narratives 77
2.5 Key terms cited in Ontario students' narratives by region 79
2.6 Key terms cited in Quebec students' narratives by region 80
3.1 Key pronouns by gender and province 93
3.2 Social and cultural key terms by gender and province 95
3.3 Military and political key terms by gender and province 98
3.4 Key terms used by students by language group in Ontario 107
3.5 Key terms used by students by language group in Quebec 109
4.1 Key terms in relation to identification with Canada for Ontario students 118
4.2 Key terms in relation to identification with Canada for Quebec students 122
4.3 Key terms in relation to identification with French Ontario for Ontario students 126
4.4 Key terms in relation to identification with Quebec for Quebec students 132
5.1 Narrative plausibility in reference to historical thinking concepts 142

Foreword

For more than two decades, the realm of history teaching has been cut across by two important ideas:

1 Young people do not know much about the past, nor are they really interested in its subject content.
2 The reason for this is that we do not know how to teach them history. If we followed the principles of historical thinking, we could greatly improve this situation and kill two birds with one stone: spark their interest in the past and raise their awareness to a critical appreciation and understanding of history.

Such claims are partly true and partly false, and partly illusion, too. The book we are to read here sets the record straight.

Saying that the young care not about the past whilst being ignorant of it is inaccurate. Evidence lies in the research I conducted for about ten years with more than five thousand young Quebecers, during which I asked them to recount the history of Quebec as they knew it: only a few of them would admit to not caring about the past or having knowledge of the past. On the other hand, many said they were disappointed to know so little about the history of the society they live in.

"Knowing a little" does not mean "not knowing at all," yet some readers will lament the low level of historical knowledge among youth. But we need to be realistic regarding the historical erudition of young people. Do we really expect, in people who do not intend to spend their life serving Clio, an accumulation of knowledge on their country or their society akin to that of a historian in academia or a keen collector of antiques? Generally speaking, students take in as much on any given subject as they deem necessary to their personal well-being or social efficiency (passing a test, for example, would fit in both categories). In human beings, learning is never devoid of a practical and instrumental goal.

One could say, thus, that what "my" young research subjects know about the history of Quebec is fundamental albeit not substantial. By "fundamental" I mean that this knowledge they possess actually refers to their intake (their appropriation, even) of the main tropes, recollected topoi, narrative structure, and keywords of the community to which they belong – Franco- or Anglo-Québécois, depending on their individual sense of identity. This knowledge is not anecdotal or superfluous; it is nothing short of paramount. Clearly, young Quebecers master the essential elements of the narrative (national or societal, it doesn't matter here) that allows them to be part of a historical experience and to position themselves as heirs whose predecessors acted on this experience and carried it through. All things considered, the only thing missing in this metahistorical skeleton of theirs is the factual meat!

It is quite tempting to say, then, to all those nationalists great and small – in Quebec, Canada or elsewhere – for whom each young person should aspire to be a memorialist: Do not worry about the state of our teenagers' historical knowledge. They might not know all the details they ought to in your vision, but they certainly got the message you want them to spread.

Building on my research, refining its methodology and applying it nationwide, Stéphane Lévesque and Jean-Philippe Croteau carry further the study of the development process of young people's historical consciousness. I am not going to spoil the results and conclusions you will read in the following pages. Let me only say that the authors clearly illustrate how present and vivid the mythistories articulating their identity communities are in young people's historical consciousness; how we cannot think of educating youth in the matter of historical thinking by treating them like empty shells only needing to be filled by enhanced knowledge in order to move forward; and finally, how difficult it is to partition or separate learning places, as people have a finger in every pie when it comes to learning – this being education's salvation as well as its damnation.

The interest of Lévesque and Croteau's research also lies in the second question they tackle in this book, which stems from their initial results. Here's one way to put it: if students learn history through their socializing in a culture that educates its members wherever it can, in schools naturally, but in many other cultural venues as well, what can we do – in a world where the possibilities of strengthening the acquired knowledge of the past are much more numerous than the possibilities of escaping it – to lead teenagers out of a state of historical knowledge deemed unsatisfactory and into a state that would be, let's say ... more satisfying?

For some, the solution is obvious: training in historical thinking (which is similar in many ways to scientific thinking, but for a few specificities such as the fight against anachronism). To say it clearly: teach the youth how to question the past, how to consider its multiple sides from different angles, how to empathize with actors of the past, how to grasp the endless dynamics between change and continuity, causes and consequences ... and the job is done. Students will acquire the reflexes needed to turn the past into a limitless field of questioning, one that does not teach any lesson to coevals, but leads them to a nuanced and compassionate understanding of the human condition. Isn't this after all the goal of teaching history, of educating through history?

One would hope that they were right. But nothing is simple in the realm of education, especially since young minds are not to be confined as laboratory rats to a cage where teachers could control all learning variables as they see fit. Picture a young person, listening intently to all three classes where you explain, with varied and appropriate references and primary sources, that history is not clear-cut, that reality is dense, and that the world can be best apprehended as an open question rather than a definite answer. How are we to guarantee that this young person is not going to jump on the first interpretation that gives, at long last, clear answers to his or her questions, and meaning to his or her life? Psychologists have repeated it ad nauseam: the brain processes the information we gather or receive so that we feel safe. That is to say that the more complicated things are, the more worried people become, and if people are worried, they stop listening – and you lose them. The question haunting Lévesque and Croteau then amounts to this: how to bother, disturb, annoy, and trouble, without destroying, distressing, scaring, or terrifying? The learning scenario they imagine to help reconcile concern and completeness being also a part of this book, I will only point here to the fact that their suggestion, contrary to some mainstream ideas, is to make do with the troubling complexity rather than deny it or cast it aside. They also suggest not to unhelpfully punish the organic relation between history, memory, and identity that exists for the majority, including young people, but rather to use it skilfully. They go as far as to claim that the concept of the nation, for most people an important and convincing referential framework, should not be eliminated: it would be a better idea to use this reality as our starting point, and to present those who were socialized in its mythistories and believe them with representations that are critical of these powerful stories; for, apparently, these mythistories can only be undermined by rival narratives as powerful as they are. As powerful, but also, hopefully, more satisfying from the perspective of science – which, by the way (one has to state this explicitly, nowadays, it's important), is not something we can fiddle with as we please.

Jocelyn Létourneau
MacMillan Center, Yale University

Acknowledgments

This book represents our latest research into students' historical consciousness. It emanates from a growing body of research in a field largely informed by the influential work of Jocelyn Létourneau in Quebec. Using narrative as an instrument, we provide new evidence of young citizens' historical ideas about the collective past in the twenty-first century. This work would not have been possible without those who have greatly contributed to our own understanding of historical consciousness in education.

In particular, some individuals have provided key advice and suggestions on various ideas presented in this book. We would like to thank all those who participated in our seminar on our initial research findings organized by the Centre de recherche en civilisation canadienne-française at the University of Ottawa under the leadership of director Anne Gilbert. We also owe special thanks to participants and colleagues who offered insightful comments at presentations given at the annual meetings of the American Educational Research Association and the Canadian Society for Studies in Education, as well as at the Institute of Education at University College London, the Universidade de Santiago de Compostela, the Universidade de Murcia, and the Institute of Advanced Studies at the Collegium de Lyon.

While it is impossible to name them all, we would like to acknowledge the following individuals for their comments and feedback on various drafts of this book: Arthur Chapman, Penney Clark, Catherine Duquette, Anne Gilbert, Cosme J. Gomez, Kevin Kee, Andreas Körber, Jocelyn Létourneau, Jean-François Lozier, Christopher Martell, Sabrina Moisan, Gabriel Reich, Tania Riveiro Rodriguez, Jorge Sáiz Serrano, Peter Seixas, Sarah B. Shear, and Paul Zanazanian. We would further like to thank our research assistants, Raphaël Gani, Marc-André

Lauzon, and Maxime Saumure, for their invaluable assistance on the development and realization of this research.

This book could not have been completed without the excellent editorial and administrative assistance from the staff at the University of Toronto Press, in particular Meg Patterson, Robin Studniberg, and Matthew Kudelka.

This book is dedicated to all the Canadian participants who have so graciously volunteered for our study and generously shared their narrative ideas about the collective past. The future belongs to them.

BEYOND HISTORY FOR HISTORICAL
CONSCIOUSNESS

Introduction

> Few skills serve citizens better than to be able to sort through the historical contexts that set the stage for the present and the future.
> – Conrad et al., *Canadians and Their Pasts* (2013, 10)

Setting the Stage

Everyone embodies a narrative about the world and their place in it.[1] These narratives structure how individuals and communities think, define themselves, and act in life. Recent theories of historical consciousness focus on the role narration plays in contemporary people's attempts to give meaning to the past and orient themselves in time. Relying on German historian Jörn Rüsen's theory of historical consciousness, this book presents the results of a comprehensive study conducted with more than 600 French Canadian students' narratives of the collective past. It offers new results on how young citizens think about their national history in the twenty-first century and what impact education, historical culture, and the "real-life" curriculum of meaningful personal experiences have on the formation of memory, identity, and historical consciousness. Our project emerged from the wake of several investigations recently conducted in Quebec, New Brunswick (NB), Ontario, and Europe on students' narrative representations of the past. Inspired by the influential works of Quebec historian Jocelyn Létourneau, these studies have challenged popular stereotypes of young people's apparent lack of historical knowledge – their abysmal "trou de mémoire" (memory hole) – and offered more authentic findings using narration as a research instrument.[2] They have shown, among other things, that students are far more knowledgeable about and interested in history than has been publicly decried in polls and media headlines. They can mobilize a great deal of historical knowledge in story-form, and indeed, their narrations offer coherent synthesises of the past, the present, and the envisioned future, visions that can hardly be captured by traditional assessments of factual knowledge. As Sam Wineburg and his colleagues put it, quizzes and standardized tests continue to dominate public attention but "tell us precious little about the development of historical understanding in contemporary society or about the knowledge widely shared by citizens." These assessments, they argue, "cannot tell us what is common, shared, and widely understood by young people about the past that inhabits their present. Moreover, by restricting notions of history to the canonical knowledge of the state-sponsored curriculum, these tests keep at bay the myriad forces that act to historicize today's youths."[3]

Recent Canadian investigations have also revealed the interpretative frameworks that students use to create narrative representations of the collective past. Students, no less than adults, tend to construct stories of the nation in the context of culturally mediated frameworks that strongly affect how they think historically and how they connect emotionally with communities of memory. Political, cultural, and identity contexts are important real-life factors in shaping students' narrative visions of the past.

Yet these studies all suffer from the same flaw: they have been conducted in isolation and without consideration for comparative analysis, regional differences, and collective identification. These shortcomings have led to a host of questions: Do young French-speaking Canadians from different regions tell the same stories of the national past? Does identity affect their narrative visions of the past? Are gender, language, and cultural experiences important factors in structuring a historical narrative of the nation? How do young people situate themselves in national history and construct a story of the past that they can use in the present? To answer these questions, we felt that a new study was necessary. The timing was right.

Indeed, recent large-scale national surveys conducted in Canada, the United States, Australia, and Europe point to the central role that history plays in the lives of citizens. Whether it is watching history television networks, doing online genealogical research, visiting museums, collecting heirlooms, engaging in family histories, or participating in or debating commemorative events, people actively engage with the past in their daily lives. As the authors of the *Canadians and Their Pasts* national study confirm, "a vast majority of people everywhere in the country have turned to the past to help them situate themselves in a rapid changing present, to connect themselves to others, to fill their leisure hours."[4] In many ways, people's engagement with the past responds to fundamental human needs: it shapes their sense of identity, their understanding of the world, and their own vision for the future. In Rüsen's words, history is "an essential cultural factor" in people's lives precisely because it offers an orientation over the course of time, telling them who they are, where they came from, and where they are headed.[5]

But history is a contested domain of knowledge, and public education is a disputed field on which contenders advance their own visions, their own agendas. People seem to agree on the value of history in society, yet there is no public consensus as to what should be taught in school or how it should be taught. As history educators Keith Barton and Linda Levstik rightly observe, "no one likes the way history is taught."[6] For cosmopolitans, history is too traditional and too focused on the nation's past. For nationalists, it is too multicultural and too vested in issues of citizenship rights and globalization. For Indigenous people, it is too racist and colonialist. For members of settler societies, it is dangerously close to losing its Enlightenment values and scientific principles. At the core of all these contentions is the role of history in shaping a political community – a people.[7] Indeed, while these various contenders offer different stories of the past (and of history education), they all aim to convey the *right* story for their own people. Conservative and liberal Canadians, for example, do not want young people to become ahistorical citizens; rather, they want public schools that teach them their own distinctive form of community-building. The question then reverts to what kind of people do we want?

Like historical narratives, nations are never static and are constantly rebuilding. More than thirty years ago, Benedict Anderson argued persuasively that the complex "imagined communities" in which we live depend on various sociocultural forces, including print literacy and public education, through which individuals are socialized to imagine themselves as members of the nation. "Members of even the smallest nation," he contended, "will never know most of their fellow-members, meet them, or even hear of them, yet in the minds of each lives the image of their communion."[8] Yet in these accelerating times, the relationship between individuals and the nation is changing. The imagined community is a source of tension in Canada and around the world. For some, the links between imagination and social life are increasingly "global and deterritorialized one[s]," making the nation either too small or too big to deal with world-scale phenomena such as global warming, mass migration, multinational corporations, terrorism, social media, and the Internet.[9] Globalization would thus be the antithesis of nationalism.

But globalization is a double-edged sword, one that drives individuals in opposite directions. With the increased mobility of people and the rapid changes that globalization has brought to societies, various nationalities around the world, from Quebec through to Catalonia and England, have awakened and become more aware of the threat it poses. This has led to an "increased national sense" as a response to the forces of market capitalism, transnational lobbies, trade associations, and world news services that threaten local cultures, traditions, and histories.[10] If cultures speak particular languages, commerce and social media increasingly speak only one. For many, the future looks both hostile and undemocratic; they sense that forces for integration and uniformity are pressing nations into a single commercially standardized global network driven by transnational banks and corporations. As Ruchir Sharma recently argued in *The Guardian*: "Globalisation as we know it is over – and Brexit is the biggest sign yet."[11] Globalization lacks the democratic mechanisms to protect local culture, community, labour, and rights. Perhaps Canadian historian Michael Ignatieff best summed it up when he contended that "cosmopolitans like myself are not beyond the nation; and a cosmopolitan, post-nationalist spirit will always depend, in the end, on the capacity of nation-states to provide security and civility for their citizens."[12]

For others, however, including those whose identities have been marginalized within traditional nation-states, globalization represents a golden opportunity to express their plight on the global stage. The promotion of human rights in general and of collective self-determination in particular has encouraged minority groups to voice their own self-interest and to participate in organizations that have conventionally excluded them (e.g., l'Organisation internationale de la Francophonie, the Organisation for Economic Co-operation and Development). According to Michael Keating and John McGarry, "rather than eroding minority nationalism, globalization has occurred alongside their emergence or re-emergence."[13]

History Wars à la Canadienne

Canada offers an interesting site for studying the transformations affecting young citizens and their relationship to the nation. Born out of a nineteenth-century compact between the "founding nations,"[14] the Canadian federation is *de facto* a multinational state in which historical groups (French Canadians, Indigenous peoples) claimed nationhood long before the federation was created in 1867.[15] Many of the pivotal moments in Canadian history have centred on political and cultural divisions between these groups. In particular, the French/English divide has been expressed in historiographical narrations and ways of conceiving the Canadian nation as "two solitudes."[16] Public education, which the constitution has separated between French-speaking and English-speaking schools, has mirrored these historical interpretative differences. As a consequence of this, the emplotment of Canadian history as found in school curricula and approved textbooks differs significantly between the two school systems, which emphasize distinctive forms of community and national identification.[17]

The recent politicized controversies over the purpose of national history in French-speaking schools offer an interesting case study of the "history wars" *à la canadienne*. In the province of Quebec, the implementation of the History and Citizenship Education (HCE) curriculum in 2007 provided the pretext for debates over the future of the national community. Quebec nationalists viewed the new program of study as a means to "denationalize" the history of Quebec and Canada and to promote multiculturalism, citizenship, and cultural diversity. Long-standing issues of the past, notably between French and English Canadians, were being displaced by the study of rights, social justice, and current events. According to the former education minister, Marie Malavoy, "with the reform of education, the program wrongly places on the same pedestal Quebec's national question with feminism, capitalism, and Americanism."[18] Similar arguments were made by various historians and sociologists, who accused their colleagues of being indifferent to the political and national history of Quebec in their own teaching. One of the most vocal critics was the historian Eric Bédard, who declared that this reform would lead to a catastrophe: "Without adequate knowledge of our national history, our heritage, how is the younger generation supposed to exercise their full citizenship rights? How can the sons and daughters of recent immigrants integrate [into] their host society?"[19]

The reaction was such that minister Malavoy struck a working committee to study the future of national history education in the province. Led by professors Jacques Beauchemin and Nadia Fahmy-Eid, the committee held several public consultations and produced in 2013 a final report titled *The Meaning of History*.[20] In that report, the authors reaffirmed the need for history to be taught within a clearer "national framework" that would serve as "the space within which collective debates can be understood and rendered meaningful."[21] Reconciling history with its national framework also meant, for the authors, reconnecting with the Québécois collective memory. Narration was to be the backbone of this project. For the authors, the history program would require a "more continuous narrative structured around clearer narrative threads, all within the context of Quebec's national framework."[22] Reinstating a national narrative, and with it the idea of knowledge transmission, would mean designing a new program of study that would offer a clearer chronology (i.e., story) of the facts pertaining to Quebec and Canada.

The Meaning of History did not go unnoticed. Several scholars and educators quickly responded publicly to what they perceived to be an orchestrated return to conservative nationalist education. The HCE program, history educator Christian Laville from Université Laval argued, was contributing to the development of crucial competencies and habits of mind necessary for "young Québécois who will be called upon to be active citizens capable of judging complex issues and participating [in] the democratic process."[23] Brushing aside the question of national identity, the proponents of the HCE program emphasized its focus on critical inquiry skills and thinking historically.[24] Stéphane Lévesque, who has written extensively on historical thinking in Canada, declared that if we want students to become critical thinkers who can craft their own evidence-based narratives of the past, then we need to provide them with the means to develop historical thinking and literacy.[25] In many ways, Quebec's HCE program was in continuity with North American curricular revisions that had been taking place since the 1960s.[26] Perhaps Marc-André Éthier, history educator at the Université de Montréal, best summed up this perspective: "History education requires scientific rigour, which in turn demands that educators not impose their own sociopolitical narrative vision but instead encourage students to think more critically about the world, to transform their own commonsense representations (including those of the nation) into more reasoned conceptual ideas founded in the discipline."[27]

The intensity of the national history debate was such that the Quebec government decided to progressively replace the current HCE program with a new History of Quebec and Canada (HQC) curriculum in 2017. In line with *The Meaning of History*, the new program of study is more attuned to the "national framework" of Quebec nationalism and is structured around key episodes in the French Canadian collective memory[28] so as to facilitate narrative intelligibility among young citizens and introduce them to the collective adventure of the Quebec people "from its earliest days, when the community was discovering its uniqueness, to modern times, which require it to deal with the complexities of the 'national issue' as it currently defines our conflicts and agreements."[29] As the program is just now being implemented across the province and was not available at the time of this study, we have very little information about its current application in schools.

In the neighbouring province of Ontario, where francophones are a linguistic minority, the debate has revolved less around the national history program itself than around the broader mission of French-speaking education and its future in the context of increasing diversity. Since the province's founding in the nineteenth century, Ontario's French-speaking schools have embodied the foundational construct of French Canadian memory, identity, and community. Throughout the province's history, supporters of francophone schools have justified their existence on the basis of the need to promote and preserve French Canadian identity in the face of English Canadian assimilation and cultural supremacy. The right of francophones to receive an education in their mother tongue – the so-called "schools question" – is still regarded as a core element of French Canadian identity (along with the Catholic religion), at least in Ontario.

In the present day, a number of critics are questioning the historical mission of French-speaking schools in the face of twenty-first-century globalization. In particular, a vocal group of scholars at the University of Toronto have argued that factors such as ethnocultural diversity, mass migration from rural to urban communities, and the changing identities of young French Canadians, who are increasingly defining themselves as "bilinguals" – that is, not exclusively francophones or anglophones – are making it necessary to redefine the school system.[30] According to these scholars, it is now urgent that public schools adapt their mission to the "new realities of Ontario" by embracing a renewed vision that is less "homogenizing" and "folklorizing" and better suited to the diverse linguistic and cultural practices of young francophones.[31] As Diane Gérin-Lajoie, professor at the Ontario Institute for Studies in Education of the University of Toronto, puts it:

> I strongly believe that Ontario French-language education has to be redesigned in the context of today's reality. French-language schools can no longer operate as if they were places of dominant French-language speakers. While it is essential to promote French language and culture, French-language schools must take into account the linguistic and cultural diversity of their population. Furthermore, these schools must better recognize the impact of English Canadian culture on the social practices of students in these schools.[32]

This vision of education from an urban, multicultural perspective has not gone unchallenged. According to sociologist Joseph-Yvon Thériault of the Université du Québec à Montréal and geographer Anne Gilbert of the University of Ottawa, French Canadians from Ontario (i.e., Franco-Ontarians) are on a dangerous, slippery slope, in that they are compromising community-building and identity formation for the sake of pluralistic individual accomplishment. For them, today's multicultural schools view their student populations as aggregates of learners from all walks of life, who see their sense of belonging to the francophone community as a matter of personal, linguistic choice. As a consequence, Ontario's French-speaking schools are renouncing their historical mission. These schools no longer aim to develop French Canadian culture or to share a sense of collective identity over the *longue durée*.[33] According to Gilbert, today's schools are promoting a pluralistic notion of identity based solely on individual life experiences and success in the Canadian economy, with little heed to the collective rights and struggles of this "founding nation" of Canada:

> The current French-speaking school project of Ontario, as found in the new ministry policy, does not include community-building, or barely so. Instead, we privilege an individualist vision of the group, making French language and its defence a matter of individual success and integration, thus retaining from the notion of community its sense of diversity and fragmentation in light of international immigration and globalization. We now face a story of Canadian multicultural nation, with its emphasis on diversity and individual rights, with all the consequences of this cultural assimilation.[34]

Similar educational debates have taken place in English Canada. As historian Ruth Sandwell explains in her study, the most recent episode in the Canadian history wars was precipitated by Jack Granatstein's polemic book *Who Killed Canadian History?*, in which he argued that history education is now literally dead as a result of misguided bureaucrats and child-centred progressives, academic specialists and social historians, and advocates of multiculturalism who celebrate the cult of victimhood and diversity.[35] Following that book's release, various scholars, educators, and stakeholders across the country engaged in heated arguments over the nature of Canadian history and the purpose of education. According to Tim Stanley, historian of racism and anti-racism at the University of Ottawa, the new social historians have "killed Canadian history" precisely because their research approaches have "the potential to be more successful in capturing the multiple pasts of this time and place than nationalist frameworks have proven to be."[36] In the face of grand narratives of Euro-Canadian colonialism, Stanley calls for contextualized narratives, for small pictures of the collective past that recognize the varied experiences of people(s) and that can be written in multiple ways, thus acknowledging the historical agency of both the privileged and the oppressed. Similar arguments have been voiced in social science education, calling for reconciliation with different forms of knowledge, including Indigenous ways of knowing, so as to engage learners with the moral dilemmas associated with "Canada's colonial legacy, silenced histories, and multiple, shifting identities in the present."[37]

Interestingly, these scholarly debates were not confined to the academic tower; they found their way into the national media and soon reached the public. Journalists, editors, polling firms, and organizations dedicated to history have taken up the arguments and offered provocative responses. The headlines are telling: "The end of history"; "Assisted suicide"; "Collective ignorance"; "Amnesiac generation"; "French assimilation"; "Memory hole"; and "I don't remember."[38] Faced with a public outcry, politicians and public servants soon felt the need to respond with their own remedies: official excuses, public consultations, the renaming of official sites of memory, commemoration ceremonies and celebratory events, the creation of historical sites, and, finally, revisions of policies and curricula.

But what is most striking about the current situation in Canadian history education is how little policy has been informed by empirical research about *students*. Indeed, we still have relatively limited data on how students acquire and respond to national history, what stories of the collective past they internalize and tell, and what attachment and sense of national identification they have. We recognize that scholarly research cannot in and of itself solve societal questions over contested national histories in Canada; but we do believe, with curriculum specialist Larry Cuban, that our work can contribute significantly to the broader national conversation – and ultimately to educational reform – provided that it addresses more directly students as active agents of historical learning and change. Too often, research is being conducted on official policies, curricula, and standardized testing without considering the impact of theory and research on what Cuban calls the "learned curriculum," that is, the curriculum a learner acquires or makes sense of as a result of formal and informal learning experiences.[39] In this regard, our work concerns itself with how empirical study can probe students' sociocultural learning and help shape their historical consciousness, with the goal of better understanding how narratives are constructed, disseminated, and used in society to legitimize particular aims, from social cohesion and belonging to critical evaluation of narrative interpretations.[40]

As both Quebec and Ontario are now implementing revised history programs, we will be presenting additional evidence about the kinds of narrative ideas students hold and the role that history education can play in challenging collective memory and in promoting more critical understandings and uses of the past in contemporary Canadian society. Our study also offers a new research perspective for other countries comprised of multinational communities or "nations within," such as the United States, the United Kingdom, Spain, Belgium, Switzerland, and Australia, which have restructured themselves to accommodate substate groups claiming distinctive historical cultures and collective rights. Our approach and findings will thus be able to help educators in complex societies think about ways to study historical consciousness and envision history education programs that contrast with traditional nationalist approaches, which are unresponsive to collective narration as a research instrument and to the sociocultural context in which students learn national history.

From Mythistories to Historical Consciousness

The questions that drive this research lead us to reflect on the important relationship between memory and history consciousness. Both memory and historical consciousness have to do with uses of the past. But there are subtle differences between the two. Memory is the residue of life, says French historian Pierre Nora, because it is embodied in living societies.[41] It takes root in the concrete, in spaces, objects, monuments, and lived experiences. Collective memory is by nature multiple and specific, plural yet individual. According to Maurice Halbwachs, all our memories are, in one way or another, tied up to the group because what we choose to remember (or forget) is dependent on social interactions.[42] So for Halbwachs, each personal memory is a unique perspective on collective memory, a perspective that changes according to the particular role and place the person occupies within the group.

From this perspective, memory is not a vast reservoir of unlimited personal experiences. Rather, it is a more or less organized "stock of information" as well as representations of the past that involve both the individual and the group. Létourneau refers to this as "mythistories" – sets of references including teleological schemes, clichés, reified characters, and fragments through which the past, the present, and the future are not only decoded but also anticipated.[43] The following is a memory example largely shared among French Canadians: "I remember that in 1534 Jacques Cartier discovered Canada." This statement from French colonial history links personal memory (I remember) to the collective memory of Cartier as the first French explorer to "discover" this country. This well-known Eurocentric mythistory has been transmitted over time, from one generation to the next, and constitutes a form of simplified historical knowledge with which it becomes possible to create grand narratives of the collective past. As Stanley puts it, collective memory gives voice to "a particular interpretation of the past best characterized as 'nationalist grand narrative.'"[44]

Historical consciousness, by contrast, places the emphasis on the mental reconstruction and appropriation of historical information as brought into the mental household of an individual.[45] Collective memory nourishes the recollection of mythistories (Jacques Cartier discovered Canada), whereas historical consciousness views memory as a more complex process of mental reflection and appropriation into personal life.[46] As history educator Paul Zanazanian sums it up, "historical consciousness constitutes an entryway into how individuals perceive, explain, and give meaning to (past) events and life experiences, as well as into how they understand their situatedness, belonging, and intentionality for living their lives."[47]

According to Peter Seixas, there are three interrelated components of historical consciousness.[48] The first aspect concerns the relationship between *historical knowledge* and *daily life*. For Rüsen, historical knowledge is a necessary condition for human life. "The cognitive structure of historical thinking," he contends, "cannot be explicated without systematically taking into account its constitution and function in practical human life."[49] History, including disciplinary history, is driven by contemporary issues and the humans' cultural needs. Historians work with specialized theories and methodologies, but their research interests are contextualized and driven by present-day circumstances, and the scholarly representations of the past they produce "become available to the larger culture to help reshape contemporary issues in light of the past."[50] Second, historical consciousness is concerned with *temporal change*. It combines the past, the present, and the future in such a way that "human beings can live in the tense intersection of remembered past and expected future."[51] This temporal sense enables people to orient their own lives over the course of time and guide their own daily activities by this synthetized perspective. For Rüsen, the past and the future are "merged into an entire image, vision or conceptual temporal change and development that functions as integral part of the cultural orientation in the life of the present."[52]

Finally, historical consciousness is *expressed through narrative*. With narration it becomes possible to organize the internal unity of the dimensions of time according to the concepts of continuity, coherence, and intelligibility. As French philosopher Paul Ricoeur contended, it is through narration that time becomes "human time."[53] Narration also fosters a sense of direction and purpose (including a moral dimension) and establishes the identity of the narrator. In Rüsen's model, narrating history plays an essential role in shaping consciousness. As he puts it, history is a particular mode of thinking in which the emphasis is "on developing historical consciousness, and learning history as a process of gaining narrative competence."[54]

Matrix for Making Sense of Historical Consciousness

Historical consciousness is a complex theory, originally devised in German scholarly literature, and the organizational structure of historical consciousness has been expressed over the years in terms of different models. Recently, Seixas has proposed a history/memory matrix based on the initial diagram of Rüsen (see figure I.1).[55] Seixas contends that Rüsen's ideas about the importance of history in daily life were devised "before memory studies had come into their full flowering." In this new model, questions of memory and life practice and disciplinary history are in constant relationship through a self-sustaining circular process. Community interests and public memories contribute to group-building and identity formation. As communities change and cosmopolitan societies develop over time, they give rise to societal questions that "might be constructively taken up by the critical, evidence-based, truth-seeking methods of history." Following this, new scholarly interpretations of the past emerge and feed back into popular memory. Over time, new challenges, ideas, and people generate needs for different kinds of orientation in time, thus "giving rise to new modes of historical investigation."[56] In Seixas's matrix, history education finds itself at the nexus of the two zones, between historical practices and memorial beliefs, where students can learn in a scholastic environment to develop their critical historical consciousness.

Seixas's contribution is both timely and significant because scholars have struggled with the transposition of these conceptual ideas onto education. As Peter Lee observes, "Rüsen's account of historical consciousness is – even in the brief works translated into English – a sophisticated and complex theoretical account, covering many different conceptual and empirical matters."[57] By superimposing onto Rüsen's initial matrix an additional layer of memory/history practices, he offers an alternative model for looking at how history education can be integrated into the scheme.

But the challenge with this new matrix is on two related grounds. First, Seixas redefines the matrix by adding procedural features to the history zone and overall purpose to the memory zone. These additions

Figure I.1 Seixas's history/memory matrix

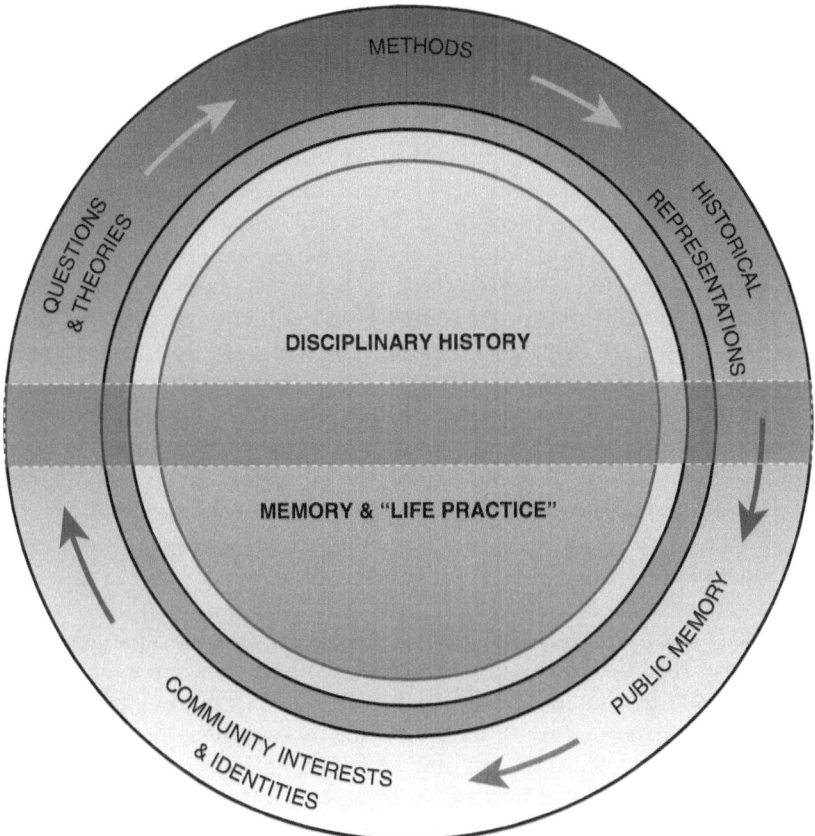

From Peter Seixas, "A History/Memory Matrix for History Education," *Public History Weekly* 4 (2016), DOI: dx.doi.org/10.1515/phw-2016-5370.

are extremely important on their own because they explain how disciplinary history is practised as well as what functions memory plays in daily life. But the combining of the two zones in a progressive, circular model is, in our view, problematic. On the one hand, it is misleading to claim that scholarly knowledge, developed through the scientific, evidence-based history method, directly informs the needs of daily life and public memory. Historians generate interpretations within a community of specialists, thus producing a vast "theoretical surplus" beyond people's needs for life orientation and identity-building. This surplus is not reinvested in public memory and most often remains dormant or even ignored by society at large.[58] At the same time, the history zone addresses a specific practice of historical scholarship, known as historical investigation, whereas the memory zone is about general contexts in which history lives in practice. In the current model, it is thus unclear how history education is supposed to bridge the two zones, given that they are conceptually distinct.

Second, Seixas's model places history education right at the intersection of history and memory in the middle zone. While this arrangement helps explain the potential influence of both zones on education, this is equally problematic because it implies that history education is equally informed and governed by these two realms. In real life, as Finnish scholar Sirkka Ahonen observes, history education is "a part of the public culture of history. It is not a spin-off of academic history, as its contents are influenced by political powers and its form of knowledge by pedagogical considerations."[59] This is why some European scholars such as André Cherval prefer to talk about "school disciplines" so as to make the distinction between scholarly and scholastic domains more explicit.[60] All of this means that we need to find a better way of recognizing the role and influence of history on educational practices.

As an alternative to Seixas's matrix, we propose a modified version that responds to some of these shortfalls and also encapsulates the essence of historical thinking and narrative competence in a larger cultural context that includes public education (see figure I.2).[61] First, this modified matrix will allow us to see how these diverse communities are related in society and how they can potentially inform one another without being conflated into a one-dimensional loop. Disciplinary history, cultural and daily life, and history education subscribe to distinctive approaches and practices to generate narrative representations. Indeed, historians do not study the past and engage in research activities in the same way that lay people do in their daily lives. "Historians," as John Tosh puts it, "are members of a profession one of whose principal functions is to enforce standards of scholarship and to restrain waywardness of interpretation."[62] Much has been said about this disciplinary process, and perhaps Sam Wineburg is the one who best explained how historians differ from students and lay people in using sources and thinking historically.[63]

But history, as Rüsen reminds us, is much more than a matter of historical studies. It is an essential cultural factor in people's lives because "human life needs an orientation in the course of time which has to be brought about by remembering the past" through narrative acts.[64] One function of this cultural, public memory is to reaffirm

Figure I.2 Lévesque's historical culture matrix

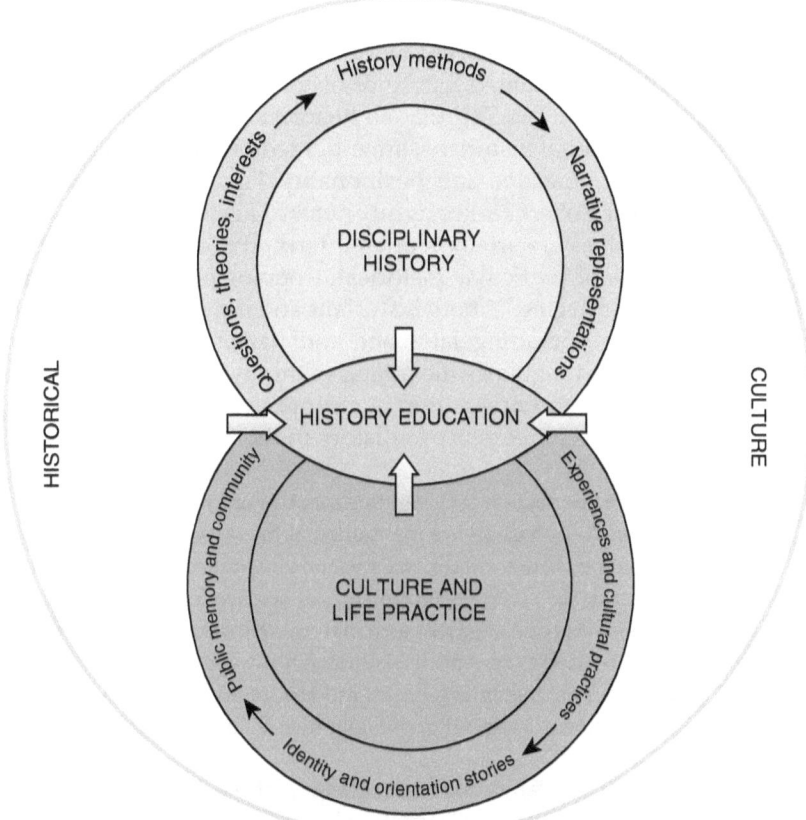

connections with the past and shape people's sense of belonging and community-building. The goal of these practices is to establish "continuity and connection over time canda their successes are coherence and homogeneity across community."[65] Disciplinary history, by contrast, is a scholarly way of performing this function through established norms and principles. While a distinction between these two sets of practices serves useful conceptual purposes, it is important to remember that the two often overlap and coexist in the lives of citizens, including historians, as indicated in our revised matrix.

Indeed, these various historical practices do not operate in a vacuum; they take place in the larger context of historical culture, that is, within the totality of discourses whereby a societal community understands itself and its future by interpreting and narrating the past. This is extremely important, for communities of practice – whether scholarly, scholastic, or cultural – are contextually situated and subjected to important power relations. Recent works on the philosophy of history have highlighted the situated nature of historical knowledge production and convincingly revealed that all historical narratives, including the ones of professional historians, are moulded by the narrator's own epistemological perspective and positionality. For Hayden White, as Australian scholar Robert Parkes rightly notes in his review of his work, "historical narratives are artefacts of an interpretive act constituted by an historian's use of particular rhetorical, tropological, narratological, and ideological strategies."[66] Both historians and lay people are shaped by cultural forces, including language and narrative structure, and this fosters and even regulates the milieu within which it is possible to study the evolution and orientation of culture over time. As historian David Carr contends in reference to history in the European context:

> We can now see a connection between this account of historical narration and the other two key concepts we mentioned at the outset: historical culture and orientation. If the former is a society's awareness of the past in the broadest sense, the emergence of historical science in the nineteenth century represents Europe's way of articulating its historical culture in a systematic and focused way. And if historical culture is society's way of orienting itself in time, the emergence of modern history responds to the need for reorientation arising out of the immense changes wrought.[67]

In Rüsen's conceptualization, narrating history and understanding historical narratives are structural competences of historical consciousness. Our revised matrix provides a distinctive model for analysing current debates over national history in education. It makes it possible to understand the contested goal of school history beyond the simple dichotomy of "telling national narrative" versus "teaching historical thinking," as is too often the case, at least in Canada. It also makes it possible for students to learn history beyond the practical needs of collective memory by making use of scholarly methods and tools of history so as to understand the nature of narrative and generate usable stories of the past that better respond to the needs of today's complex cultures.[68]

Our revised model is also consistent with Rüsen's progression in that it develops forms of historical consciousness through the effective use of the forces of historical culture. According to him, several conditions must be met if human life is to find its way over the course of life, and these can be defined in terms of types of historical consciousness, ranging from "traditional" through to "exemplary," "critical," and "genetical."[69] While these types are not mutually exclusive and do not naturally progress into an ideal type, they nonetheless serve useful analytical purposes. They illustrate how individuals and societies alike engage in and use the past for the purpose of contemporary life.[70]

For example, the traditional type corresponds to persons who view historical traditions and memory as necessary conditions for their human existence. Past time is equated with present time in a sense of eternity. Traditional narratives are constructed as fixed knowledge and remind people of their origins and destiny in a continuous course of action. Traditional-type persons often justify present-day decisions on the grounds that "things have always been like this" or "you don't fix what's not broken." The exemplary type is more analytical and considers the past in terms of useful lessons for present-day purposes. Stories of the past are more than fixed traditions to be remembered as they account for specific temporal and human experiences. Identities are shaped by these experiences and lessons are learned. Exemplary-type persons typically look at past cases for explaining or justifying today's actions. For example, from the failed policy of appeasement toward Nazi Germany, exemplary-type persons will take the lesson that we should be assertive and uncompromising when dealing with ruthless leaders and regimes such as Syria. The genetic type of consciousness is for Rüsen the most advanced. It uses traditions and memory along with analysis and critical interpretation to transform historical and contemporary realities into diverse, complex narratives. The dimensions of time are connected with the notion of temporality through which the "alteration of forms of life is necessary for their permanence."[71] Identities are not fixed but rather are mediated by continuity and change in an ongoing process of self-definition. Stories organize life understanding as a temporal dynamic process, polythetic in nature and open to revisions and multiple perspectives. Genetic-type persons appreciate that their society is the result of decisions made by predecessors but at the same time acknowledge that the future is open to different ways of thinking about the continuity of society over time. For example, a genetic-type person will recognize that Quebec represents a distinctive community of memory with a societal project going back to New France but question or reject the determinist view that there is a "community of destiny" with an established path toward national independence and sovereignty. While the purpose of our study was not to analyse students' narratives using this typology, we believe it can serve as a useful delineation model for understanding structural change in dealing the capacity to digest the complexity of past and present realities – an educational aspect we will address in the last part of our study.

Finally, our revised model situates learning in the broader sociocultural context, thus reminding us that educators are among a diverse group of historical agents in the formation of students' historical consciousness yet too often act as if they were the only ones. We need to reconceptualize the development of students' historical ideas, not exclusively as a practice of public memory or a set of scholastic competencies of historical thinking, but also as the effective result of the interplay among historical culture, public memory, practical life, schooling, and the practice of history. How we conceptualize the rationale for history education should thus be informed by the study, influence, and interplay of these forces.

Perhaps sociologist Philippe Perrenoud's notion of *curriculum réel* (the "real-life" curriculum) best encapsulates the distributed nature of students' learning in society.[72] For Perrenoud, learning is the result of coherent and meaningful life experiences that take place in both formal and informal settings. Students do not learn historical knowledge solely in the controlled environment of the classroom. They also develop significant historical memories, mythistories, and emotional connections, as well as narratives of the collective past, in diverse and distant places that we, as educators, often deem irrelevant to students' scholastic experiences, from field trips to YouTube and social media. This curriculum, as Perrenoud reminds us, is so much part of our cultural life that we no longer see it as an essential educational force. As he puts it, "this anthropological approach to real-life curriculum takes us away from the standard reference to formal learning instruction, to a deliberate educational purpose. It forces us to take into account what hyper-schooled societies often forget: we learn through recurring, meaningful experiences, whether or not these are under the control of an educational intention."[73]

Perrenoud's ideas teach us a valuable lesson: unless we engage the meaningful learning experiences of students, it is unlikely that our formal history teaching will disrupt the powerful memories, emotions, and experiences that they acquire in practical life and too often take for granted. History education needs to problematize this cultural knowledge so as to help learners develop more complex types of historical consciousness – particular ways of conceiving the world as a complex, multidimensional space open to changes and new forms of traditions, memories, identities, and narrative representations.

Probing Historical Consciousness

Our project was developed in the wake of similar investigations.[74] While these studies rely on a common narrative methodology and offer highly instructive results regarding students' historical consciousness, they also have their shortcomings. First, they have been designed as distinctive case studies, each with a unique research question focused exclusively on the history of its own regional community (Québécois, Anglo-Québécois, Acadians, Franco-Ontarians), not the Canadian national past as a whole. Second, all of these studies were conducted in isolation without consideration for comparative analysis. As such, they do not tell us whether students from different regions share similar narrative visions of the collective past.[75] Nor do they tell us whether French Canadians from different provinces have preserved over time common historical memories, histories, and experiences in their own respective historical cultures. As historian Gérard Bouchard contends, a key advantage of comparative analysis is that it offers the opportunity to study empirically apparent singularities or even deterministic beliefs about the future of a given community.[76] Third, only one of these studies (Ottawa) looked at the role and impact of identity on students' historical consciousness. Its findings suggest that national identification is a determinant factor in understanding how young people relate to the collective past and ascribe significance to particular moments in national history. Yet no other study of students' narratives has confirmed these conclusions.[77] Finally, our study aims to offer an alternative way of conceiving history education beyond the simple dichotomy of "teaching narratives" versus "learning historical thinking" as it is often presented in educational circles. From our perspective, the justification for history in schools (and in the wider society) is in terms of its contribution to historical consciousness, to the construction of our mental structure and competence that "underlies our dealing with collectively important aspects of past, present, and future."[78] This competence articulates itself via narration, that is, the telling and understanding of historical narratives.

Our study was funded by the University of Ottawa, the Centre de recherche en civilisation canadienne-française (CRCCF), and the Quebec Ministry of Intergovernmental Affairs. It was conducted by our research team during the winter and spring of 2016, in the wake of the 400th anniversary of the founding of the first French settlements in Upper Canada (Ontario). Our team consisted of four senior researchers who worked to design and launch the project. Geographer Anne Gilbert and history educator Stéphane Lévesque are from the University of Ottawa; historians Jocelyn Létourneau and Jean-Philippe Croteau are, respectively, professors at Université Laval and Sichuan University in China. To support our team's work, three research assistants contributed actively to the collection and analysis of data: Raphaël Gani and Maxime Saumure from the University of Ottawa, and Marc-André Lauzon from the Université du Québec à Chicoutimi.

We chose to probe the historical consciousness of French Canadian students from the provinces of Quebec and Ontario. These two original provinces of Canada offer interesting cases for comparing the development of historical consciousness in two related sociopolitical contexts of French Canada: a French-speaking majority setting (Quebec) and a French-speaking minority setting (Ontario). The study reached out to 635 volunteer participants who had completed their national history courses in their respective province of residence. In Quebec, students have to complete two years of national history (grades nine and ten), while in Ontario, national history is covered over a three-year period (grades seven, eight, and ten). To ensure better demographic representation of the population, we visited thirteen different public high schools (seven in Quebec, six in Ontario) located in various geographical regions with distinctive characteristics: rural/urban, French-speaking majority/French-speaking minority, homogeneous/multicultural (see Tables I.1 and I.2).

In terms of demographic information, we found the following characteristics for each student population (see Table I.3). In Quebec, 385 students volunteered for the study. Of these, 174 (45%) were female and 210 (55%) were male.[79] A total of 332 (86%) participants identified French as their mother tongue, 5 (1%) participants identified English, and the remainder (13%) another language (in order: Spanish, Arabic, Creole, Rumanian, Russian). In terms of the language most frequently spoken at home, 316 participants (82%) indicated French, 8 (2%) English, 6 (2%) English and French, and the remainder (14%) another language (in order: Spanish, Arabic, Creole, Rumanian, Portuguese). Regarding ethnocultural identity, 264 participants (69%) identified themselves as "Québécois," 77 (20%) as "Canadian," 14 (3%) as "Québécois-Canadian," and 4 (1%) as "Franco-Ontarian," with the remainder (7%) identifying with one of the following (in order): Haitian, Acadian, Lebanese, Afro-American, Mexican. The average age for participants was 16.3, with 35% of the participants being seventeen years old, 48% sixteen years old, and 14% fifteen years old at the time of the study.

The Ontario sample was made up of 250 participants: 137 females (55%) and 113 males (45%). Overall, 120 participants (49%) identified French as their mother tongue, 86 (35%) English, and the remainder (16%)

Table I.1 Location of participants in Quebec

Regions (no. of schools)	N	%
Montreal (1)	85	22
North of Montreal (1)	65	17
Quebec City (1)	68	18
Gatineau (2)	43	11
Central Quebec (1)	62	16
Saguenay (1)	62	16

Table I.2 Location of participants in Ontario

Regions (no. of schools)	N	%
East (3)	116	46
Northeast (2)	59	24
South (1)	75	30

Table I.3 Demographic data for each student population

Population	Quebec	Ontario
Male	45%	55%
Female	55%	45%
Average age	16.3	16
French mother tongue	86%	49%
English mother tongue	1%	35%
Other mother tongues	13%	16%
Born in Canada	89%	86%
Born outside Canada	11%	14%

another mother tongue (in order: Arabic, Creole, Spanish, Kirundi, Greek). With regard the language most spoken at home, 87 participants (35%) indicated French, 85 (34%) English, 32 (13%) English and French, and the remainder (18%) another language (in order: Spanish, Arabic, Creole, Chaldean/Armenian). In terms of ethnocultural identity, 137 participants (55%) identified as "Canadian," 64 (26%) as "Franco-Ontarian," 14 (6%) as "Franco-Ontarian-Canadian," and 14 (6%) as "Québécois," with the remainder (7%) identifying with one of the following (in order): French Canadian, American, Lebanese, and Haitian. The average age was sixteen, with 28% aged seventeen years old, 40% sixteen years old, and 26% fifteen years old.[80]

Please Tell Us the History ...

The questionnaire for this study included two different items: a two-page narrative task and a series of personal questions. To avoid the limitations of previous studies, we first presented a common narrative task to all participants: *Please tell us the history of French Canadians in this country as you know it*. We used this particular task for three reasons. First, the instruction to "tell us the history" places students in the strategic position of narrators: they have to mobilize historical knowledge in the form of a personal narrative of the collective past, not a short-answer justification or a chronological list of historical happenings. This performance, as we discussed earlier, is highly important from the perspective of historical consciousness because it invites students to create a coherent story from the past to the present and thus make decisions about what is most significant to tell about the collective past. This narrative approach has proven to be an effective strategy in previous studies of people's historical consciousness. Second, we focused the task on the "history of French Canadians" because national history in Canada is taught from the perspectives of the distinctive linguistic groups that make up the country. French Canadians, whether they live in Quebec or in Ontario, have developed their own French-speaking school system, dating back to the nineteenth century, with its own distinctive curriculum. That is to say, English-speaking and French-speaking students do not learn the same national history in school. While the general objectives are the same, the specific focus and content knowledge is unique to each language group. Finally, we purposely stated "French Canadians in this *country*" so as to leave it for students to interpret what "country" means to them. Would students from Quebec or Ontario view their country solely in provincial terms? Or would they instead consider Canada to be their country?

The second part of the questionnaire contained a series of demographic, educational, and identity questions so that we could learn more about participants' ethnocultural background, linguistic practices, and sense of identification. For the identity questions, students had to choose on a scale (from 1-weak to 7-strong) their identification with various collective groups in Canada (Quebec, French Ontario, and Canada). This strategy, well known in social psychology, made it possible to identify students' own sense of belonging and membership in particular historical groups, that is, their sense of collective identification.

The questionnaire was presented to students in class during the school year. Students were instructed *not* to use textbooks, classroom materials, or the Internet. We indicated in our instructions that we were fishing neither for correct facts nor for their ability to search online information. Our goal was broader: we sought to understand what historical knowledge and stories of the national past could be used for structuring a narrative of the historical experiences of French Canadians. Students could write their narrative in whatever form and structure they preferred for sixty minutes. In short, our study was conceived as an investigation in school context, not as a school activity for evaluating students on a series of prescribed learning outcomes.

All data collected from the questionnaires were coded by three separate raters using an inductive/deductive method of analysis. General categories of narrative orientations – or "schematic narrative templates," in James Wertsch's original terms – were initially informed by a literature review in Canadian historiography. As Wertsch explains, "specific narratives are organized around particular dates, settings, and actions, whereas schematic narrative templates are more generalized structures used to generate multiple specific narratives with the same basic plot."[81] A central element of narrative templates is what Vladimir Propp called in his study of the morphology of folk tales the "recurrent constants" that can be found in multiple narratives and that serve as backbone features, or *functions*, for structuring the organization of templates (in Propp's study, these recurrent constants included abstention, violation, complicity, struggle, punishment, and victory).[82] Perhaps more importantly for Propp, these functions could be arranged in a particular sequence, an emplotment (e.g., starting with function A to end with function W through the use of functions B, C, and D) to form a general narrative template with which multiple specific stories could be created. Wertsch, who applied Propp's model to the study of the collective past, demonstrated that vernacular narratives of certain communities of memory subscribe, at a certain level of abstraction, to larger narrative templates.[83] Wertsch also suggested that these templates evolve over time and are inspired by forces of historical culture.

Through an iterative process, in which Canadian historiography and students' own narratives were scanned to identify possible recurrent constant features (e.g., discovery, struggle, adversity, revolution) and larger narrative templates, we revisited the initial categories to see how they were reflected in the dominant themes and narrative visions expressed in students' narratives. This process was applied first to a representative sample of participants and then to the entire corpus. Stories were coded on two separate levels: intra-narrative (sentence) and overall narrative (dominant orientation). As narratives can be polythetic in nature, and borrow from different perspectives, the overall orientation was determined by the preponderance of internal sentence coding combined with a synoptic analysis of the dominant vision expressed by the narrator in the story. Table I.4 presents the different categories and descriptors used for the analysis. To illustrate how we coded the stories, we present below a narrative excerpt from an Ontario student. The overall text was coded under "Adversity," but each sentence received a specific coding according to its own orientation and meaning. The predominant message of "Adversity" stems from a big-picture analysis of the narrative in light of the various sentences presented by the narrator, which contain both negative aspects (French was forbidden in school) and positive ones (today this regulation is no longer applied).

> French was always relegated to a marginal language. [Francophone negative]
> English was taking over, but Francophones always fought and struggled to keep their language. [Francophone adversity]
> At some point, French was forbidden in school, so classes were taught in English only. [Francophone negative]
> But today this regulation is no longer in application and great many schools are French-speaking. [Francophone positive] (0112A03-East)

Because of the non-probabilistic sampling strategy we used and the regional differences between francophone groups across the country, the results of our study do not claim to represent all young French Canadians' historical perspectives. Also, our results provide a specific portrait of young French Canadians at a given moment in time and cannot offer evidence for change over time. That being said, the study offers new and rich findings on students' historical consciousness in the twenty-first century and raises key issues that are critical for the future of history education in Canada, and possibly in other multi-national countries that have nations "within" a state (e.g., the United States, the United Kingdom, Spain, Belgium, and Australia). Given the large amount of data generated, it is not possible to present the entire set of narratives produced by students. Results and conclusions are thus based on a combination of descriptive tabulations and excerpts from students' narratives that provide examples of evidence upon which our conclusions are based. As the participants produced their narratives in the French language, all excerpts presented in this book have been carefully translated by the authors to respect the specific context, vision, and literary style of the original narrative texts, keeping in mind that some words, ideas, or expressions such as "les filles du Roy" have no direct English equivalents. In these instances, we maintained the original wording with some further explanatory notes for the reader. Finally,

Table I.4 Categories and descriptors of narrative orientations

Categories	Descriptors
Story of French Canadian experience	Narrative vision centred on the historical development of French Canadians in Canada. This vision presents four possible variations: *Francophone affirmation*: Narrative vision centred on French Canadian positive struggles for nationhood. Focus is placed on activism and militancy and the collective desire to construct a distinctive national community over time. This narrative orientation highlights the exploits of (past/current) figures who have played a vital role in the survival of French Canadian culture and identity. The future of the community is presented in positive terms (e.g., "We fought for our rights and we are now recognized in Canada"). *Francophone adversity*: Narrative vision centred on French Canadian difficulties (struggles, threats) and successes (wins) over time. This story emphasizes the various challenges and contradictions pertaining to the historical development of French in Canada. The future is unclear and uncertain. Vigilance is *de rigueur* for collective survival (e.g., "French Canadians have displayed a lot of courage but the threat of assimilation still weighs on our shoulders"). *Francophone defeat*: Narrative centred on a pessimistic vision of French Canadian historical development. Focus is placed on stories of collective oppression, marginalization, and victimization. The narrative presents either a negative vision for the future (assimilation) or a radical solution (rebellion) to resolve the collective faith of French Canadians (e.g., "English is the dominant language in the country and French Canadians continue to be assimilated"). *Francophone presence*: Narrative centred on a description of French Canadian historical development. This narrative often presents facts and events without a clear (positive, negative, or mixed) vision (e.g., "The history of French Canada started about 400 years ago when French explorers discovered America").
Story of Canadian nation-building	Narrative vision framed on the historical development of Canada from colony to sovereign nation and focused on Canadian institutions, rights, economy, and/or geography. Canada is presented as an independent North American nation-state made up of different provinces and groups, including French Canadians. Little emphasis is placed on distinctive memories and identities, which are subsumed under the Canadian historical community. Contemporary views can also include references to Canadian democracy, peace, and way of life (e.g., "Leaders such as Baldwin and Lafontaine played a key role in the establishment of Canadian institutions and responsible government that are symbols of Canada today").

(Continued)

Table I.4. (Continued)

Categories	Descriptors
Story of modernization	Narrative vision of the collective past inspired by social history and presenting the development of Canadian society in terms of social interactions and/or progress. Emphasis is placed on processes of industrialization, urbanization, immigration, unionization, schooling, and so on. In this narrative, the state plays a key institutional role in economic prosperity and social justice through various mechanisms (taxation, redistributive policies, health care, public schooling, etc.) (e.g., "Canada was strongly affected by the Depression and the two world wars, industries were transformed, and women took a greater place in the workforce").
Indigenous perspective	Narrative vision of the collective past presenting the experiences of Indigenous peoples in America. This vision may be shaped by postcolonialism and/or antiracism. This narrative perspective presents a positive, negative, or contested assessment of the relations between Europeans and Indigenous people (e.g., "Early contacts between European explorers and Indigenous people led to commercial treaties and partnerships").
Descriptive/ presentist story	Narrative presenting various events from the past without any coherent or explicit interpretative vision of history. This type of narrative can also offer a *presentist* perspective that looks solely at present-day developments in Canada (e.g., "Canada is a large country made up of ten provinces, and Ottawa is the national capital of Canada").
Life story	Narrative centred on personal/family history, often in reference to larger historical developments such as immigration or schooling. This type of story not only presents life experiences but also serves to define the personal identity of the narrator. The story becomes a way to express who the person is (e.g., "I was born in Mexico and came to Canada with my parents. French is my second language").
Undetermined	Texts presenting no narrative information, or information irrelevant to the task of telling the history of the nation (e.g., "I don't remember anything!").

it is important to mention that for assessments of the impact of identity on students' narrative orientation, we combined results from questions on identification with overall narrative orientations using QDA Miner, a flexible and highly effective software for mixed methods.

This Book

The five chapters of this book present different aspects of our study. In chapter 1, we present the historical context for this study. As the narrative task for students was on the history of French Canadians, it is important to situate the development of French Canada in reference to its evolving memory, identity, and geography. Quebec and French Ontario offer two different but complementary cases for studying the development of historical consciousness in French-speaking majority and minority societal settings. We then analyse students' narratives using our established categories of narrative orientations presented in the introduction. We demonstrate that Ontario and Quebec students tell narratives of their national community entrenched in distinctive sites of memory but that they also tend to rely on shared narrative frameworks that present French Canadians' historical struggle for their rights in a predominantly English-speaking country.

In chapter 2, we present the various geographical orientations of students' stories. These results reveal how the participants envisioned the collective past and focused their stories on particular aspects they considered significant for them. As the task made reference to the broad notion of "country," these results also help us understand the geographical environment in which they placed their narratives. We show that Quebec and Ontario students, despite common visions of the past, do not have the same narrative imaginings of their country.

In chapter 3, we look at students' narratives using two additional variables: gender and mother tongue. We reveal the significant differences in how male and female students narrate the history of French Canada. Young men are more likely to present stories of wars and conflicts while young women tend to emphasize personal and social history. Female students are also more inclined to offer first-person narratives in which they situate themselves as active narrators. Mother tongue is another important variable in understanding students' narrative views. This is more particularly the case in Quebec, where the gap between francophones and non-francophones is most significant.

Chapter 4 is devoted to another key variable: identity. Following our pilot study in Ottawa, we postulated that students' sense of national identification seriously affected their narratives of the collective past. Given that our participants were from two different provinces and various regional settings, we were interested in whether identity would be a determining factor and, if so, whether the place where they live affected this sense of identification. Our results are conclusive. In both cases, collective identification played a key role in shaping students' visions of the past. Interestingly, there were important differences between Quebec and Ontario students, with the former group far more likely to strongly identify exclusively with their own province as opposed to Canada.

In chapter 5, we return to some of the key issues we took up in this study and address more specifically the challenge of teaching and learning historical narratives. We explain in more educational terms how our strategy and our results can be understood in terms of narrative competence. We argue that the current Canadian focus on "historical thinking" is incomplete and misguided. We believe that if students are to graduate with a more critical understanding of history, useful for their practical lives as citizens, school history needs to move beyond a disciplinary model of discrete key concepts of historical thinking that pays limited attention to the broader narrative frameworks and the historical culture within which individuals live their daily lives. So we propose the inclusion of "narrative" as a metahistorical historical concept – and ultimately a competence – that shapes how we make sense of the past and do history.

In the conclusion, we put into perspective the value and significance of such a study for understanding the development of historical consciousness in twenty-first-century multinational countries such as Canada. We contend that if history education is to play a major role in shaping the historical views and representations of the next generation of citizens, it needs to find better ways of engaging the various forces from the "real-life" curriculum that affect their uses of the past, their sense of identity, and their visions of the communities in which they live.

1
Narrative Orientations

Historical consciousness is structured according to a vision of the past that takes the form of narration. In constructing a narrative representation, young people draw on past experiences to define the present and reflect on the future of their community. Tracing the historical path of their community over time allows them to forge a sense of identity and define their place in society. Narrative orientations thus refer as much to a vision of the past as to an anticipation of the future. For the purpose of this comparative study, we deliberately selected schools located in various regions of Quebec and Ontario to account for and compare the possible differences in students' narrative representations of their country. Each region was selected for its distinctive social, cultural, demographic, and economic characteristics; when considering the significance of lived experiences for students' learning, this approach can help us understand more about the impact of those characteristics on students' narrative orientations. But before looking at these, it is necessary to understand French Canada as a sociopolitical community that traces its origins back to New France.

French Ontario and Quebec: Two Geographical Entities[1]

Historian Marcel Martel writes that "French Canada" was initially a cultural concept, one that expressed a common identity for French-speaking Canadians.[2] It symbolized a national ideal of a country made up of "founding nations" and "became an institutionalized space in which many organizations expressed a desire for collective action and evoked the solidarity that was supposed to exist among all French Canadians."[3] French Canada was also inscribed in collective memory as a glorious colonial enterprise in North America, with references to bold-hearted French explorers, missionaries, and military heroes who helped develop this vast, non-territorial nation.[4]

This concept was propagated by the defining élites of French Canada, who included politicians, intellectuals, and of course the Catholic clergy. Among these men were Henri Bourassa, politician and founder of *Le Devoir*; Lionel Groulx, renowned historian and priest; and Napoléon Belcourt, Canadian senator and first president of the Association canadienne-française d'éducation d'Ontario (ACFÉO), a provincial association founded to defend French Canadian educational rights in Ontario. As French-speaking Canadians settled throughout the country and even in the United States, the French Canadian élite developed a vast network of organizations to protect their common good and to alert them to the importance of preserving their distinctive historical experience in Canada. The Ordre de Jacques-Cartier (OJC), a clandestine society founded to promote the interests of French Canadians and their access to political power, served as an expression of solidarity and collective will.

But French Canada has never been a sovereign nation with its own territory and government. From the start, it was an assemblage of communities, most of these founded by French settlers, who encountered various historical experiences and faced equally varied challenges. French Ontario and Quebec are two of these cultural communities that trace their origins back to New France.[5]

Quebec

In the French language, Quebec represents – at least for its people – three different entities: a city, also known as the Old Capital (in reference to the original capital of the colony); a province in the Canadian federation; and perhaps above all an "imagined community." French Canada was invented in the province of Quebec, although it is difficult to identify the exact moment in time when local French settlers began defining themselves as "French Canadians." Historian Guy Frégault suggests that the inhabitants of colonial New France in the early eighteenth century were sufficiently distant and different from those of France for a distinct national sentiment to exist. Michel Brunet argues that the conquest of New France by the British transformed the French in the colony into a "conquered people," which triggered a collective defence mechanism that has endured ever since.

However, Quebec nationalism is not a static phenomenon.[6] According to some historians, it would have first experienced a political and liberal form during the parliamentary struggles between the Parti canadien, originally the Parti patriote, led by Louis-Joseph Papineau, and the British colonial administration. Inspired by the American Revolution and French Republican ideas, this new nationalism aimed to form an autonomous (or independent) political nation, whose citizens regardless of language and religion would share the same sense of belonging to the political institutions and democratic values of French Canada.

The defeat of the Patriotes rebellions of 1837–38 announced the failure of this political conception of the nation. The Catholic Church, with the support of conservative leaders, took advantage of the new political situation to propose a new definition of the nation based on a community of shared language, religion, laws, customs, and traditions, whose survival was threatened and must be defended. Catholicism and the French language became the two main elements of French Canadian cohesion; both were seen as necessary to avoid being culturally assimilated by the dominant English-speaking Protestant majority.

The years after the Second World War set the context for a redefinition of the nation. French Canadian traditionalism was criticized by many liberal thinkers such as Pierre Elliott Trudeau (in public outlets such as *Cité libre*) and nationalists like André Laurendeau (in the newspapers *Le Devoir* and *Action nationale*), who called for a democratization of political institutions, the secularization of society, and the modernization of the state. These nationalists decried, among other things, the gap in education rates, living standards, and participation in the economy between francophones and anglophones in Quebec, but also elsewhere in Canada. They claimed that the province of Quebec, the only political jurisdiction that francophones fully controlled, ought to intervene through affirmative public policies that would put an end to social inequalities.

The most drastic changes took place in the 1960s during the so-called Quiet Revolution. Inspired by the political slogan "Maîtres chez nous" (Masters in our own house), the province of Quebec entered a vast and accelerated period of modernization and "rattrapage" (catch-up) with the rest of Canada. From the nationalization of hydroelectricity (Hydro-Québec) through to the secularization and democratization of the school system, the government of Quebec greatly expanded the role of the state in the province's economic, social, and cultural life. This unleashed forces that would have major consequences for French Canada.

The Quebec government's expanding influence in provincial and national affairs led to disputes over the place of Quebec, and francophones in particular, in Canada. The Canadian government established a Royal Commission on Bilingualism and Biculturalism in 1963 to examine Quebec's dissatisfaction with its status in the Canadian federation.

As the commission observed, "Canada, without being fully conscious of the fact, is passing through the greatest crisis in its history. The source of the crisis lies in the Province of Quebec."[7] French Canadian nationalism, which was becoming more and more Québécois in nature, was exacerbated by the lack of recognition of Canada as an "equal partnership," in the sense of equal opportunity for francophones and anglophones to participate in the institutions affecting their lives. For many in Quebec, Canada was still operating as an Anglo-dominated society that disrespected the founding nations.

French Canadians from Quebec became increasingly concerned about being a minority in English-speaking Canada. Attempts to abolish French-language education in various provinces during the nineteenth and early twentieth centuries (in New Brunswick, Manitoba, Alberta, Saskatchewan, and Ontario) offered clear evidence that French Canadians would need to acquire their own political power in order to preserve their rights. Many in Quebec turned to their own provincial government for state protection and national recognition. The neonationalist discourse, as Gérard Bouchard argues, reimagined the survival of French Canadians in the context of a modern territorial nation within the province of Quebec.[8]

Martel contends that defining Quebec as the political expression of French Canada had two major consequences. First, it led to a drastic redefinition of the non-territorial nation of French Canada, which included historical communities across the country, from Bouctouche in New Brunswick to Maillardville in British Columbia. New, territorialized identities emerged as a result of this redefinition process. French Canadians from Quebec gradually became "Québécois," those of Ontario "Franco-Ontarians," those of Manitoba "Franco-Manitobans," and so on. Perhaps the only exception was the Acadians from the Maritimes, who already had a well-established sense of identity going back to the eighteenth century. Second, the government of Quebec established itself as the official voice for defending French Canadians. The neonationalists installed a power dynamic between the Quebec nation-state and the Canadian nation-state, thereby replacing a federal state with two founding nations. French Canadians' interests were now equated with those of Quebec. For some nationalists, independence as a sovereign nation-state ("le pays du Québec") became the motto of this new nationalism. This nationalist movement was viewed as a direct outgrowth of the decolonization revolutions taking place elsewhere in the Americas as well as in Africa. In this neonationalist context, French Canadian communities outside Quebec were no longer seen as part of the new, modern nation.

Of course, not everyone in Quebec agreed to this national project. Twice in its history, in the 1980 and 1995 provincial referendums, a majority of the Quebec population rejected separation from Canada. According to Jean-Marc Léger, Jacques Nantel, and Pierre Duhamel, "Québécois are a moderate people in perpetual search for consensus," be it within the Canadian federation or not.[9] But Quebec nationalism is not simply consensual; it has resulted in prominent divides among French Canadian communities that have endured to this day. As Martel observes, the "break-up of French Canada" meant that the pan-Canadian institutional network created over the past two centuries was no longer a locus for the expression of collective will and action.[10]

As a result, some intellectuals have recently proposed that Quebec nationalism be revisited from its broader North American perspective. According to sociologist Joseph-Yvon Thériault, in their attempt to define Quebec as a modern society, nationalists have occluded an important aspect of their history and their memory: the national will of all French Canadians to create a distinct society in the New World.[11] According to him, the constant variable throughout the history of francophones in America, be they Québécois, Acadians, or Franco-Ontarians, is their "intentionalité" (their will) to invent a new society in America with a distinct societal culture different from the Anglo-Saxon one, and to purposely inscribe this collective aspiration on future generations. In his view, Québécois have attempted to redefine their national project in the mould of American modernity (the "Américanité") without understanding that their vital aspiration has in fact been in continuity with the enduring French Canadian project – a national project that he refuses to see as folkloric, colonialist, and pre-modern. As Thériault puts it, "French Canada has never been, strictly speaking, an ethnic group (as it is too often called in our day to assert more strongly its fading away) but a culture-nation, a grouping of human beings behaving at a second level of culture, with reference to history, literature and institutions, often within a State, and also sometimes within a Church."[12]

For others, like Jocelyn Létourneau, Quebec nationalism should be understood in continuity with its traditional aspiration for "quiet change" over time.[13] Unlike American and French *révolutionnaires*, French Canadians in general, and Québécois in particular, have always rejected drastic revolutions, the *tabula rasa* theory, in favour of resistance and rebellion, which in the view of Létourneau allow a group to strategically reposition itself in a place that is more workable between extreme political positions. Located between the burden of collective *survivance* (inscribed in tragic memories of the Conquest transmitted over time) and an uncertain national future (of political ambivalence between federalism and sovereignty), Québécois prefer "the life of a conformable and reassuring, peaceful and serene present, which largely nourishes their own consciousness."[14] For Létourneau, the reconquest of French Canadians can take place within the current Canadian federal framework through the appropriation of narratives of "canadianité."[15] This unique concept refers to the Canadian historical experience as the expression of ongoing tensions and frictions, sometimes positive and sometimes negative, that have resulted in the founding of a complex Canadian society – a society that does not neatly fit a common narrative denominator but instead (re)creates multiple ones, including Quebec's own. Létourneau refers to this as the "Canadian ambiguity," the challenge of maintaining a democratic sovereign state through collective ambivalence as opposed to collective memory conformity. For him, the future of Canada thus resides in the ability of Canadians to make effective use of dialogue, conciliation, and accommodation of various cultural forces and narrative representations that have historically contributed to shaping Canadian society.

In the circumstances, how do young Quebec citizens understand their place in the current Canadian context? To answer this question, we visited schools in various regions of the province. A first set of regions lies between the two metropolitan centres surveyed, Montreal and Quebec City. The Gatineau region, close to Ontario, is one of this set, as are the regions north of Montreal, as well as and Central Quebec and its regional capital of Victoriaville. A second set of so-called peripheral regions, historically dominated by national resource exploitation, are characterized by a more fragile demography and economy and are also more subject to cyclical fluctuations. However, they stand out for their strong regional awareness. Saguenay is the best example owing to its geographic isolation and cultural homogeneity.

The statistical portrait of immigrant students produced by Quebec's Ministry of Education, Recreation, and Sports offers an overview of these ethnocultural communities and their representation in Quebec regions. First- and second-generation immigrants account for more than half the student population in Montreal, one quarter in Gatineau, and below 15% in the other regions surveyed. However, the situation varies greatly from school to school, reflecting the residential distribution of immigrants. The presence of anglophones also adds to the context. In Montreal and Gatineau schools, the percentage of anglophones in the student population is above 10%.

French Ontario

Trying to locate French Ontario on a map of Canada can be a daunting task. French Ontario is an imagined territory that corresponds to the various spaces where French-speaking Ontarians live or have lived. In Ontario, where French Canadians have always been a linguistic minority, francophones could not count on demographic factors and power dynamics to influence politics in the same way as did their neighbours in Quebec. They would have to maintain an effective institutional network in order to protect their collective interests; their survival as a collectivity would also depend on successful relationships with provincial and federal authorities. Educational language rights, in particular, have been central to their claims and their existence as a distinct people in the province.

The first Ontario school acts of the nineteenth century allowed for French-speaking education, as well as German and Gaelic education. French Canadians could create or maintain their own French-language schools or classrooms depending on the region and the demand. But in the late nineteenth century, growing nationalist feelings among Anglo-Protestants coupled with strong anti-French sentiments in various regions of Ontario led to more restrictive regulations aimed at cultural assimilation. French-speaking schools were accused publicly of being "the nurseries not merely of an alien tongue but of alien customs, of alien sentiments, and ... a wholly alien people."[16] Following a provincial report that concluded that the quality of education in francophone schools was largely inadequate, the provincial government of Premier James Whitney issued a regulation in 1912, known as Regulation 17, that limited the use of French as the language of instruction to the first two years of school. The goal was to gradually assimilate French Canadians into the mainstream. But French Canadians had no intention of remaining quiet. Already in 1910, the Association canadienne-française d'éducation de l'Ontario (ACFÉO) had been founded to protect French-language education. With the support of other French Canadian organizations across the country, as well as that of influential moderate English Canadians, who helped create a lobbying group called the Unity League of Ontario, the francophones of Ontario forced the provincial government to revisit its decision in 1927. But this particular battle was not over. Regulation 17 was officially withdrawn only in 1944; it then took forty more years for French-language public schooling, from elementary to high school, to become a reality. Indeed, Franco-Ontarians had to wait until 1997 to have full governance rights over their own school system. Even today, Ontario is not officially bilingual and French-language services are provided unevenly across the province to its French-speaking habitants. Furthermore, the recent attempt to create a Franco-Ontarian university in Toronto was initially abandoned in 2018 under the newly elected Progressive Conservative government of Premier Doug Ford. This drastic political decision has led to an unprecedented national movement of solidarity among francophone communities, even in the province of Quebec. Some have even proposed convening a national dialogue on new Estates General of French Canada.[17]

The struggle for educational language rights has been only one aspect of the survival of French Canadians in Ontario, but in many ways it is the one that has shaped most strongly their sense of identity.[18] According to some historians, French Ontario developed gradually on the foundations of French Canada, using collective memory and local traditions to position itself in the *longue durée* of French settlement and community-building in North America.[19] In their book *L'Ontario français: des Pays d'en Haut à nos jours*, Gaétan Gervais and Michel Bock offer a detailed account of the origins and development of Franco-Ontarians as a unique collectivity anchored in more than 400 years of local presence on the land.[20] In 1610, explorer Étienne Brûlé was sent on a reconnaissance mission by Samuel de Champlain in the Upper Ottawa River region. He was the first European to visit "Les pays d'en haut" (what would become Upper Canada). Three years later, Champlain himself visited the region in search of a western passage, travelling as far as Huronia on Georgian Bay to meet with the local Indigenous people, the Hurons. The records he kept of his travels offer the first European accounts of the lives of the Indigenous peoples in what would later become the province of Ontario. But it took another half century for the French to establish trading posts and garrisons across this vast territory ranging from Hudson Bay to what is now the US border. As Paul-François Sylvestre puts it, "*coureurs des bois* and *voyageurs* travelled the territory, while Jesuit missionaries evangelized in Huronia."[21] Fort Pontchartrain (near what is now Détroit) became the first permanent colony in the region; it was home to the first Catholic parish (1767) and the first French-language school (1786).

Today, French Ontario represents a vast cultural territory with more than 450 schools serving more than 550,000 French-speakers (slightly less than 5% of Ontario's total population in the 2011 Canadian census). This population is geographically dispersed across the province. Eastern Ontario has the largest population of francophones in Ontario (42%); they have settled in various rural and urban communities and have the most concentrated French-language programs and services in the province. French is a well-recognized public language in Eastern Ontario, thanks to its close proximity to and ties with Quebec.[22] Also, Ottawa, the federal capital, provides a rich political, cultural, and educational milieu that has contributed to the stability and prosperity of francophones in the region.

As a natural resource region, Northeastern Ontario presents a contracting setting. Highly vulnerable to economic fluctuations in the lumber and mining sectors, this region has experienced profound demographic shifts over the decades and now a significant decline. Northeastern Ontario now holds 22% of the total francophone population. Still, it can count on the vitality and activism of its local population, which has long been a hotbed for cultural life and creativity as well as a stimulating source of identity-building. It is in this region that the Franco-Ontarian flag was designed by historian Gaétan Gervais and his student Michel Dupuis, both at Laurentian University. Officially raised for the first time on 25 September 1975, the flag, which includes a fleur-de-lys and a trillium (the two emblematic flowers of French and English Ontario), now represents Franco-Ontarians across the province and is celebrated annually on 25 September.

Southern Ontario is the most heavily populated and economically diverse region of Ontario. It is also the provincial region that attracts the highest number of immigrants. Southern Ontario is home to 36% of the total francophone population. The region's growing ethnocultural diversity has resulted in a new "francophonie," a multicultural French-speaking population drastically different from the traditional French Canadian old stock families originally from Quebec, who have lived in Ontario for centuries. This cultural development has generated significant challenges, including how to recast the French Canadian and Franco-Ontarian organizations that have traditionally served the francophone population. Southern Ontario now faces an important assimilation challenge. Representing less than 5% of the regional population, francophones are a marginal group in a sea of ethnocultural communities struggling for their own recognition. Equally challenging, Southern Ontario cannot count on the same level of francophone resources and educational institutions as found in other regions such as Eastern Ontario. The recent provincial decision to initially cancel the Franco-Ontarian university project illustrates the vulnerability of the francophone community, in the south in particular.

Data from the Education Quality and Accountability Office of Ontario (EQAO) provide additional linguistic information pertaining to the three regions we visited for our study.[23] In the schools of Northeastern Ontario, only 20% of francophone students say they speak another language at home as frequently as French, thus indicating that French is still the dominant language used in school and at home. The situation is the opposite in Southern Ontario, where 80% of the students speak another language at home. These findings are comparable to those for the urban schools we visited in the city of Ottawa.[24] Schools in other Eastern Ontario communities occupy an intermediate position, with 60% claiming to speak another language at home.[25]

As indicated in the introduction, we analysed students' narratives in terms of schematic templates or "narrative orientations" that represent big picture frameworks informed by French Canadian historiography. These can help make sense of the collective past on the large scale.[26] Below we look at each narrative framework as found in Quebec and Ontario participants' texts.

French Canadian Experience

As indicated in figures 1.1 and 1.2, the dominant narrative orientation for both Quebec and Ontario students is the *French Canadian experience*. This big-picture orientation privileges a story of the historical experience of francophones in Canada, one that touches on their origins, their political and cultural struggles, and their future prospects. More than four fifths (81%) of Ontario students and three quarters (77%) of Quebec students place the francophone historical experience at the centre of their story. Given the historiographical and curricular emphasis on French Canadian history in these two provinces, these results should come as no surprise. However, this narrative orientation is polythetic in nature; people can offer a variety of historical voices and interpretations of the French Canadian experience, ranging from the most optimistic to the most pessimistic. For this reason, we have divided this category into four specific orientations: affirmation, adversity, presence, and defeat.

The *francophone affirmation* orientation is used by 13% of Franco-Ontarian students and 8% of Quebec students. This narrative framework structures the history of French Canada as an epic filled with collective challenges and upheavals, determination and resilience, and a final victory for the future of francophones. For the authors of this type of narrative, French Canadians can look back on their past with a sense of accomplishment and envision the future with confidence. Surprisingly, Franco-Ontarian students tell more optimistic stories than their Quebec counterparts. The implementation of French-language schools across the province, bilingual public services from the federal government, and, to some extent, the recent victory to protect French-language health

Figure 1.1 Narrative orientations for Ontario students

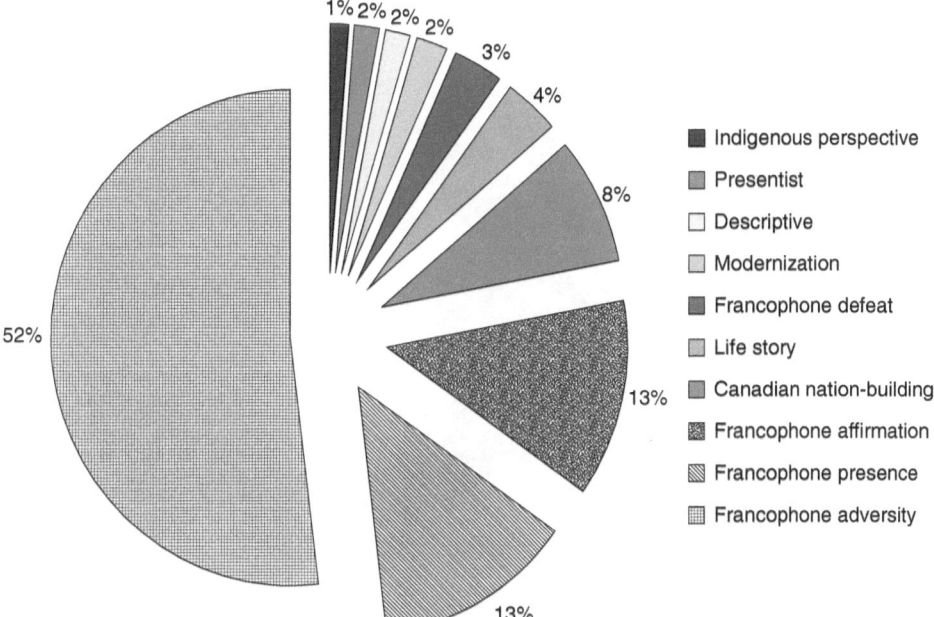

care (Montfort Hospital) constitute a collective achievement, an "end of history" that ensures the cultural security of francophones in Ontario. In Quebec, it is the time-honoured resistance to British overlords and the recent progress in political and social matters (opposition to the Durham Report, the Quiet Revolution, Bill 101) that offer a positive vision of history.[27] The following narrative excerpts present the views of students who do not hesitate to refer to celebratory events (e.g., Flag Day) or even acts of rebellion to express their optimism:

> When we are celebrating the Francophone Flag Day, it's a day to honour our beautiful French language. We wear white and green colours to show our joy as Franco-Ontarians. Francophone is important for the history of the country since the French language people has had to fight for the right to speak and have French courses and schools, hospital, etc. in French. (0111A6-East)
> Quebecers were not assimilated by the English despite what Anglophones wanted to do. They even deprived them of their religion and said that

Figure 1.2 Narrative orientations for Quebec students

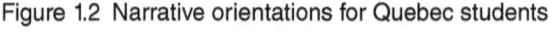

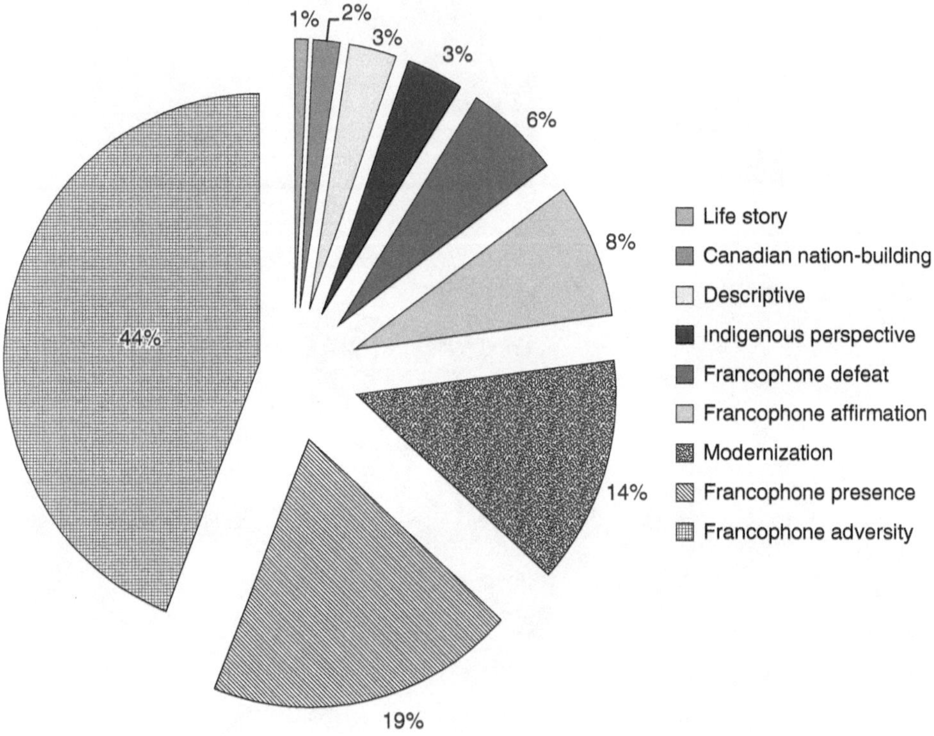

French was a dirty language. We were even called "fool" in the Durham Report [?]. But, we French Quebecers have resisted, survived this attempted assimilation. We are strong and even rebel. All this for the protection of own culture. All those people who fought to keep everything that belonged to us now. We must never give up this rich and strong culture for another one that is for others. (105A16-Gatineau)

At the opposite end of the spectrum, the *francophone defeat* orientation frames the past as a pessimistic narrative focused on the losses of French Canadians in the face of the dominant English (*les Anglais*), who often take the form of a ruthless oppressor. The future is rarely viewed with optimism. The authors of this type of narrative are most often fatalistic, believing that the French fact in America will inevitably disappear. This narrative orientation is relatively marginal among

Ontario participants (3%) but slightly more popular in Quebec (6%). This is a strange paradox. Franco-Ontarians find themselves a minority in Ontario and do not benefit from the institutional and cultural resources that Québécois enjoy, yet they express a more favourable vision of the past and conceive the future of their culture in more positive terms than in Quebec, as we noted in the previous discussion on *francophone affirmation*.

The following two students, the first from Ontario and the second from Quebec, offer a vision of national history that is fairly tragic, positioning themselves as victims, as an oppressed people dominated by the English Canadian majority:

> The first true foundation of the Francophone comes with Samuel de Champlain and the founding of Quebec. French colonization was challenged by the English colonization, which even led to a series of wars and conflicts. "New France" is about wars and conflicts. "New France" surrendered/was conquered by the British forces. An English majority makes up Canada and begins to stifle the French minority. Francophone habitants gathered in small communities to preserve their culture. Driven by a desire for political and religious purity, the English majority tries to eradicate French language in various ways (Regulation 17). (0112A17-East)
> After a while, the English take possession of our territory. It is the beginning of the end. From that moment on, we are seen as a minority, and they try to dominate us, our culture, language, laws, etc. We are a detested people in the eyes of the English who see us as a pain in the back. (GR0213-Quebec City)

For the Quebec proponents of this negative historical interpretation, the Conquest occupies a central place. It appears as the tragedy that has caused irreversible damage to French society in America. The British regime is slowly but surely compelling a long descent into political marginalization, economic dispossession, and ultimately cultural assimilation. In the narratives of *francophone affirmation*, the Conquest is also present, but the situation of French Canadians is more positive, thanks to their resilience and to their will to resist that allows them to win important victories and ensure their cultural survival over time. Stories of *francophone defeat*, in contrast, present the Conquest as the beginning of a long series of collective failures confirmed by other successive events such as the failed rebellions of 1837–38, the union of the two Canadas, the FLQ (Front de libération du Québec) nationalist-terrorist movement and its repression by the federal government, the failure of the two Quebec referendums on sovereignty, and the decline of French as a mother tongue in Canada:

> The people of Quebec simply wants a right granted to all other nations in the world, to have a country for its people. There was the FLQ, an electroshock for Quebec, the October crisis during which Quebec was scared. Then there was for the first time in modern Quebec a political party in opposition to the liberals (I don't remember the name). The referendum of 1980, lost by far, the failed accords on the constitution, which led to the second referendum of 1995, when the people of Quebec was scared to secure its right: to have its own country. (GR0632-Montreal)
>
> The political system was unequal to French Canada which gradually led to patriotic rebellions in 1837–38 to preserve their rights. The French never got everything they wanted and still want today ... In sum, the French were manipulated and never had it easy in their history. (GR009-Montreal)

These negative visions of the nation are not dominant. The vast majority of students in both groups tell stories along the lines of *francophone adversity*, a narrative orientation that is neither entirely positive nor totally negative but instead nuanced. This type of narrative is favoured by over half (52%) of Franco-Ontarian students and almost half (44%) of Quebec students. These stories present a vision of the past filled with pitfalls and obstacles, but also with important victories often won in difficult historical circumstances. However, these historic gains remain fragile, and students often call for vigilance in the face of an unpredictable future. The following narrative excerpt from a Quebec student suggests that, despite the trauma of having been conquered, of "being the main target," past struggles should make francophones alert and responsive to the will of the people to stay alive and "continue our struggle":

> The French-speaking people has never had an easy task, since they are the minority, they are not only less "strong" against their main opponent (the English-speaking people) who threatens them all the time so that the French language disappears and that its Catholic religion does the same. This small people has always been the main target of other peoples, but despite everything, it has always kept its place through its many "confrontations." Take the Revolution of the Patriots, the Quebec Act or even the ultramontanists, these "events" have all played their small role which showed that we fought to obtain the same rights as the others, which should have been be assigned right from the beginning equally and justly. We, as former French colonists, have the right to say with pride that we are

a people able to affirm itself and that despite the inconveniences, we will continue our struggle for success. (105A18-Gatineau)

The following passage from an Ontario student is another typical example of *francophone adversity*. The author acknowledges the gains made by the Franco-Ontarian minority, which strengthen the status of French in the province, but adds that their language is at risk in the face of the dominant influence of English culture. This situation, in the student's view, may lead francophones to use English-speaking institutions and services instead of their own:

> Today, even though Canada is officially bilingual, most citizens do not speak French. Government services, such as schools, hospitals, and police are offered in French, but they are less common. We have to force ourselves a lot to use our language, because the media is often in English. It is more difficult to pass this language and culture on to future generations because the world around us is predominantly anglophone. (0211B04-East)

Finally, the *francophone presence* orientation is a descriptive narrative template that presents the history of French Canadians without ideological orientation or particular narrative position with regard to the past and future of the community. It should be noted that 19% of Quebec students and 13% of Franco-Ontarian students offer such stories. Why do students choose this descriptive type of narrative? It is difficult to answer this question, but our analysis suggests that it may be related to a sense of personal indifference, a lack of interest in our project, or simply an undeveloped historical consciousness. The following Franco-Ontarian student confesses his ignorance of the subject of our project but agrees to give it a try. He admits candidly that "I don't remember how French Canadians became Franco-Ontarians":

> The history of the Francophones in this country, as I know it, was that there were Aboriginals, Jacques Cartier came to Canada, where the Aboriginals were, he changed their religion, how they spoke, and he discovered Canada, but after the English arrived, and the English and French went to war because the English did not want the French language in the school, but the English won the war ... So I don't really remember how French Canadian became Franco-Ontarians and how the French kept French language and religion in schools. (011A20-South)

For students in both Quebec and Ontario, the beginning of French Canadian history starts with the "discovery of Canada" by the French navigator Jacques Cartier (sometimes confused with Christopher Columbus) and the arrival of French settlers, who established a French colony in America. Students often begin their story with an account of origins that traces the presence of francophones in the country and the existence of francophone communities in Canada today. For this Quebec student, the founding of New France was the beginning of a collective adventure that continues to this day:

> In 1608, Samuel de Champlain was the first Frenchman to settle in America. He founded New France and Quebec City. More and more New France will expand its territory until the British settle in North America too, and start to wage war against the French until the English triumphs and seize the territory of the New-France and it becomes little by little the Canada of today. Francophones have had to fight to keep their language and they will become French Canadians and then Quebecers and today French is still the dominant spoken language. (04B11-Quebec City)

Differences do emerge between the two provinces. For Ontario students, the story of the French colony aims to situate the origins of their community over time, showing how francophones have inhabited this land for centuries. For this participant from Northeastern Ontario, French colonization was responsible for the presence of francophones in Ontario:

> The French wanted to establish a great French empire so they settled in Northern Ontario to the West. This is why there are more French cities in the North (Cochrane, Timmins, Sudbury). The French have stayed in what is now Quebec. Here near Ottawa we are French thanks to our French ancestors. (0110A01 North)

For Quebec students, the history of the colonial period has a more emotional tone; it describes something of a golden age – an epic tale of colonial expansion crushed by the British Conquest, which presages the marginalization of francophones and their political struggle for survival. The British victory is depicted as a tragedy that has blocked the natural evolution of French Canada. This student from Montreal argues that the War of Conquest put an end to French Canada, which is now a reality only in Quebec, where most citizens speak French:

> The first settlers here were French-speaking, Canada at the time was a complete French territory until the British tried to take the territory and make it English-speaking, Canada was divided into two parts Upper and Lower Canada, Lower Canada being the French-speaking part of the

country. There were also the Patriots who fought for their Quebec culture and the language, they also wanted to resist the English. With time, Lower Canada becomes what Quebec is, the only French-speaking province in an anglophone country. To protect this language and the culture that comes with Bill 101 and 2 referenda. Some French-speaking communities live in other Canadian provinces, but Quebec remains the only province supposed to be entirely francophone. (GR0606-Montreal)

This story of origins is important for many students in Quebec and Ontario, as it roots their cultural difference and the unique trajectory of their linguistic community in the *longue durée*. History becomes the central element with which they can demonstrate how French Canadians are culturally different from English Canadians:

French Canadians are citizens of Canada who have French origins. They form an ethnic group, most of their ancestors are settlers who arrived in the colony of New France. Together with the Acadians, they make up the entire group whose origins go back to the colony of the N.F. They are part of the founding communities of Canada. (0211B12-East)

In the eyes of many students, history serves as an identity marker that defines a particular society with its own values and ways of being and that distinguishes them from other Canadians. Sometimes students do not hesitate to profess the permanence of their culture and their language:

With Jacques Cartier they settled and we share this culture. Now it is important and it represents a lot Ontario. (0210A04-East)
Why do Quebecers still speak French? Because they do not want Quebec dependent on Canada. So they use language and culture to establish the differences between them and the Canadian people. (0205A11-Gatineau)

The notion of struggle is central to stories of *francophone experience*. Struggles help explain the survival of their culture and their language against the English-speaking majority that has attempted to assimilate them. The Conquest, from this viewpoint, is important in that it embodies the greatest challenge faced by French Canadians. If, for some, Quebec has lost its capacity to act as an autonomous community, for others francophones have managed to find imaginative ways to live their lives as French speakers:

Francophones in this country have been very important in the history of Quebec and the world. Francophones have been important in many fields, whether socio-cultural or economic. All francophones are proud of it and that will forever be engraved in our memory. Francophones and Quebec have all had difficulties, but they have been able to succeed. They had problems, political, economic and many other unspoken ones. We can be proud of who we are and what we will be. (04B06-Quebec City)

In Ontario, as we saw in the previous chapter, the pivotal moment in students' narratives was the Regulation 17 crisis. This episode plays a fundamental role in the identity construction of Franco-Ontarians, as does the Conquest for young Québécois. In many ways, the fight against Regulation 17 marked the birth of their own community. It allowed French Canadians from Ontario to overcome their minority situation and to acquire the right to exist as an official community. For many, notably in Eastern Ontario, the second most important act of collective resistance was the saving of Montfort Hospital in the 1990s:

Francophones were persecuted because they were (and still are) a minority in the country. I am not sure how many years later Regulation 17 was created by the Department of Education. This law prohibited the use of the French language as a language of communication and education. Despite this fact, francophone teachers continued to teach in French and defended their right. When the police came, they barricaded the door and chased them away (Gisèle Lalonde). A more recent event that had to do with francophones and the Montfort Hospital. In recent years they wanted to change the hospital from French-speaking to English-speaking. But francophones "fought" to keep the only francophone hospital in Ottawa and that worked. To conclude, for a long time, francophones have tried to keep/defend their place in Canada and this continues even today. (0211B09-East)

Interestingly, young Franco-Ontarians frequently mobilize the experience of the Regulation 17 crisis to explain their own presence in Ontario today, and to legitimize their past and future claims for a bilingual province or to acknowledge their contribution to Ontario's history:

When we are celebrating the Francophone Flag Day, so it's a day when we honour our beautiful French language. We wear white and green colour to show our joy as being a Franco-Ontarian. The Francophonie is important for the history of the country since the French language has had to fight for the right to speak and have French courses and Schools, hospital etc in French. (0111A6-East)

Finally, the stories of the *francophone experience* reflect a sense of hindered progress, of an unfinished journey for the francophone communities in Canada combined with a vision of an uncertain future for French Canadian culture and language. Their stories often end by recalling the historical struggle for survival as an endless one.

Quebec students in particular tend to describe their national community as an unfinished society that missed its rendezvous with history and that is unable to achieve complete independence as a sovereign French-speaking country. Quebec remains a community on the margins whose destiny has been usurped by the British and that has been deprived of its capacity to act independently as a nation within or outside Canada. The following student tells a fairly dramatic story of Quebec society, ending with a defeatist look at the future of his community – a community that is unable to live up to its motto "Je me souviens" (I remember):

> Without the support of France, Quebec was too weak to fight against British power and their loyalists. As the 1837–38 revolutions show, taking up arms will not work and they will find other ways to reclaim our lands occupied by anglophones. After these years the anglophone threat will be more discreet but still present. Quebecers relegated to simple workers living in poverty exploited by the Anglo bosses did not improve the chances of survival of our language. Politicians like René-Lévesque or Jacques Parizeau intervened to wake up the public with their referenda, but the results show that there is still work to be done. Even today a minority of the population is concerned about our language. I'm sure the motto "I remember" is not appropriate. (GR0631-Quebec City)

Students in Ontario do not have this sense of a lost destiny but still describe a fragile community with an uncertain future due to persistent assimilation pressures. The following student is worried about the decline of the French language in Canada, but this concern does not prevent him from being proud of his language:

> I think over the years, French in Canada is decreasing. It's sad to see. However, there are still many persons who identify themselves according to French and they keep the language alive. I am proud to be francophone and to be able to speak this language. (112A02-South)

Of course, this sense of fragility is not shared by all student participants. Many others envision their community in more positive terms, especially when taking into account all past victories of French Canadians. Young Franco-Ontarians have a particularly positive view of the recent past due to some important gains for French-language services:

> In Quebec, it's a little more relaxed, being a French-speaking province. But in Ontario, which is an anglophone province, we had trouble just keeping our only francophone hospital in Ontario, Montfort Hospital, we had to fight to keep it. Today we can find francophones across Canada, in Ontario, Manitoba, Alberta, etc. We have come a long way to have our freedom of language, because of these brave people proud to be francophone, we are bigger and prouder than ever. (110A16-East)

While Quebec students tend to tell less positive narratives, most of them still take a favourable view of the collective past. According to this student, the contribution of French Canadians to domestic and international affairs has led to the creation of a "Quebec nation" with a distinctive way of life:

> Several other events such as the rebellions, world wars and the Cold War occurred, which greatly contributed to defining themselves as the "Quebec" nation rather than "French-Canadians." All these events have made us who we are. We have developed our way of thinking and our Quebec identity thanks to what we have experienced. (GR0233-Central Quebec)

Canadian Nation-Building

The *Canadian nation-building* orientation is a pan-Canadian narrative framework that does not place the historical experience of francophones at the forefront. Instead, it refers to Canada's historical development as a whole. This narrative orientation transcends cultural, social, and geographic affiliations so as to provide a grand narrative for all Canadians. In total, 8% of Ontario students tell stories reflecting this vision of the nation. For Quebec students, the proportion is barely 2%.

The *Canadian nation-building* narrative framework is characterized by the prevalence of the Canadian space and attachment to the country. Regional and provincial experiences are not rejected, but they acquire significance only when they reinforce the national character and contribute to the image of Canada as a mosaic of cultures and languages living together. Students who support this view talk about multiculturalism, open immigration policies, the building of the transcontinental railway, and Canada's contributions on the world stage (e.g., peacekeeping) as elements of their grand narrative. Some also emphasize that Canada is a bilingual country, with French and English recognized as the official languages of Canada:

> There was the construction of the railway across all of Canada in order to populate the west. The population has grown. There was the Gold Rush that attracted many immigrants to Canada who grew up a lot and formed various provinces and then joined and formed Canada. We were under the command of Great Britain. We fought for our independence. We had to fight for French and French rights. Various groups came together to form Canada and we had to accept different cultures. Populate the great North and the Prairies (West). We have grown a lot thanks to wheat/cereal market. We continue to welcome many immigrants who make us grow. (110A06-East).
>
> The history of the Francophonie begins with (Christopher Columbus 1492) the colonization of New France by France. The language quickly spread with the fur trade (Aboriginals). Later, the 13 colonies fought to gain territory from New France, which became a colony of England. English people arrived on the territory. Over time, the territory was divided in two: Upper and Lower Canada. The French then split to divide English-speaking Canadians (part of Ontario) and French-speaking Canadians (in Quebec). Today, Quebec is a province of Canada. So we are all Canadian but with different origins. (05A14-Saguenay)

As we will see in chapter 4, collective identification plays an important role in structuring a narrative vision of the collective past. As such, students who identify strongly with Canada are more likely to tell stories of Canadian nation-building. Yet this narrative orientation is clearly not the dominant one. Both cultural and educational factors can help explain these results.

Modernization

The *modernization* orientation provides a narrative framework for stories about society's economic mechanisms and social transformations. This framework also places great importance on marginalized social actors often forgotten in national history, such as women, immigrants, workers, and cultural minorities, who have also contributed significantly to society. In students' narratives, there are several references to social actors such as the famous "Filles du Roi" (or "Filles du Roy" as sometimes written in old French) who were sent to New France by the

French king at the request of intendant Jean Talon to help restore gender balance and stimulate population growth:

> The history of francophones begins with the arrival of the French. Indeed, they are the ones who transmitted their language, their religion and their culture. They made it possible through various measures, like the Filles du Roy, to increase the population and to create a colony. They also created the economy in the colony with mercantilism. (04A13-Quebec City)

Overall, 14% of Quebec students chose the *modernization* perspective, compared to only 2% for Ontario students. This framework is clearly not a preferred orientation for telling the history of French Canada, particularly for Ontario students. The discrepancy between the two groups is possibly explained by the impact of the Quebec HCE program, which is more sensitive to, and structured around, social and economic history than the Ontario program, which is still largely focused on political history and national identity-building. The following excerpt from a Quebec student presents the history of francophones in the context of urbanization and industrialization with reference to the impact of these on women and demography:

> New France or Province of Quebec is industrializing and it lead[s] to rural exodus. People leave the countryside to go to cities for work (mainly in factories). After that there were the 1st World War and the 2nd. This allowed women to finally enter the job market. The Church was very present and with Mr. Duplessis, this period is called "the great darkness." There were in the same years the baby boom (after the 2nd World War), which explains the aging of the population today. (GR0101-Gatineau)

Other Narrative Orientations

The other narrative orientations – *life experience, Indigenous perspective, descriptive/presentist, undetermined* – are extremely marginal in our corpus, representing no more than 3% each. As we will see in the next section, these types of narratives are not without interest for our study. The proportions for *life experience* and *Indigenous perspective* are extremely low at the provincial level, but they also vary somewhat among regions. As for the small number of *descriptive* and *undetermined* stories, there is every reason to celebrate. These stories often reflect students' indifference, their lack of interest, or even their historical ignorance. The low frequency of these stories shows that, contrary to popular expectations, the young citizens in our study have visions and representations of the past that they use in the production of historical narratives.

Narrative Orientations by Region

In Ontario as in Quebec, the dominant narrative orientation is *francophone adversity*. However, there are variations across regions (see figure 1.3). It seems that in more anglo-dominant areas where francophones have less diversified institutional resources, the story of adversity is prevalent. It is the most popular category in Southern Ontario (67%), as well as in the Northeast (58%). These regions, especially Southern Ontario, are characterized by the fragmentation of the French fact and by the difficulty finding francophone public spaces outside the school environment. While this is less the case in Northern Ontario, the question of French in the public sphere is still a daily-life issue, notably in urban communities such as Sudbury:

> When an explorer discovered the country of Canada, it became French. Meanwhile, suddenly the British came to Canada with their language – English. So, there were linguistic conflicts between French and English. The country has been divided in Upper and Lower Canada (divided by language). In my opinion the English have always seen themselves as "superior" and French does not get a lot of credit. This language had to overcome several challenges. (0110A06-South)

Results from Eastern Ontario differ from those in the other two regions: there we find a smaller proportion of stories of *francophone adversity* (39%) and a higher proportion of *francophone affirmation* (17%). The latter orientation attracts the interest of barely 7% of students in the North and 11% in the South. It appears that students in Northeastern and Southern Ontario have mixed views of the past, more so than students in Eastern Ontario. The optimism of Eastern Ontario students is possibly due to what Gilbert calls the cultural comfort of the Ottawa region, which is characterized by a large, active francophone population, an institutionalized network, and bilingual services and job opportunities offered by the federal government. The close proximity of Quebec is also an important factor for Eastern Ontarians, who encounter Québécois in the course of many activities. These conditions ensure that francophones in that region have greater cultural security, which leads them to make a more positive assessment of their past. From this perspective, the Franco-Ontarian community sees the battles over Regulation 17 and the Montfort Hospital as tangible victories. Also, the presence of the federal government in Ottawa reinforces the idea that francophones have fully acquired the collective rights that are necessary for their community to thrive. The following student from

Figure 1.3 Narrative orientations of Ontario students by region

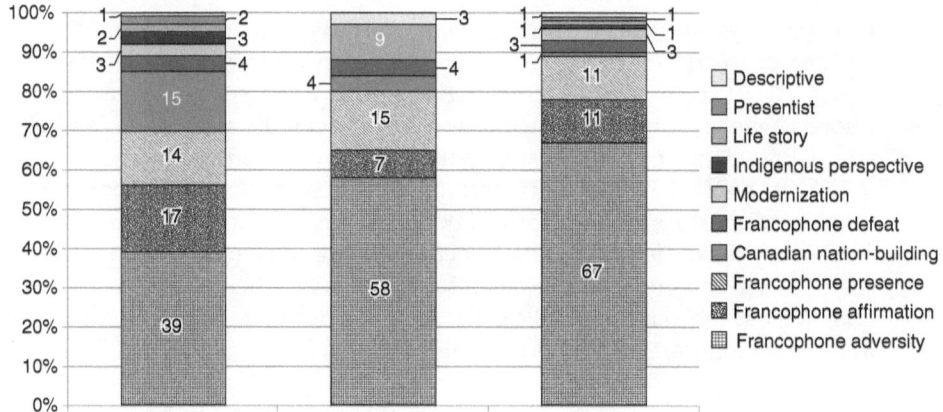

Eastern Ontario expresses his optimistic pride in francophone victories with reference to the Franco-Ontarian Flag Day:

> Francophones fought for several years to keep their language. Anglophones and Francophones continued to fight to keep their language. Francophones were able to keep their language. They are found everywhere in Ontario ... Each year we celebrate the Franco-Ontarian Flag Day. (112A01-East)

Interestingly, it is also in this Ontario region that the *Canadian nation-building* perspective is most popular (15%). The presence of the federal government, whose institutions and symbols are omnipresent in Ottawa's urban landscape, and the fact that Canadian public services employ a large number of bilingual citizens (possibly the students' own parents) are additional factors that encourage greater attachment to Canada. The following is a good example:

> People from Europe/Great Britain came for fishing. At one point, a sailman to explored further the continent. He discovered Canada. Another one wanted to populate the new country. He led the construction of the railway across all of Canada in order to populate the west. The population has grown. There was also the Gold Rush that attracted +++ immigrants to

Canada. Growing up a lot and formed various provinces to join Canada. We have been under the command of Great Britain. We fought for our independence. We had to fight for French and French rights. The various groups joined to form modern Canada. We had to accept different cultures to settle the North and the Prairies (West). We have grown a lot thanks to the wheat/cereal market. We continue to welcome many immigrants who make us grow. (0110A16-East)

In addition, stories of *francophone defeat* are relatively few in Ontario compared to Quebec. In total, they account for 4%, 4%, and 3% respectively for Eastern, Northeastern, and Southern Ontario. We can say with some confidence that young Franco-Ontarians have a fairly positive or nuanced view of the historical experience of their community, particularly in Eastern Ontario. In contrast, students from Northeastern Ontario are more likely to tell stories along the lines of *life experience*. These students tell personal stories related to schooling or their family situation as a way to explain the historical experience of their community:

> I do not think I've learned anything about Francophones in the past or maybe I do not remember it. But I participated in a play that came to my city and my school. This play was about this very topic but I only remember the part that I was in. I believe this is regulation 17: when francophones finally got rid of a law that did not allow teachers and students to learn in French language. (2010A10-North)

As seen in figure 1.4, Quebec students offer stories that are less supportive of *francophone adversity* (between 37% and 49%) than those of their counterparts in Ontario, and more sympathetic to the *francophone presence* (between 13% and 28%). Gatineau students present a special case. It is in this region that the stories of adversity are fewest and those of *francophone presence* most prevalent:

> The "territory" after several conflicts and regimes became English and French with New France, then Upper Canada and Lower Canada, the Province of Quebec. Finally, those who wanted to be closer to the English-language way of working were going to Ontario. That is why there are Franco-Ontarians today. (0105A06-Gatineau)

The economy of this region, which straddles the Ontario border, is closely intertwined with that of the federal capital. The inhabitants

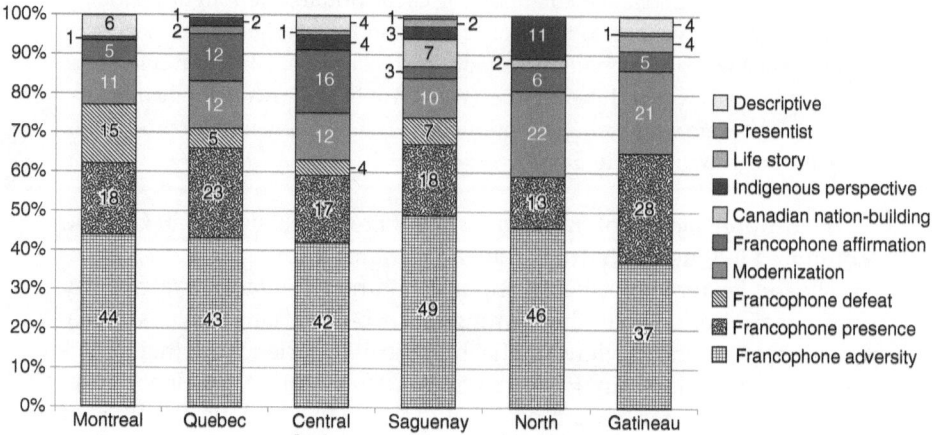

Figure 1.4 Narrative orientations of Quebec students by region

of Gatineau cross interprovincial bridges on a daily basis to work, study, visit, and shop in Ottawa, rendering the notion of borders relatively vague. In addition, the citizens of this region have, along with Montreal, the highest rate of bilingualism in the province. It may be that bilingualism and interprovincial interactions make local students moderate in their national views and more descriptive in their stories of the collective past. This does not, however, lead them to tell narratives of *Canadian nation-building*, as in Eastern Ontario. From this perspective, Gatineau students do not embrace the same visions as those from across the Ottawa River. As we will see in chapter 4, their national allegiance is to Quebec, not so much to Canada, even if their stories undoubtedly reveal less nationalist feelings than elsewhere in the province.

The same phenomenon can be observed in stories of *modernization*, which are encountered primarily in Gatineau (21%) and to the north of Montreal (22%). For students, this narrative orientation may be a strategic way to escape traditional nationalist narratives, with their emphasis on the English "Other," which has very little resonance for them. Students from Gatineau have their views rooted in Quebec, and this leads them to take refuge in narrative orientations of the *francophone presence* or *modernization*, both frameworks deemed more nationally neutral and less emotionally charged:

About 500 years ago, Christopher Columbus discovered North America. Around the 17th century, the first French who travelled to America founded the city of Quebec. His name is Samuel de Champlain. The King of France sent an explorer to look for resources, but the king was disappointed to learn that there were no resources he could exploit. Yet settlers learned to use wood to do a lot of things and lumber became the world's largest market at the time. In the same century, the King of France sent the *Filles du Roy* to New France so that French settlers could repopulate. Today we inherit these settlers who formed our society. (205A02-Gatineau)

Surprisingly, the *francophone defeat* orientation is not frequently used in Quebec, except in Montreal (15%), which stands out from the rest of the province. This pessimistic view of the past possibly draws on the urban multicultural environment, where francophones rub shoulders with different cultures and where the status and influence of the English language is more visible in the public space. Under these conditions, young francophones fear that English will inevitably supplant the French language and that cultural diversity will threaten the identity of francophones, as stated by the following student:

Culture, language, traditions have changed because of adaptation. Today in Quebec, laws have been passed to protect the language and culture of Quebec because they are threatened by multiculturalism. (GR0512-Montreal)

This vision of the past and fear for the future was not found elsewhere in the province. In fact, when combining results for *francophone defeat* with the low number of positive *francophone affirmation* stories (5%), we find that students from Montreal have the least favourable view of the past and vision for the future:

With the arrival of English-speaking immigrants we begin to worry about the survival of French, the language that distinguishes Quebecers from the rest of Canada and its culture, we want to preserve it and measures are taken, Bill 101 is applied. Today, French is still one of the official languages but English continues to expand and enter our lives (work, business, friend), part of Quebec now speaks almost English only. (GR0518-Montreal)

In contrast, stories of *francophone affirmation* are favourably expressed in two of Quebec's most francophone regions, Quebec City and Central Quebec. However, students from Saguenay, another culturally francophone region, do not follow this pattern. These participants challenge certain preconceived ideas about francophone culture and the national narrative. Indeed, it is in this region that the orientation of *francophone adversity* receives the highest support (49%) and *francophone defeat* some of the lowest support (7%). Students in Saguenay do not convey an optimistic view of their past. Barely 3% of their stories support the *francophone affirmation* orientation. Another surprising element regarding this traditionally nationalist region is the presence of stories of *Canadian nation-building* (7%), the highest percentage in the province. The following student from Saguenay describes the historical experience of francophones in the development of Canada:

> The British won in 1763 and took over the francophone colony of New France. Until 1848 when the francophones finally get a responsible government. On the other hand, this will not prevent many anglophones, such as the Loyalists and citizens of countries devastated by the war, from coming to settle ... This territory will then split into two parts in 1791 called Upper and Lower Canada, now called Ontario and Quebec. In addition, the rest of Canada today is mainly anglophone, making Quebec the only French-speaking province in Canada. (04A17-Saguenay)

Finally, students from the North of Montreal region present a high percentage of stories of *modernization* (22%) and, surprisingly, stories of *Indigenous perspective* (11%), which is a unique case in the province. This type of narrative pays particular attention to Indigenous peoples by expressing understanding of their historical perspectives in the context of European colonialism, and also by trying to rehabilitate their place in national history. Interestingly, these students are the only ones in our study who open a place for Indigenous citizens in modern Canadian society. Other students prefer to talk about Indigenous peoples in the colonial period as if they had disappeared from contemporary history. Their experiences are relegated to past times:

> In −33,000 BC arrived the Aboriginals. The Aboriginals bartered, their religion was called animism and they lived in long houses that contained several families (5 and more). Later, thanks to Christopher Columbus (1492) and Jacques Cartier (1503) who discovered America, the Europeans traded with the Aboriginals (rifles, spices, alcohol, etc. against fur). Then, the Europeans tried to assimilate the Aboriginals so as to take over their

land and exploit natural resources (mining) and expand their commerce using the river way. (GR0632-Montreal)

The French found Canada. Because of fish and fur, they traded with the Aboriginals. They killed Aboriginals to colonize Quebec as they did not want to assimilate. Then the English colonized the French. Today, Aboriginals are not recognized. (GR0601-Montreal)

The analysis of the data per region indicates that important regional variations exist within each province. It appears that the historical consciousness of young people is built not only on a larger, global scale at the national level, but also according to historical roots in particular local settings. This regional positionality leads them to create representations of the past through social, economic, and cultural lenses, and even sometimes to distance themselves from official grand narratives. In the process, they narrate a story of the past that reflects the reality of their own living environment.

Conclusion

Francophone students from Ontario and Quebec share a Canadian state and make references to a collective memory. Yet they inhabit different provincial territories with distinct political authorities, cultural practices, and history programs. These divergences are evident in how they have interpreted the notion of "country" in their narratives. While most young Franco-Ontarians have defined it in reference to Canada, their peers in Quebec have instead focused their stories on the francophone experience in the province of Quebec.

Interestingly, students in both groups tend to share the same narrative framework of the historical experience of adversity and struggle of French Canadians in a predominantly English-speaking country. The defining moment in this narrative for Franco-Ontarians is the Regulation 17 crisis and, to a lesser extent, their successful opposition to the closing of Montfort Hospital in the 1990s. For Quebec students, their national narrative is a series of struggles and contests, with the Conquest of New France as a defining moment, much like Regulation 17 is for Ontario. The Conquest serves to define their community in reference to the English "Other" who reminds them of their status as a conquered people and of their long struggle for collective affirmation. Regulation 17 plays a different role in Ontario. Students exploit this dramatic event as a catalyst for community-building. In doing so, they remember Regulation 17 as a useful lesson for present-day struggles. This view is reinforced by cultural and curricular references in Franco-Ontarian education.

Finally, the vision of the future is relatively similar for both groups. There are no clearly marked differences between francophones in Quebec and Ontario in this regard, except perhaps that Franco-Ontarians are slightly more optimistic about their future, particularly in Eastern Ontario. It is a strange paradox that students from French-speaking Quebec seem to be more fearful of their future than their colleagues living in a minority situation in Ontario. This unexpected finding reminds us that students' own narratives of the collective past are not primarily devised by scholarly canons of historical thinking and writing; rather, they are crafted in reference to experiences, emotions, schematic representations, and even mythistories that structure their historical understanding of the country. By neglecting the important impact of historical culture on young French Canadians, history education can easily ignore students' preconceived ideas of the nation and their uses of the past. In many ways, students' narrative representations reflect the ideologies of current political orders among francophone communities, with limited attention to marginalized groups within society. The negligible place given to Indigenous peoples in students' narratives of the country is one obvious indicator of the need to engage their oversimplified perspective, which continues to uphold dominant, stereotypical representations of the "Others."

2
History, Territory, and the Nation

Attachment to land plays an important role in shaping a sense of collective identity. The homeland establishes the milieu within which it becomes possible to imagine sites of remembrance and realms of memory.[1] Attachment to land can also generate important emotional ties to what the French language refers to as "terroir," a particular cultural understanding of land, including its human capital and histories. This attachment to land may be considered in two distinct ways: as an attachment to *place*, that is, specific locations of particular historical significance; and as an attachment to *space*, a more abstract type of attachment to a larger entity that has sociopolitical significance. The studies of Létourneau in Quebec and Robichaud in Acadia (NB) have revealed the importance of land, whether as a geopolitical entity or an imaginary territory, in shaping a collective memory. Québécois and Acadians have developed what we might called place-based narratives of the past. In *National Dreams*, Daniel Francis offers a similar argument with regard to English Canadians and their reference to the "True North strong and free" as in the National Anthem. For them, he argues, "north is more than a point on a compass. It is a region, a territory, a vast intimidating part of the country somewhere beyond easy comfort." The myth of the North has come to signify a vast territory different from the United States: Canadians feel themselves to be a unique northern nation with a "graspable destiny."[2] Canada's Indigenous peoples, who have inhabited the continent since time immemorial, also have an intricate spiritual, emotional, and physical connection to the land. Traditional knowledge, languages, cultural practices, and oral traditions built up over time are all, one way or another, connected to the land. As Indigenous scholar Michael Marker observes, oral traditions and mental maps of the landscape are always "recycled from the past into the present consciousness."[3]

This process, Marker argues, is important for connecting the landscape with the mindscape.

In a context of increasing mobility and diversity of perspectives, how do twenty-first-century students connect with their country? What geographical references and historical symbols do they use to tell their stories? This chapter considers students' narratives from a geographical perspective. More specifically, we look at how participants interpret the notion of "country" and how territory and space serve to define the geographical locus of their stories. This leads us to examine in the next section students' histories in relation to their place of residence. We are interested in ascertaining whether the particular places students live affect their visions of the past, of their country.

Imagining the Land: The Geographical Orientations of Students' Narratives

National memories, patriotic feelings, and social claims are grounded in particular spaces. Reference to the land – the homeland – is central to national history. People remember particular battlegrounds, they visit dedicated sites of memory, and they attend local celebrations. But what happens in a multi-national country like Canada in which the nation and state do not naturally correspond? Our study asked participants to tell the history of French Canadians in this "country." How did students interpret the notion of country? Where were their narratives located? Would we find differences between students from different regions?

According to our analysis (see figures 2.1 and 2.2), Quebec and Ontario students do not have the same definition of the country. Over half (52%) of Quebec participants concentrate their histories of French Canada on the Quebec territory, while slightly more than one-third (38%) focus on Canada. Interestingly, the third most important space for situating their stories is America (6%). This last group of students is more likely to present the history of French Canadian development in the larger continental context of North America. The following excerpts present examples of geographical orientations of students' narratives. Note that for many students the country represents not only a historical piece of land but also a political space for collective attachment. Our findings corroborate the views of the national study *Canadians and Their Pasts*, which confirms that Québécois are far more likely to identify with their province than residents of Canada are to identify with their country as a whole.[4]

Figure 2.1 Territorial orientations of Quebec students' narratives

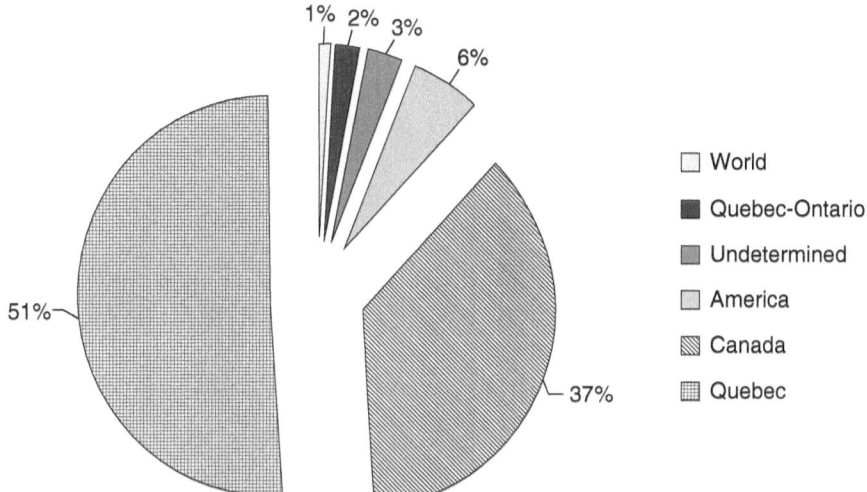

Quebec
The history of Quebec begins when French Europeans arrive in Quebec City by boat. They will then colonize this territory in their own way as well as make it bigger. Later, the English invade the territory and take control. So there are rebellions and many constitutions are put in place. There is subsequently the idea of Quebec sovereignty as an ideology for the Quebec people. (105A13-Gatineau)

Canada
Following the conquest of America there was a war and the English took over the territory of the French. The English established new laws and imposed their regime on the entire population. A few years later, Canada was split into Upper Canada and Lower Canada, one Canada for the English and the other for the French. (05A06-North of Montreal)

America
The French were in Europe and Christopher Columbus discovered America so they colonized it. The English were also part of the colonization of America and there were wars for control over the territory. (GR0608-Montréal)

In Ontario, students' results are the opposite. Over half (52%) of their narratives present a story situated in the country of Canada while

Figure 2.2 Territorial orientations of Ontario students' narratives

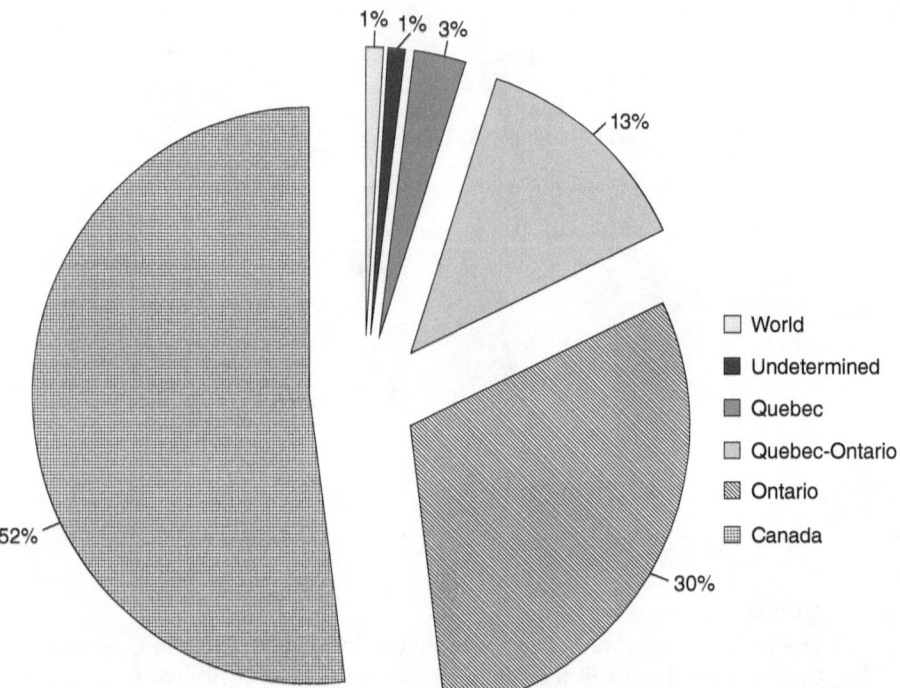

slightly less than one third (30%) are located in the province of Ontario. A significant minority (13%) tell stories situated in both Ontario and Quebec, referring to the colonial territory of Upper Canada (Ontario) and Lower Canada (Quebec). For Franco-Ontarian students, Canada is *de facto* the geographical space for situating the history of French Canadians. Unlike the Québécois, the majority of Franco-Ontarians do not use the province as the symbolic space for telling their national history. Canada continues to serve this important function to them.

Saying this is not to say that Ontario participants invariably present stories of *Canadian nation-building* from coast to coast. In fact, the majority of Franco-Ontarian students used Canada as a conduit for telling the history of French Canadian development *within* Canada. This is an interesting nuance. Canada is interpreted at different space levels. It can be seen at a larger state level (country) but possibly at some higher levels of resolution where the focus in on a particular collectivity such as French Canadians or Franco-Ontarians, as stated by the following students:

Canada
Since the arrival of the French in Canada we had to fight for equality and even today Ontario is a province where speaking in French can be difficult. During the Regulation 17 crisis we did not give up our rights and we fought back to get what we wanted, to speak our language. (011A112 North)

Ontario
The Francophonie began about 400 years ago when the French explorers came to our country. One of the most outstanding explorers is Étienne Brulec [sic]. He explored southern Ontario. The French were also the first to arrive and take the exploitation of natural resources. (012A08-East)

Quebec and Ontario
The history of francophones begins in France, which then spread to New France, including part of Canada (Quebec), the root from which Canada's Francophonie originates. While the root is in Quebec, Quebecers also moved to Ontario, which contributed to the Franco-Ontarian identity. (210A08-South)

Still, an significant minority of participants place their narrative focus on Ontario and even on French Ontario with reference to key French/English struggles or French explorers like Étienne Brûlé, sometimes referred to as the first Franco-Ontarian. At least two factors can help explain students' attention to provincial spaces, whether it is Ontario–Quebec or Ontario. First, many students evoke the memory of New France and its colonial development in the Saint Lawrence Valley and the Great Lakes region. In many ways, New France continues to represent for them a common heritage and collective venture that all French Canadians share. Second, Ontario students typically start their story with the French colonial past in much the same narrative way as Quebec students. The voyages of Jacques Cartier and the influential roles of Samuel de Champlain, French explorer and colonial administrator, and Jean Talon, French intendant of New France, are common to both student groups; they do not belong exclusively to Québécois. Divergences in narrative appear later in text when Franco-Ontarians focus on subsequent events such as the Ontario schools question. Interestingly, Quebec students rarely (2%) raise in their narratives events or memories from Ontario or other Canadian regions. Their stories are located primarily within the Quebec imagined community. French Canadian collective historical memory seems to flow in one direction, from Franco-Ontarians to Québécois, not the other way around. In fact, Quebec students are more likely (6%) to refer to America than to other Canadian regions.

As we noted earlier, Ontario and Quebec are vast provincial territories comprised of multiple distinct regions. Some are urban and culturally diverse; others are rural and homogeneous. Does a sense of regional belonging influence how our participants see their country?

Regions of Ontario

The seven public schools chosen for our study were located in three Ontario regions. As indicated in figure 2.3, Eastern Ontario students are most likely to focus their narratives on Canada (64%) and less likely to refer to the province (21%). For many, their sense of national belonging is to the Canadian state, not the province. The prominence of Ottawa as the federal capital and the political influence of the various federal institutions in the region (which employ more than 145,000 local workers) helps explain students' preference for Canada as the geographical space for their stories. As this Ontario student puts it:

> In 1867 Canada finally became a unique and autonomous country. The first French Canadian prime minister we had was Wilfrid Laurier and this man did a great job, but people in those times had a problem with that because he was French ... Today, the Prime Minister is bilingual because of the wonderful impact of Wilfrid and many others who had an impact on Canada and helped to develop this wonderful country, Canada. (110A112-East)

The situation in Northeastern Ontario is different. More than half (55%) of the participants prefer to focus on the province of Ontario; fewer than one third (29%) emphasize Canada. Only 12% identify the region of Ontario/Quebec as the locus of their stories. The historical culture of Northeastern Ontario plays a significant role in students' narrative orientations. Culturally homogeneous and far from Ontario's metropolitan centres, Northeastern Ontario has developed among its local residents a distinctive sense of self and a strong local attachment to cultural activities and realizations (festivals, concerts, exhibits, etc.).

> The French wanted to establish a great French empire so they settled in Northern Ontario to the West. This is why it has more French-speaking cities in the North (Cochrane, Timmins, Sudbury). (110A001-North)

Figure 2.3 Territorial orientation of Ontario students' narratives by region

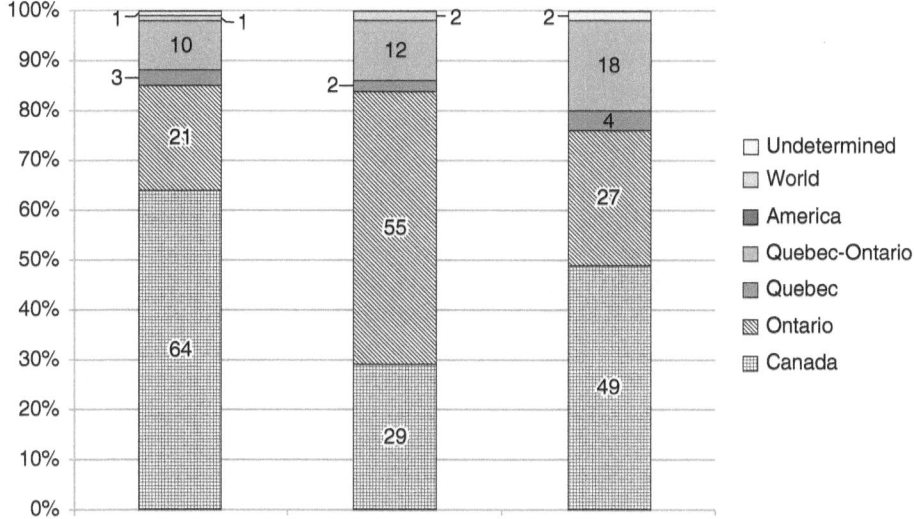

Southern Ontario students occupy a transitional position between the East and the North. Almost half (49%) of them focus their narratives on Canada, roughly one quarter (27%) on Ontario. Interestingly, a significant number of students (18%) tell stories of Ontario/Quebec history. This unique result might be explained by the historical context of Southern Ontario. As noted earlier, some border communities such as Windsor can trace their origins back to eighteenth-century French settlements. Locals continue to take great pride in this historic presence in the region:

> The history of the country's francophones began when Europeans arrived by boat. Samuel des Champlain, one of the first Europeans to come to Canada and settled in Quebec. From there, after Samuel founded the country we live in today, many French immigrants came to the country. Little by little, the French began to populate different regions. Many francophones used canoes and sailed the St. Lauren River all the way to southern Ontario. Immigration has continued, and the francophone population has continued to expand in the country. (112A15-South)

Regions of Quebec

Participants from Quebec schools were located in six regions: Montreal, Quebec City, Central Quebec, Saguenay, North of Montreal, and Gatineau. As noted in figure 2.4, the percentage of narratives focused on the province of Quebec varies significantly from one region to another, ranging from 33% to 63%. We also find important variations with regard to Canada (between 29% and 47%). Interestingly, it is in the multicultural region of Montreal that the emphasis on the province is most significant, and in Saguenay, a highly homogenous and traditionally nationalist region, that it is the least significant. In many ways, the focus on the Quebec provincial territory is not a simple geographical decision but a highly political one, with ample references to French and English struggles in the province. From that point of view, the French/English cultural context of Montreal underscores for local students their difficult circumstances as francophones. Daily contacts with anglophone and immigrant "Others" remind them of their precarious situation.

> The first French speaker was a person from France ... The first francophones were of course not people of our country. After a few years, French became our first language and English our second language in Quebec. We struggled for our language, that's why we still have it today. Today, we accept many people from foreign countries so that one day we could lose our language, French, it would be replaced by English, because the majority speaks English in our country. (GR0413-Montreal)

The struggle for the French language in Quebec is not exclusively a concern for native French-speaking Montrealers. Several students from immigrant backgrounds support the claims of Québécois. The following participant, originally from the United States, believes that the Québécois, like the Indigenous peoples, are distinct peoples in Canada who have historically faced oppression and assimilation. They want to be recognized as nations, but in her view, national history is still unfolding in a way that is perpetuating linguistic pressure and collective anxiety:

> The French arrived here a long time ago, when we made Quebec a colony ... There was a lot of Anglophone influence and that tell us what we know today as Quebecois. At a certain point, "Quebec" passed under the influence of the English and they tried to assimilate everyone (Francophone + Native Americans). There were a lot of battles, because the francophones

Figure 2.4 Territorial orientation of Quebec students' narratives by region

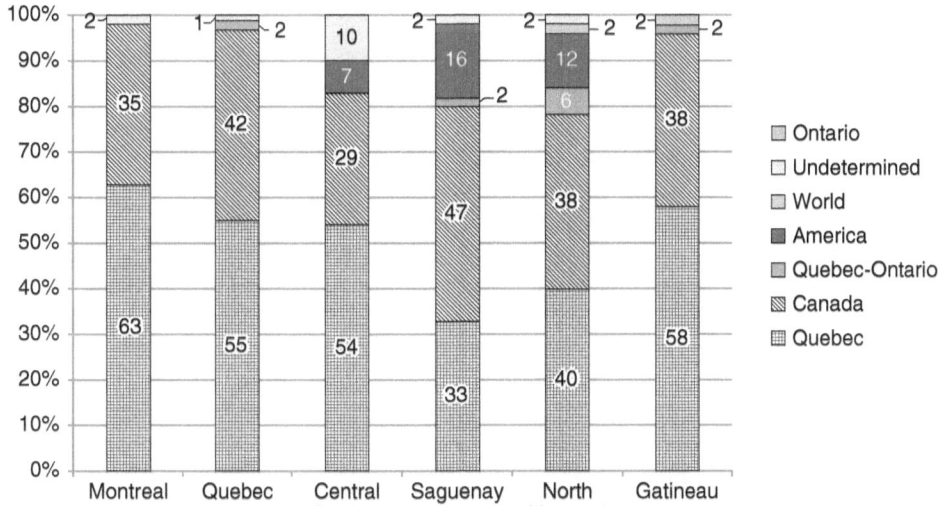

did not want to be under their control anymore. The history of the francophones, in my opinion, is still going on today. Quebecers want at all costs to be recognized as Quebecers, their culture as well, and they are active for the preservation of French. (GR0505-Montréal)

Results from the Gatineau region are also surprising. A majority of students (58%) from this border region with Ontario position their narratives in the province of Quebec. Despite strong economic ties and countless cultural encounters between the two provinces, Gatineau students do not display a stronger interest in telling a national history in Canada. The provincial border between Ontario and Quebec runs deep through the consciousness of these students:

In my opinion, the most important moments are during the Quebec revolt against the British. Despite their defeats and the dead, Quebecers have not been assimilated and have preserved the French language. (105A05-Gatineau)

The Saguenay region has long been a nationalist bastion. But surprisingly, our participants offer contrasting results. Almost half (47%) of students' narratives are focused on Canada compared to only one third

(33%) on the province of Quebec. What could account for this unusual finding? Three reasons come to mind. First, the number of participants (n = 62) is relatively low. It is always a challenge to generalize from a small sample. It is possible that these students offer narratives that do not represent local students' ideas about national history. As such, our results should be interpreted carefully.

But other factors lead us to think that our participants are not necessarily outliers. Indeed, like the Quebec sovereigntist movement itself, nationalist feelings among the younger generation of Québécois have changed drastically, especially in traditionally nationalist regions. Quebec nationalism seems to have gradually given way to other allegiances and claims (e.g., to international trade, the environment, and social programs) that transcend the traditional antagonism between Quebec and Canada. The region's economic situation is clearly an important factor in explaining this shift. Like Northeastern Ontario, Saguenay is a resource-based region. In this regard, the recession of 2008 was an eye-opener. While many left the region to seek work, others took the opportunity to reposition the regional economy on the global stage, with an emphasis on new media and technologies. The recent arrival of Ubisoft, a leading international computer games developer (e.g., *Assassin's Creed*), is an example of technological innovation that has had an impact on how young citizens imagine their future.

The third reason pertains to the possible influence of the History and Citizenship Education (HCE) program on students' narratives. As noted in the introduction, Quebec nationalists have criticized the HCE curriculum for "denationalizing" Quebec's national claims and focusing instead on social history and citizenship education. Students from Saguenay offer narratives much in line with that of the HCE program. Whether this a direct effect of school history is unclear. But as we will see in chapter 4, the strong focus on Canada, and to a certain extent America, is linked to additional social factors that students take into account when telling the history of French Canadians. One of those factors is colonialism and its negative impact on local Indigenous peoples and their ancestral land, which, as the following student puts it, was "stolen." The establishment of a reserve system governed by the Indian Act of Canada is sometimes acknowledged by Saguenay students as a damaging legacy of French and British colonial policies that has endured to this day:

> Francophones are people who speak French, francophones arrived in Quebec during an exploration trip by Christopher Columbus. When he arrived on the soil of this beautiful province, he realized that they were not the first ones to discover this magnificent territory ... After many years of war and conflict, the French have stolen almost all the territory from the Aboriginals,

so today there is a law for First Nations and reserves, but still we stole a good part of their land. Several political party leaders later tried to separate Quebec from Canada, especially the Parti Québécois. (04A20-Saguenay)[5]

What Themes and Characters Do Students Refer To?

Narratives have an internal structure with sentences and keywords that provide meaningful units for creating a structured vision of the past. What concepts, terms, characters, and events do students use to structure their stories of French Canadians? Are there convergences and divergences between Quebec and Ontario participants?

As noted in Table 2.1, the top key terms used by students in their narratives refer to common concepts such as French, English, Quebec, France, and Canada. While the order is somewhat different between the two groups (Canada comes second for Franco-Ontarians and France third for Québécois), the variations are not significant. But as we go down the list, more important differences emerge. Quebec students privilege elements more closely associated with New France, while Ontario students choose concepts related to the Ontario schools question.

New France in Quebec Narratives

We indicated earlier that New France is a vital historical reference and the starting point for students' narratives both in Quebec and in Ontario. That being said, Quebec participants are far more likely to refer to it. Whether this is an effect of the HCE program, which places greater emphasis on this historical period, or a manifestation of French Canadian collective memory, is not clear. What *is* clear is the significance of New France for orienting students' visions of the past. When looking at Table 2.2, we see that the key terms most associated with New France, such as "colony," "fur," "trade," "Filles du Roi," and "discovery," are cited far more frequently by Quebec students, representing on average over 80% of all citations per key term.

In many ways, New France is an inescapable element in Quebec students' narratives. It is, in Propp's words, a recurrent constant in the larger narrative template of French Canadian history. It is the defining feature for explaining the presence of francophones in Quebec, well before the references to the Conquest or to Confederation. The following two excerpts highlight its significance in Quebec students' narratives:

> As I know it, the story of the francophones in the country is like this: after the discovery of North America, France made the decision to send its citizens to populate the "territory," for them, New France. (GR0625-Montreal)

Table 2.1 Key terms most frequently mentioned in Quebec and Ontario students' narratives

Rank	Key terms	Quebec (frequency)	Rank	Key terms	Ontario (frequency)
1	French	935	1	French	833
2	Quebec	517	2	Canada	434
3	France	512	3	Francophone	420
4	English	494	4	English	299
5	Canada	416	5	Language	237
6	Francophone	410	6	Country	198
7	We	376	7	I	194
8	Territory	314	8	School	190
9	New France	307	9	Quebec	186
10	Colony	296	10	War	185
11	War	256	11	We	164
12	Language	253	12	France	130
13	Our(s)	195	13	Rights	119
14	King	187	14	Ontario	119

Table 2.2 Key terms associated with New France cited in Quebec and Ontario students' narratives

Key terms	Quebec (frequency)	%	Ontario (frequency)	%
New France	307	83	62	17
Colony	296	94	19	6
America	176	94	12	6
Aboriginal/Indigenous	169	91	16	9
Fur	137	97	4	3
Jacques Cartier	103	70	45	30
Filles du Roi	87	84	16	16
Trade	79	96	3	4
Settler	73	88	10	12
Samuel de Champlain	48	49	49	51
Jean Talon	43	75	14	25
Discovery	33	79	9	21

At the origins a land of trade and furs, French settlers create a new country, New France. (GR0631-Montreal)

The references to historical characters offer a more palatable portrait of students' emphasis on New France. French navigator and explorer Jacques Cartier, who is sometimes confused with Christopher Columbus, is the leading figure in Quebec. Students refer to him extensively when discussing the European explorations of the sixteenth century that would lead to the settlement of New France. As this student puts it: "The history of French Canadians starts with the arrival of Jacques Cartier in Quebec in the 16th century" (0105A04-Gatineau).

Jean Talon is another symbolic figure among Quebec participants. The first intendant of New France, he is most remembered by students for his leading role in bringing the "Filles du Roi" – unmarried women sponsored by the French king to immigrate to New France between 1663 and 1673 – to populate the small colony in the seventeenth century. "The number of women was so low," writes one Quebec student, "that Jean Talon brought in the Filles du Roi to populate the colony which will later become the Province of Quebec" (04B09-Quebec City). Another female student from Quebec City recounts the context of the time: "The king establishes the royal government and sends the filles du roi as well as poor families from France. He gives monetary incentives to large families and fines those who are not married by the age of 18 years old" (05B15-Quebec City).

Samuel de Champlain is an emblematic person in French Canada and is shared almost equally by students from both groups. He established the first permanent settlement in Quebec (1608); he was also an explorer who ventured into the interior of the continent as far as the Great Lakes. His prominence is such in collective memory that an imposing statue of Champlain, his famous astrolabe in hand, is strategically placed in Ottawa, overlooking the river. So it is no surprise that Champlain is also recognized among Ontario students (cited forty-nine times) even more that Étienne Brûlé (cited eleven times), the first recorded European to visit Upper Canada:[6]

> The first fishermen were not exclusively French. They came from Spain and England (Basques, Normands, Britons) but Samuel de Champlain arrived and founded Quebec in 1608 (or slightly before that), "Canada" is officially French [and] that is why Francophones trace their ancestry back to France. (04C02-Québec)
>
> In 1608, Samuel de Champlain is the first French settler in America. He established New France and the permanent settlement of Quebec by the same occasion. Gradually, New France will expand its territory. (04B11-Quebec City)
>
> The King sends more and more people to Canada. Among them are Samuel de Champlain and Étienne Brûlé. Samuel establishes Quebec City and Etienne explores the vast territory of New France. (0112A14-East)

Interestingly, the importance given to New France by Quebec students has a broadening effect on the spatio-temporal framework of their narratives, placing Quebec history in a global geopolitical context. As indicated in Table 2.3, "France," "Great Britain," "Europe," "Asia," "India," "United States," and the "American Revolution" are cited far more frequently by Quebec students. In using these concepts, students situate the history of French Canada in reference to wider

Table 2.3 Key international terms cited in Quebec and Ontario students' narratives

Key terms	Quebec (frequency)	%	Ontario (frequency)	%
France	512	80	130	20
British	103	83	21	17
England	69	71	28	29
Great Britain	46	71	19	29
Europe	43	74	15	26
United States	40	58	29	42
Asia	40	98	1	2
Revolution (Fr./Am.)	40	70	17	30
India	37	90	4	10
European	28	64	16	36

international movements such as European colonialism, international trade, and other great transformations including wars, migrations, and revolutions.

> England took possession of New France and in our cities the English made their appearance and a large part of their migration was due to the war of independence of the 13 colonies which deported hundreds of subjects of the Queen. (05A10-Saguenay)
>
> Following the American War of Independence, many English Loyalists immigrated to the country now called Canada. They established their culture, their religion and their language. (04A06-Quebec City)

Note, however, that Quebec students' attention to the larger global context is largely limited to the colonial period and to European history, without much consideration for Indigenous presence, treaties, and land claims. Indeed, after the Conquest of New France, their narratives gradually fall back on the Quebec political territory as if the land had irreversibly been settled for good. References to First peoples, Europe, the United States, and Asia become negligible except when referring to major international conflicts such as the two world wars.

The Conquest: The Untold Defeat

One striking element when looking at students' narratives is the lack of explicit mention of the "Conquest." This is all the more surprising when we consider how this tragic event in the history of French Canada has led to a collective sense of *survivance* and sparked heated debates among Canadian historians and politicians.[7] When examining students' narratives more closely, we find that the Conquest is still present in the text but without that specific term being used. Indeed, several ideas refer to this event without explicitly naming it – for example, the "Battle of the Plains of Abraham," the "British war," the "English war," the "takeover," or simply "the war." In fact, the word *war* ranks eleventh among the terms most used and refers most frequently to the "War of the Conquest," which, in students' terms, signifies the Seven Years' war in North America. It is mentioned no less than 256 times by Quebec students (58%) compared to 185 times by Franco-Ontarian students (42%):

> It was in the 1500s that Jacques Cartier landed for the first time on what would become Quebec. Unlike the inhabitants already installed, he speaks French. Years passed, New France, a colony belonging to France, spread French throughout America. After two and a half centuries, the colony will have roughly 63,000 inhabitants, all French-speaking. These habitants and their descendants will face a major cultural challenge because the British will take over the territory in 1760. (GR0101-Gatineau)

As with the references to New France, the Conquest represents a constant in students' narratives, most particularly among the Quebec City participants. For them it is a turning point in history, a moment in time that set French Canadians on a radically different course. For students, the Conquest opens the door to visions of the past marked by collective struggle and continuous adversity. For some, it is located in the colonial aspiration for French expansion on a vast, hostile continent already populated by local Indigenous people and dominated by British forces and their ambitious merchants. For others, the Conquest marks the abrupt end to the dream of a continent-wide French-speaking society possessing immense territories and rich economic ties extending from Hudson Bay in the north to the mouth of the Mississippi in the south. After the Conquest, French Canada faces a completely different reality. Francophones are now a small minority under the British Crown, swimming for survival in an English-speaking ocean. Assimilation becomes the dominant threat.

> Everything shifts during the conquest of France (New France) by Great Britain (Thirteen Colonies). This is the capitulation of Montreal. Suddenly the French are under the influence of the King of Great Britain. (04B19-Quebec City)
> Years went by and New France lost the Battle of the Plains of Abraham and ultimately the whole territory after the Conquest. They were under the military regime until the end of the war between France and England.

Since then, francophones are under the authority of the Queen of England. (04A08-Quebec City)

Then the War of the Conquest. The French lost all their territories and colony. There were numerous attempts to assimilate [them]. (GR0426-Quebec City)

Regulation 17: The Other Turning Point

Québécois consider the Conquest the pivotal event in French Canadian history. Franco-Ontarians have established their own history marker – the infamous Regulation 17 of 1912, which restricted the use of French as a language of instruction. Franco-Ontarians reacted with public outrage to this decree. The response in francophone communities was such that the conflict extended to the élites of French Canada and the entire Catholic clergy, who mobilized the population to side with Franco-Ontarians.[8] Henri Bourassa, editor of *Le Devoir*, a prominent French Canadian newspaper, and a strong supporter of the "founding nations" principle, used the context of the First World War to denounce what he called the "Prussians of Ontario" for their far-reaching decision and offered his support to the national cause of Franco-Ontarians.[9] The Franco-Ontarian cause also came to the attention of the Judicial Committee of the Privy Council, the highest court of appeal in the British Empire.[10] Unable to fully enforce Regulation 17 due to strong local resistance, the government of Ontario introduced a new policy in 1927 intended to improve bilingual instruction in schools.

As we can see in Table 2.4, students use several key terms when discussing the Ontario schools question. References to "school," "Regulation 17," "teaching," and "rights" are extremely frequent among Franco-Ontarian students. These are not neutral terms in students' narratives. They are associated with the resistance movement and the need to "fight" for French-language rights. In the minds of participants, Regulation 17 remains to this day a traumatic event for the Franco-Ontarian community:

There was the deportation of Acadians in Louisiana and several other atrocities such as Regulation 17 which prohibited the teaching of French in schools. (112A16-East)

There is also the Regulation 17 which prohibited French language instruction. Because French Canadians were a minority, they could not teach in French and there are anglophone inspectors who visited schools to control language, and if they were found to be speaking French they were punished. (0211A16-East)

Table 2.4 Key terms associated with Regulation 17 cited in Quebec and Ontario students' narratives

Key terms	Quebec (frequency)	%	Ontario (frequency)	%
Francophone	410	49	420	51
Language	253	52	237	48
School	8	4	190	96
We	376	70	164	30
Rights	60	34	119	66
Ontario	26	18	119	82
Franco-(On./Can.)	15	11	116	89
Regulation 17	0	0	111	100
Teaching	0	0	63	100
Ontarian	0	0	60	100
Fight/Struggle	12	20	48	80
Hospital	0	0	45	100

The Regulation 17 crisis also serves a practical function for students: it reminds them of the need to be vigilant in the face of ongoing linguistic battles such as the provincial attempt in the late 1990s to close Ottawa's Montfort Hospital, the only French-speaking hospital in Ontario. As with Regulation 17, the Franco-Ontarian community's response to this radical political move was such that Premier Mike Harris was forced to abandon his original plan, which had been part of the "Common Sense Revolution," a conservative ideological platform whose main goals were to reduce taxes and to downsize the role of the state.[11] From this perspective, Franco-Ontario students have mobilized memories of Regulation 17, also engraved in collective memory, in the course of understanding present-day French/English realities in Canada. Some even situate Regulation 17 as part of the ongoing struggle for post-secondary education services, including the most recent demands for a French-language university:

> Franco-Ontarians have had to work and still work for our rights as francophones. I learned about regulation 17 and how women fought for the right to speak and to teach in French. (110A10-North)
> Regulation 17 was not accepted by Franco-Ontarians, and they fought for their rights. Women among others, have fought against the authorities, several heroines, as the Desloges sisters, for example, have been recognized. Regulation 17 was abolished after a few years. Another occasion where Franco-Ontarians had to fight was the opposition to the closure of Montfort Hospital, the only completely French-speaking hospital. Today, young francophones are fighting for a completely French-speaking university. (0111A05-South)

A comparative analysis of the references to Regulation 17 reveals a critical point: after the fall of New France, Ontario and Quebec students no longer tell a common history. No Quebec participant makes any mention of Regulation 17 or recent events such as the battle over Montfort Hospital. When they talk about "language," "rights," or "school," their references are exclusively in relation to events in Quebec such as the implementation of Bill 101 (the French-language charter adopted by the Quebec government in 1977 that made French the province's official language) and the growing presence of non-francophones in Quebec society. As they understand it, French Canadian history means *Quebec* history. As the following student puts it: "From Europeans to French, we then became French Canadians and Québécois from Canada, [as] the majority of francophones are in Quebec" (04C02-Quebec City).

Some Regional Divergences

As geographer Anne Gilbert reveals in her research, Quebec and French Ontario are far from homogenous geographical entities. Each has been shaped by its own social, political, economic, and cultural forces. These forces inevitably resonate in the historical consciousness of young people, who draw from their cultural environment as well as their school and life experiences when forming a vision of the past. To investigate the impact of regionalism on students' ideas, we looked at the use of key terms in reference to their place of residence.

For Ontario, the results from Table 2.5 indicate that students from Northeastern Ontario stand out for their strong historical awareness of Franco-Ontarian struggles: they refer more frequently to "Franco-Ontarian" (46%), "school" (48%), and "Regulation 17" (52%). The fact that students from this region live in very culturally active and homogeneous communities probably does much to inform their strong identity as Franco-Ontarians. In Southern Ontario, the most multicultural region, students refer extensively to "language" (39%) and "school" (34%) – two key terms that refer to the reality of their local community and to their struggle for French-language education. It may be that Southern Ontario, being characterized by high immigration and an anglo-dominant environment, has created a milieu in which they prefer to be labelled "francophone" (30%) rather than "Franco-Ontarian" (14%), the latter being a more historically and culturally loaded identity. But even the term "francophone" is mentioned less frequently than in the other two regions. In Southern Ontario, cultural diversity seems to weaken strong cultural affiliation, at least compared to the other two regions. Students from Eastern Ontario present

Table 2.5 Key terms cited in Ontario students' narratives by region

Key terms	East		Northeastern		South	
	frequency	%	frequency	%	frequency	%
Fight/struggle	26	52	5	10	17	38
Teaching	19	30	13	21	31	49
Francophones	63	47	31	23	39	30
Franco-(On./Can.)	53	46	46	40	17	14
We	100	61	34	21	30	18
Language	130	55	16	6	91	39
Rights	58	49	24	20	37	31
School	72	38	48	28	70	34
Regulation 17	24	27	52	47	35	26
Hospital	45	82	7	13	3	5

a strong sense of collective self, with frequent mentions of "we" (61%), "francophones" (47%), and "Franco-Ontarians" (46%).

> I remember learning many things in class. When I was in elementary school on every 25th of September we went outside and sang "Our Place" by the Franco-Ontarian flag. (0111A02-East)
> Now that we have fought for our language we can belong to francophone schools [built] for Franco-Ontarians. (0111A11-East)

Interestingly, students from this region mentioned "Regulation 17" less frequently (27%), even though the historic opposition to the regulation was mainly in this region. Even the emblematic Guigues school in Ottawa and Sisters Béatrice and Diane Desloges, two female symbols of Franco-Ontarian school resistance, are scarcely mentioned (ten mentions for the Desloges sisters and no mention for Guigues).[12] Eastern Ontario students seem to have placed greater emphasis on the recent Montfort Hospital crisis than on Regulation 17, as the following student observes:

> From the moment francophones became a minority in Ontario, they had to fight for their rights. One example in modern history is Montfort hospital, francophones united and fought to keep Montfort, the only French-speaking hospital in Ontario. (0112A07-East)

In Quebec, the regional environment seems to make less of a difference in students' narratives than it does in Ontario (see Table 2.6).

Table 2.6 Key terms cited in Quebec students' narratives by region

Key terms	Quebec		Saguenay		Montreal	
	frequency	%	frequency	%	frequency	%
Aboriginal/ Indigenous	33	20	36	21	33	20
Champlain	12	25	7	15	2	4
Filles du Roi	19	22	10	11	23	26
Cartier	12	12	13	13	14	14
Fur	41	30	22	16	21	15
America	40	26	8	5	30	19
Colony	73	24	39	13	47	16
We	60	16	87	23	74	20
Francophone	77	25	54	18	50	16
	North of Montreal		Gatineau		Central Quebec	
	frequency	%	frequency	%	frequency	%
Aboriginal/ Indigenous	25	15	11	6	31	18
Champlain	5	10	14	29	8	17
Filles du Roi	10	11	9	10	16	18
Cartier	31	30	13	13	20	18
Fur	21	15	18	13	14	11
America	31	20	23	15	24	15
Colony	33	11	57	19	49	16
We	22	5	37	10	96	26
Francophone	36	12	36	12	51	17

But some interesting variations exist. Indeed, local culture, museums, and historic sites, and even local street names, can trigger memory responses and influence students' own selection and uses of the past. Thus, it is in the Gatineau region that Samuel de Champlain is most cited, probably due to the local public culture – an important interprovincial bridge bears his name, and a prominent statue of Champlain overlooking the Ottawa River is visible from both sides of the river. "In 1604," as this student from Gatineau puts it, "Samuel de Champlain landed in Quebec. It is the start of the francophone presence on our territory" (0110A15-Gatineau). Champlain, as we can see, serves an important purpose in history. He helps explain why there are francophones in the region and how the colony developed in America, the land that would become "our territory." In many ways, Champlain epitomizes a dream that historian David Hackett Fischer has memorialized in his popular book: the establishment of a successful French colony in America.[13]

Other terms, such as "Filles du Roi," "Aboriginals/Indigenous," and "colony," are particularly popular in the Montreal, Quebec City, Saguenay, and Gatineau regions. No doubt these terms are familiar to students, who recognize them as part of their regional heritage and as manifestations of popular culture. The references to "we," on the other hand, seem fairly well distributed across all Quebec regions, except perhaps for the North of Montreal, which had a smaller sample of participants, which perhaps affected the findings. In Gatineau, the limited use of "we" is possibly indicative of the students' regional identity, which is influenced by an environment that is economically integrated into the federal capital region, where the two official languages coexist.

Conclusion

Several observations can be made. First of all, francophones in Ontario and Quebec refer to common aspects of collective memory even if they are aware of belonging to two separate communities. Their stories of origins begin with the same defining episode, the founding of New France, and then take two different paths to narrate the historical experience of French Canada. The importance assigned to Regulation 17 by Franco-Ontarian students, which is completely ignored by Quebec participants, is the best example of this divergence in students' historical narratives of the nation.

The same holds true for the geographical orientations of their narratives. The majority of Ontario students define the "country" in reference to Canada, while their peers in Quebec focus their narratives on the francophone experience in the province of Quebec. Following the research of historians such as Marcel Martel, we were able to observe the obvious effect of the Quiet Revolution on young Québécois, a transformation that has redefined the historical and memory space of French Canada in strictly provincial terms. For most Quebec students, narratives of the nation function in a binary mode: stories of Quebec versus stories of Canada. Franco-Ontarian students, by contrast, view the country of Canada as the space within which it is possible to narrate different stories of the nation.

The provinces serve as the default political setting for understanding regional territories in Canada, but differences also emerge within each province. In Ontario, regional identities lead Franco-Ontarian students to emphasize distinctive aspects of the collective past. Northeastern Ontarians are more likely to ascribe historical significance to the schools question, while Eastern Ontarians relate more to episodes that took place in their own region, such as the defence of Montfort Hospital in

Ottawa. In Quebec, regional differences exist but are less pronounced. It is possible that Quebec nationalism and collective memory have had a more pervasive impact on Québécois' historical consciousness, leading them to tell relatively similar stories of the nation.

Finally, the great majority of participants in both groups express Eurocentric narratives of the country that occlude the presence of Indigenous peoples as if they do not exist as individuals or nations within Canada. Those few who acknowledge the history of colonization – primarily from the Quebec City sample – stress the negative impact of colonialism on Indigenous ways of life, as well as recent land claims and the reserve system that was created after the Canadian federation was founded. Even among these participants, their narrative views convey a vision of national history in which Indigenous peoples are part of the past and insignificant in explaining modern Canadian realities, whether it is the Indian Act, the legacy of residential schools, treaties, land claims, or self-government rights. Canada and Quebec are seen as fixed, modern geographic entities emerging from a colonial past.

3
Gender and Language

Geographic and regional factors are not the only ones that can influence the construction of historical consciousness. Gender and mother tongue also have direct implications. Language is a well-known and thoroughly studied differentiator in Canada; gender as a variable is just now beginning to be studied. This study has found that even among female and male students who attend the same school system and follow the same curriculum, there are subtle differences in their understandings of the past that deserve our attention. In addition, our research results remind us that historical learning is a cultural enterprise that varies by language and also by province of residence, even if the language spoken is the same.

This chapter has two sections. First, we look at the role of gender in order to see how young women and men from Ontario and Quebec interpret the past of French Canada. To do so, we analyse students' narrative orientations by gender, which reveals that the two groups do not always share the same vision of the past. Then we consider the content and structure of their narratives. This analysis suggests that young women tend to focus on distinctive aspects of the collective past and tell more intimate historical narratives. In the second part, we conduct the same type of analysis using, this time, students' mother tongue and place of residence. The results indicate that young francophones whose mother tongue is French show less enthusiasm than non-francophones for presenting narratives of the *francophone experience*. English-speaking students (anglophones) are also less likely to tell a collective "we" story, preferring more diverse and personalized narratives.

Ontario: A More Optimistic History Depending on Gender

According to our findings, young women and men in Ontario can be distinguished by the orientation of their narratives. Female students have slightly more positive views of the past than male; they also use more frequently the narrative orientation of *francophone affirmation*, the most positive vision of the historical experience of French Canada (see figures 3.1 and 3.2). Overall, 15% of female students chose this orientation compared to only 10% for males.[1]

In students' narratives, the *francophone affirmation* orientation is closely linked to the Franco-Ontarian green-and-white flag officially raised for the first time in 1975. This symbol of Franco-Ontarian pride is displayed in every French-speaking school in Ontario. Students use it to situate francophones' collective history in Ontario in the light of past struggles for French-language rights. The following Ottawa female participant does not hesitate to call French an official language that all young Canadians should learn since "it is the easiest language and the language that everyone in Canada speaks":

> During the celebrations of the Flag Day, it's time to honour our beautiful French language. Painting white and green doors to express our joy as being a Franco-Ontarian. French is important for the history of the country since francophones have had to fight so that we have the right to speak about it and have French courses and Schools, hospital etc. in French. Also we encourage anglophones to take French courses in school since the population is more French than English [and also] because the French language is first used [in the colony] and every part in Canada is bilingual. It is an important language to learn because it is the language that everyone speaks and knows since it is learned by everyone in each country. They say that the French language is the main language, since this is the language that everyone is encouraged to learn, since this is the easiest language and the language that everyone in Canada speaks. This is the main one! It's been years since French has been made the main language in Canada. We ... recognize[d] French language and decided to make a day of celebration so we honour this beautiful language that we have the advantage to learn with our parents, teachers etc. Green and white represent the earth. How proud we are of our beautiful environment and our beautiful French language. (0111A06-East)

Male students are not so optimistic. They prefer to tell stories of *francophone adversity* (56% male vs 48% female), a narrative vision that conveys a rather mixed perspective on the past and future of the community. This vision highlights the difficulties and obstacles experienced by French Canadians and points to the fragility of their collective gains. According to the following student from Southern Ontario, francophones had to struggle against the assimilation attempts of the English Canadian majority, and collective resistance forced the provincial

Figure 3.1 Narrative orientations for female students in Ontario

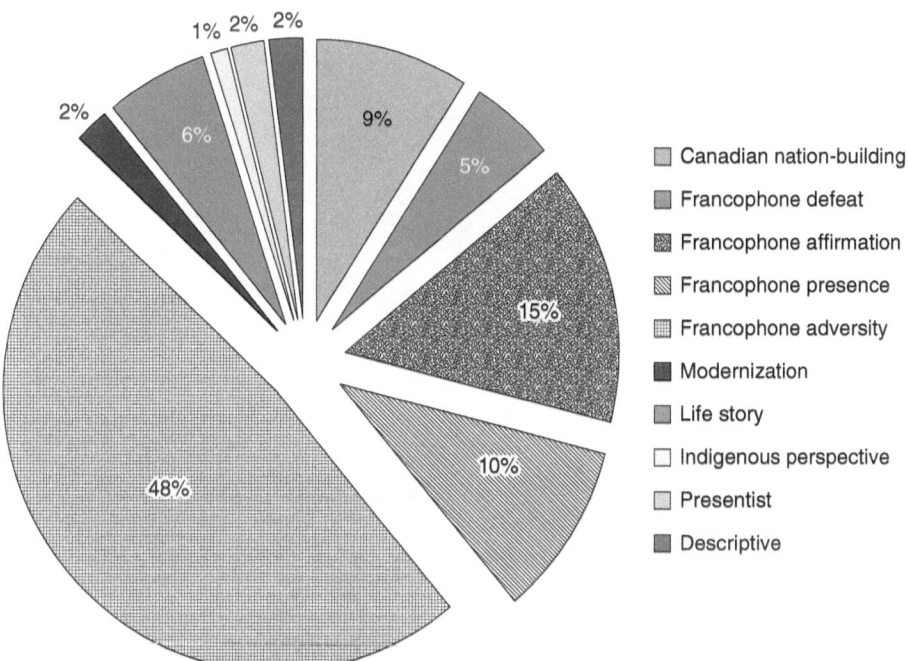

government to recognize the Franco-Ontarian community. Yet the student remains doubtful about the future of his own culture:

> The story I can remember is that the English have tried to force their way of life on the French. Their language, religion, culture, etc. However, many French individuals do not like this and revolt against the English. In Canada, many French Canadians are forced to learn and speak English. However, they wanted to continue their French traditions and cultures, and another battle exploded. After much conflict, the government has allowed people who want to speak and learn in French to have the right to do so, even though the majority of the population is English. This created what is known today as the Franco-Ontarian community. However, this culture is beginning to die I think. (0111A01-South)

A more neutral perspective characterizes the stories offered by those male participants who privilege the *francophone presence* (17% vs 10%). This orientation conveys the historical experience of French Canada in

Figure 3.2 Narrative orientations for male students in Ontario

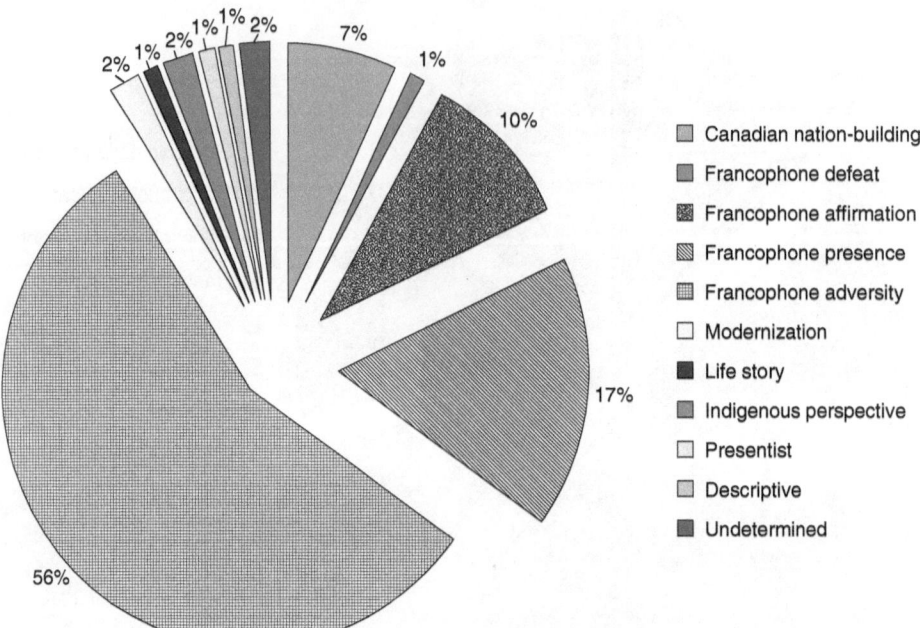

rather descriptive terms, without a distinct positive or negative viewpoint. The following male student focuses his narrative on the history of francophones without seeking to position himself with respect to the origins of the French Canadian historical experience or to express a view on its future. Instead, he tries to explain the past with factual information ranging from the European discovery by Christopher Columbus, whom he confuses with Jacques Cartier, to Canada's official bilingualism:

> The Francophone history in Canada is that the Francophonie is starting to be bigger in southern Ontario. It started when Christopher Columbus came because he was French, he was French and English. In the past we had battles between English and French and now in Canada there are several French speakers. There were French people who were in Canada at first and in the end there were English people there [as well], and now there are the two and there are two official languages in Canada. (011A11-South)

It is interesting that female students tend to place themselves at the centre of their stories and to recount more intimate experiences to explain the historical development of French Canada. The greater importance they give to *life story* narratives is telling (6% female vs 1% male). For this student from Eastern Ontario, Franco-Ontarian Day is an important celebration that offers the opportunity to get together, to celebrate and share the history and culture of Franco-Ontarians with members of other cultural communities. Interestingly, she tells this story through a personal experience with a family member originally from Africa who now lives in Ontario:

> In my opinion, what I think is important is the Franco-Ontarian day. I think it's important that we take a whole day to dress in green and white to support who we are because some people do not know where we come from or who we really are but by celebrating the Franco-Ontarian Day every year, it gives to others the chance to live it. For example, I have a family member from Africa and of course she speaks French but she did not know much about being Franco-Ontarian and learning about history. This allowed everyone to have a deeper knowledge of the French language and how easy it was to make the French language a permanent language. Not only that but also francophone artists as I learned that English music did not have the only good music. (0210A20-East)

Our results thus suggest that young women's visions of the past are slightly more positive and point toward a more optimistic future, and that they often use culture and lived experiences as means to position themselves with regard to their French-language community. Their stories also tend to be less nationalistic, with more emphasis on personal experiences. Male students, by contrast, express a mixed vision of their collective history, value more explicitly the francophone experience, and show less interest in presenting personal life stories.

Quebec: A More Convergent Vision of the Past

Two observations need to be made with regard to the Quebec results (see figures 3.3 and 3.4). First, the Quebec participants offer more varied narrative orientations than the Ontario students. No orientation receives the favour of a majority of Quebec students, though the most popular template remains *francophone adversity* (44% for the female students and 43% for the male). Second, there is no significant difference between the narrative visions of young women and young men in the province. The two groups offer quite similar narrations of the collective past.

Figure 3.3 Narrative orientations for female students in Quebec

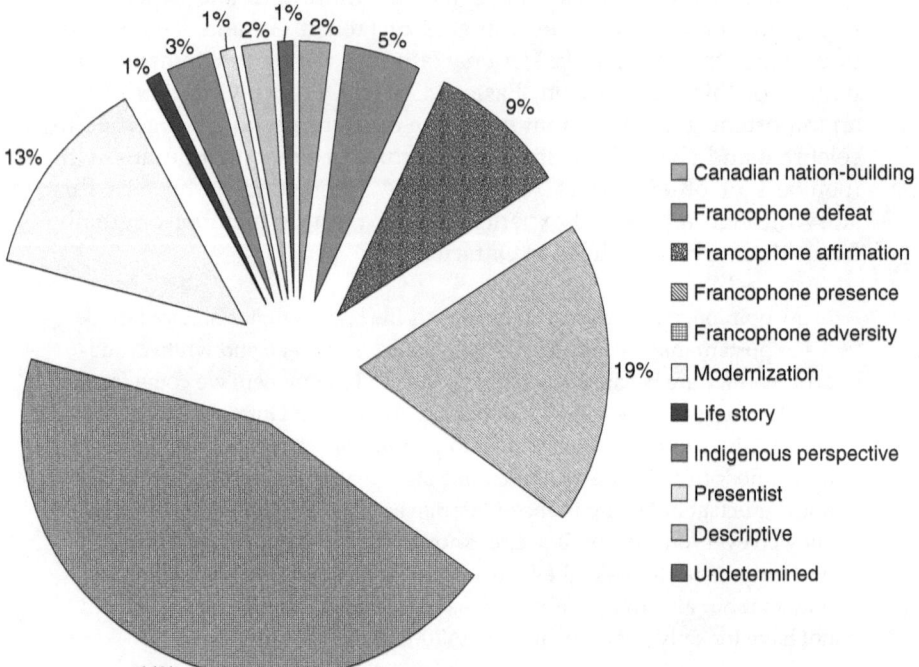

This finding supports the conclusion of Létourneau, who argues in his study of Quebec students that "similarities are more important than differences ... there is no particular way of telling the history of Québec according to boys and girls."[2]

However, certain trends found in the Ontario sample are also present in the Quebec group. Female students are slightly more optimistic and tend to favour the *francophone affirmation* orientation more than male students (9% vs 7%). This female student from Quebec City presents a story that reinterprets the history of the French-speaking majority in Quebec in light of her positive perception of today's linguistic situation in the province, which makes her believe that the Battle of the Plains of Abraham of 1759 was actually won by the French, not the British!:

> Samuel de Champlain landed on the land of present-day Quebec in 1608. He settled there and colonized this territory. Subsequently, many French came to settle, as well as British. These people, settled in the 13 colonies, wanted to take possession of the Province of Quebec, which engendered

Figure 3.4 Narrative orientations for male students in Quebec

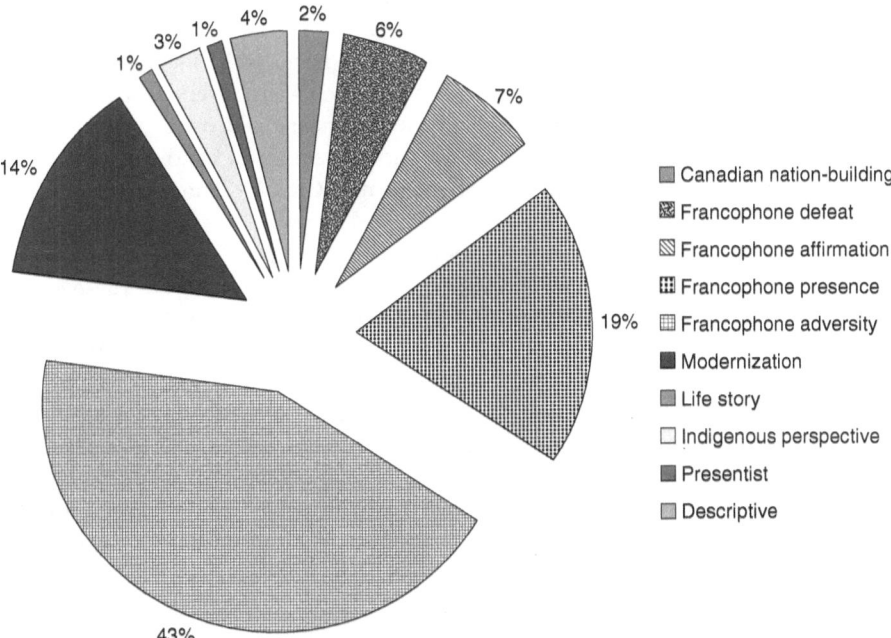

- Canadian nation-building
- Francophone defeat
- Francophone affirmation
- Francophone presence
- Francophone adversity
- Modernization
- Life story
- Indigenous perspective
- Presentist
- Descriptive

conflicts including the conquest of the Plains of Abraham. The French were victorious and in the aftermath of this conflict, a peace treaty was signed. Thus, the French language has endured and has become the official spoken and written language in Quebec, as we know it today. (05B02-Quebec City)

Young women in Quebec do not necessarily write narratives that are more sympathetic to *Canadian nation-building* (2% vs 1%) or *life experience* (2% vs 1%). In both cases, the difference is insignificant. That being said, we encountered many female students who prefer to tell less politicized stories of the national past, or who claim to have an aversion for national history because it overemphasizes politics. The following female student explains the importance of knowing history to understand society and her place in it, but at the same time she recognizes that politics is of less concern and interest to her:

> What has struck me is that a person's identity is very important to each one. It's not easy to change people as you want it. In the past, people fought to keep their language, their religion, their culture ... A good example is

the assimilation of First Nations, or when the English wanted to impose British and English laws. Also, industrialization, wars, battles, fights, treaties have affected me. I still find it important, since these have changed things and have made things like that today. I never really liked history because of politics and everything related to it, so I was not very good at it. On the other hand, I found it interesting to understand why our country or province is the way it is. I do not have a good memory, so I know that if I remember it, it's because it is important for me. (GR0225-Central Quebec)

As seen in figure 3.4, the number of stories of *francophone adversity* is roughly the same between female students and men (44% vs 43%) and is significantly lower than in Ontario (48% vs 56%). Compared to their Franco-Ontarian peers (10% and 17%), Quebec students favour more descriptive stories of the *francophone presence* (19%). When we add up all Quebec stories related to the *francophone experience* (affirmation, defeat, adversity, presence), we arrive at 76% for female students and 77% for male, while in Ontario the same proportions are respectively 78% and 84%. What can account for this difference? The discrepancy can be attributed to the larger number of stories in the Quebec sample presenting a perspective of *modernization*. This narrative orientation receives only 2% of students' attention in Ontario, regardless of gender, compared to 13% for girls and 14% for boys in Quebec. As we explained in the previous chapter, one possible reason for this significant difference is the impact of the Quebec HCE program on students' historical visions. The HCE curriculum places greater emphasis on social history, and this is particularly felt in students' narratives that describe issues of economy, commerce, and trade, especially during the colonial period.

In the following excerpt, this young man from Quebec City tells the story of New France, but from a socio-economic perspective:

Francophones arrived on the land of the Indians to fish and it was at this moment that they began to make alliances. During the French regime the French traded various products against furs with the Aboriginals. Fur has quickly become a very interesting product for Great Britain and France. These two nations started fighting for control of the fur trade. In 1760, there was the capitulation of Montreal, that is to say that the French came under British rule. At that time, Francophones became Canadians and began to work in various trades. (04b03-Quebec City)

In the same vein, we could argue that the resort to the *Indigenous perspective* is also affected by the HCE program. While relatively low in overall numbers, Quebec students (3% of girls and 3% of boys) still make use of this narrative orientation slightly more frequently than their Franco-Ontarian peers (1% of girls and 2% of boys). That being said, the overall presence of Indigenous content and perspectives in students' narratives is muted. While we recognize that our research focused on the history of French Canada, it is still disturbing to find limited references to the lives of Indigenous peoples and their encounters with white settlers and Euro-Canadians in the development of Canada. Indeed, students' mentions of Indigenous peoples relate almost exclusively to the distant past, arising when they discuss European contacts during colonial times.

> The French arrived here a long time ago, when we made Quebec a colony. The Amerindians were in the territories and they were treated very badly. There was (a little) mix between the Amerindians and the French, who, themselves, slowly saw their language change. (GR0505-Montreal)

After this period, Indigenous peoples disappear from students' narratives as if they were no longer part of national history. There is no reference to the diverse experiences of First Nations, Métis, and Inuit peoples (even Louis Riel, the French-speaking Métis leader and founder of Manitoba, barely gets ten references in students' narratives). Nor is there mention of land claims, treaties, or residential schools. In a way, the students' narratives reflect their own historical culture and schooling experience, both of which give limited place to other marginalized groups. The Truth and Reconciliation Commission of Canada (TRC) has been quite critical of the current Canadian educational system, which, in the commissioners' view, needs to be "transformed into one that rejects the racism embedded in colonial systems of education and treats Aboriginal and Euro-Canadian knowledge systems with equal respect." Implementing this system will require more knowledge *about* Indigenous peoples as well as a deeper understanding of Aboriginal ways of knowing so that "all students, both Aboriginal and non-Aboriginal, gain historical knowledge while also developing respect and empathy for each other."[3]

"I" and "We": A Question of Gender

The analysis of the internal structure of students' narratives can tell us more about the possible role of gender in telling the history of French Canada. One narrative aspect in particular is valuable: the use of first-person singular versus first-person plural. The explicit presence of the narrator in texts helps us understand how each student has positioned herself or himself with regard to the collective past. As we will see in the next chapter, the use of the collective "we" also reveals how students relate to their predecessors and establish links between the present and the past. In the same way, the use of the first-person singular can illuminate how students have explicitly adopted a narrative voice and point of view in the storyline.

As indicated in Table 3.1, female students tend to tell narratives from their own personal experience and to use more frequently the "I" form to present their history. In so doing, they affirm their narrative role more explicitly, through phrasing such as "For me history is ..." or "In this account I will tell you that ..." Regardless of the province, young women employ the first-person singular far more frequently than men (67% for Ontario and 65% for Quebec). It is interesting that Franco-Ontarian female students use this form of writing more extensively than Québécois (130 vs 70 times), even though the Ontario sample size is smaller. Perhaps Ontario female students are more prone to express their own opinions, as suggested by the following participant:

> I do not know much about the history of francophones in this country. But I remember learning about Jacques Cartier. (0210B03-South)
>
> I am sorry if this sounds like an opinion not history, but it is history, the history of how French Canadians living outside Quebec are often forgotten in the world and even today. (0112A13-East)
>
> The history of francophones before the French explorations is vague to me. So for my analysis I will start with New France after Jacques Cartier. (GR0201-Montreal)

Interestingly, Ontario female students are not the only group to use the first-person singular. We find a similar pattern among Franco-Ontarian male students. These students used the "I" form 64 times compared to only 35 times for males in Quebec. In contrast, "we" and "our" are used slightly more frequently by male students, with similar proportions in both Ontario and Quebec. We believe that the significant difference in the use of the first-person singular and first-person plural between Ontario and Quebec students is due to variables other than gender. Indeed, gender differences are neither natural nor universal but rather socially constructed and dependent on cultural context. In the case of Quebec, the majority of francophone participants, as we will see later, seem to embrace a dominant frame of reference, what psychologist Bibb Latané calls the theory of "social impact," which minimizes gender effect.[4] According to Latané, a group's influence on individuals depends on a number of factors, including the number of people in the group, their strength, and

Table 3.1 Key pronouns by gender and province

Key terms	Female (Ontario) frequency	%	Male (Ontario) frequency	%	Female (Quebec) frequency	%	Male (Quebec) frequency	%
I	130	67	64	33	70	65	37	35
Ours	19	48	21	52	28	49	29	51
Our	40	42	54	58	65	47	73	53
We	110	49	114	51	173	46	203	54

their immediacy. Latané suggests that social impact can be compared to light on a surface: the total amount of light depends on the number of light bulbs, the power of the bulbs, and their distance from the surface.

In the case of francophone Québécois, these people form a relatively strong and substantial population grouped on a common territory and with a more or less autonomous form of provincial governance. This particular geopolitical context, different from the one encountered by Franco-Ontarians, creates some converging norms, expected behaviours, and shared ideas about the past that can potentially alter the influence of other variables such as gender. Yet it is possible that the minority milieu in which Franco-Ontarians live, which is subject to strong cultural pressures, places them in a situation that reinforces their own sense of narrative identity. The story of the nation would therefore take a more personal form than in Quebec, where belonging to the community is more easily established due to social impact factors, and would also require fewer negotiations with another cultural milieu, particularly in the predominantly French-speaking regions of Quebec.

In the following excerpt, a female student from Eastern Ontario explicitly assumes the position of the narrator who tells us the story of francophones in Ontario with reference to a defining event for her – the saga of Montfort Hospital. Note that she concludes her text with a reference to the collective "we" as francophones:

> The history of francophones is a long story. But today I will talk about the most common. For example, Montfort Hospital is a French-language hospital. Several francophones have come forward to keep it. Francophones in general. Because they fought to live in a bilingual country. Because before that, francophones, we were relegated. (0210A18-East)

In this next excerpt, a student from Saguenay tells the story of Quebec history, which begins with French settlers, then assumes the collective position of "we" as Québécois to discuss the two failed sovereignty referendums. In doing so, she relates personally to the people of this historical period and positions herself as one of them:

> At the beginning, the French set foot in Quebec (in Gaspésie), it was really difficult at the beginning because of the changes of climate and the attacks of the Aboriginals. But they finally settled well and populated the colony. They offered seigneuries to the French and even sent the Filles du roi. For example at a given moment it was not so good, there was the conquest so all the French elite went to France and the leaders were now English. The English had everything in their power to assimilate the French but they were less numerous so it was a failure. Canadians remained strong. Later, there were referendums because we Quebecers did not feel good and not in our place in Canada and English speaking country but the majority of Quebecers decided to stay with Canada. (04A09-Saguenay)

Social History for Female Students and Political History for Male Students

Another important difference between the narratives of female and male students is the greater attention the former pay to social and cultural issues as opposed to military and political affairs (see Table 3.2). This preference is likely due to the fact that young women can find themselves – and their own experiences – more easily in social history, which has traditionally assigned greater importance to the life, power, roles, and agency of women in both private and public spheres. As Penney Clark observes in her analysis of Canadian history textbooks, "because women rarely contributed to political, economic or military aspects of the public sphere (at least in ways that have garnered recognition), they naturally have not figured prominently in histories of the development of the Canadian nation."[5] This perspective is evident when we look at female students' references to the "Filles du Roi" in New France and the resistance of Franco-Ontarian female teachers against Regulation 17:

> The Filles du Roi all spoke the same French dialect and hence helped standardized language in the colony and this explains our own way [of] speaking today. (04A16-Québec)
> Regulation 17 was not accepted by Franco-Ontarians, and they fought for their rights. Women among others have fought against the authorities, many heroines, like the Desloges sisters, for example, have been recognized. (0111A01-North)

In Ontario, the terms related to the schools question ("school," "teaching," "Regulation 17") are mentioned more frequently by female

Table 3.2 Social and cultural key terms by gender and province

Key terms	Female (Ontario) frequency	%	Male (Ontario) frequency	%	Female (Quebec) frequency	%	Male (Quebec) frequency	%
Anglophone(s)	41	68	19	32	50	53	45	47
Culture	30	51	29	49	54	61	34	39
Flag	37	84	7	16	–	–	–	–
Right	40	59	28	41	12	40	18	60
Rights	32	63	19	37	16	53	14	47
Schools	81	69	37	31	–	–	–	–
Teaching	33	52	30	48	–	–	–	–
Filles du Roi	–	–	–	–	47	49	40	51
Franco-(On/Can)	81	70	35	30	–	–	–	–
Francophone(s)	168	56	134	44	146	48	156	52
Language	146	62	91	38	138	55	112	45
Regulation 17	63	57	48	43	–	–	–	–
Religion	–	–	–	–	39	60	26	40

students (69%, 52%, 57%). The way in which Regulation 17 is told in history programs and transmitted in public culture gives female teachers such as Béatrice and Diane Desloges a prominent place as heroic figures who played a decisive role in the defence of French-speaking school rights. As such, Regulation 17 is more than a linguistic battle; it is often associated with women's activism in Franco-Ontarian history:

> The Desloges sisters were fired and then taught their students secretly. On the other hand, the sisters wanted more than that, and then accompanied by other women, they fought the police and the inspectors with their only defences: the hairpins. They ended up going back to school and that revolutionized francophone education in Ontario. (0211B11-East)

In the same way, Franco-Ontarian female students tend to view their history in a more progressive way and as punctuated by various social gains and cultural advances. This perspective on long-term progress leads them to favour more positive narrative orientations such as *francophone affirmation* and *Canadian nation-building*. This preference for social history, or even sociocultural history, leads female students to choose more frequently themes related to identity, language, culture, and rights: "Anglophone(s)" (68%), "rights" (63%), "franco-" (70%), "francophone(s)" (56%), "language" (62%), and "culture" (51%). The following student associates the struggle of female teachers for French-language education with the activist role of the so-called "Famous Five," a group of English Canadian feminists who, in the 1920s, successfully petitioned the Canadian government for the recognition in the law of women as "persons" with equal political rights:

> Several teachers fought to remove this rule, as for example, in my history class, we talked about the group of women called famous 5 so Nellie McLang [sic] was there. (0111A11-North)

But the theme *par excellence* is undoubtedly that of the Franco-Ontarian flag, which is discussed by no less than 84% of female students. For many, the flag is an emblematic bridge between the struggles of the past and the success of the present that Franco-Ontarians choose to celebrate annually:

> On September 25, Franco-Ontarians celebrate their victory. They fought for their language. They have raised their flag this day since they have earned their right to speak French and teach it to their children. (0211A07-East)

The flag also embodies Franco-Ontarian culture and identity and serves as a rallying symbol for a linguistic community that is welcoming of various cultures. And it is an opportunity for young women to share their experiences and to express their own sense of belonging to this community, which is now more open to the world:

> As a Franco-Ontarian, since I was a young girl, we celebrate the Franco-Ontarian flag day. (0111A03-East)
> Now every year, there are the Francophonie celebrations on September 25th. We even have a green and white flag representing us. Many people in other countries believe that in Canada the only French come from Quebec and associate us like English. (01110A02-North)

As we noted earlier, gender differences are significantly lower among Quebec participants. There is an interpretative convergence between the stories of young women and those of young men in this province. While some key terms such as "anglophone(s)" (53%), "rights" (53%), and "language" (55%) are more likely to be discussed by female students, the difference is marginal. Even the references to "Filles du Roi" are shared almost equally by female and male students (49% vs 51%). In fact, the only term that receives greater attention among female students is "religion" (60%). This is an interesting finding. Since the Quiet Revolution, the French-language civic culture has been presented as the chief constitutive element of the Quebec identity. But French Canada has, in many ways, been shaped by religion. As Martel contends, "French Canadians not only had their heavenly patron, St. John the Baptist, but they also became the instruments of a providential mission: to preserve and spread the French and Catholic heritage rich in acts of heroism that marked the history of the North American continent."[6] For some reasons, possibly associated with the prominent role of females in health care and education, young women in Quebec incorporate religion more frequently in their historical narratives:

> The history of francophones begins with the arrival of the French. Indeed, it is they who transmitted their language, their religion and their culture. (04A13-Québec)
> Then the English wanted our lands and they won them by the war, trying to impose their culture, language, religion, way of life. Thus began the interminable Franco-vs.-Anglo struggle. (GR0522-Central Quebec)
> As the years go by, the French and English arrive to live in community. The region is very present in Quebec and the church is at the centre of education, healthcare and morality too. (0105A03-Gatineau)

As might be expected, male students use far more frequently concepts related to battles and military conflicts (see Table 3.3). In Quebec, the "Battle of the Plains of Abraham" (52%), "war" (56%), "Patriots" (67%), and "revolution" (67%) are dominant themes in young men's narratives. Male students also express greater interest in territorial and political terms, such as "America" (66%), "England" (62%), "France" (53%), "Lower Canada" (58%), and "Upper Canada" (58%). In many ways, politics and the military are still a male business in school history. The dominant figures of Canada, either as victims or heroes, are mostly represented by men who rebelled against, or governed, the colony and later the country:

> In Europe the war between England and France has begun. After several years, the war came here in 1754. The English wanted more territory, so they took to New France. The battle took place on the Plains of Abraham where the English claimed New France. (0205A06-Gatineau)
> One of the important elements of our history, probably the most important, is the rebellion of the patriots. This has proven to us that francophones are badly treated, that anglophones have the advantages. (GR0632-Montréal)

The following students' excerpts offer additional examples of dominant themes addressed in their narratives. Focus is placed on empires, countries, and conflicts over questions of language, culture, and education:

Table 3.3 Military and political key terms by gender and province

Key terms	Female (Ontario) frequency	%	Male (Ontario) frequency	%	Female (Quebec) frequency	%	Male (Quebec) frequency	%
America	–	–	–	–	59	34	116	66
England	9	32	19	68	26	38	43	62
Lower Canada	–	–	–	–	37	42	52	58
Battle	22	56	17	44	15	48	16	52
British	–	–	–	–	44	43	59	57
Colony/colonies	–	–	–	–	118	40	178	60
Settlers	–	–	–	–	27	38	44	62
Europe/Europeans	19	61	12	39	27	39	43	61
France	60	46	70	54	241	47	270	53
French	84	17	411	83	458	48	468	52
War(s)	88	48	97	52	113	44	142	56
Upper Canada	4	31	13	69	32	42	46	58
Patriots	–	–	–	–	13	33	27	67
Regime	–	–	–	–	34	71	14	29
Revolution	9	52	8	48	13	33	27	67

Following these events [the taking of Constantinople by the Turks], four great powers (France, England, Spain, Portugal) get themselves into the exploration of new passages to Asia, the king of each country finances the voyages. (05A11-Québec)

France, Spain, England, both wanted their possession of this new land. They were surprised to meet on this land the indigenous peoples. (GR0234-Centre of Québec)

Everything started when Europe came to take the territory of Aboriginals to create New France. Europe used our territory to get wood and fur. (05C01-North of Montreal)

In Ontario, results are similar but less pronounced. Male students are more likely than female ones to refer to "England" (68%), "France" (54%), "Upper Canada" (69%), and "War(s)" (52%). Yet one important difference between Quebec and Ontario male students relates to the more limited emphasis Franco-Ontarians place on the colonial era – an era that corresponds to intense military and political conflicts over the destiny of New France, as stated by the following student from Eastern Ontario:

We waged wars to keep our tongue, like the battle of the Plain of Abraham, which we lost against General Wolfe and against the country, England. (0110A16-East)

In brief, the narratives of young Quebec and Ontario men present political and military perspectives, often more defeatist in outlook as well as less optimistic about the future of French Canadians. Female students adhere to more sociocultural and affirmative visions of the past, focused on the social dimension of French Canada. This reveals the significant yet still marginalized role of women in shaping society.

French Ontario: A Story Shared by Language Group

Language is often presented as a distinguishing factor, even a factor in social divisions. But schooling also plays a determining role in the socialization of young citizens and the sharing of a common culture and set of values. How do students from increasingly diverse linguistic backgrounds tell the stories of French Canada?

Our student samples reflect the sociocultural and linguistic realities of the two provincial environments we studied. In Ontario, fewer than half the students have French as their mother tongue (49%); for more than one third it is English (35%), and for less than one fifth it is another language (16%). Our Franco-Ontarian school sample is more culturally and linguistically diverse than the Quebec one. The minority nature of the francophone community in Ontario and its dispersal throughout the province foster cultural diversity, variations in linguistic practices, and mixed identity affiliations.

As shown in to figure 3.5, *francophone adversity* is the dominant narrative orientation for Ontario's English-speaking (58%), French-speaking (48%), and other-language (allophone) (55%) students. Interestingly, students whose mother tongue is either English or another language besides French are more likely to tell stories of linguistic tensions and adversity. The following excerpt, from a Métis student from Eastern Ontario, presents the history of French Canadians from the perspective of collective struggles centred on two major events: conscription during the First World War, and Regulation 17:

> I know that the history of French Canadians is that they are separated from the English. In Vimy Ridge, they all gathered and worked together to win this battle. They did it. And after this battle, Canada became a united country. Canada has become a complete/independent country. But they announced that there were no soldiers (England), so there was not enough volunteers. They started to put propaganda, but it was not enough yet. The government introduced conscription. Conscription is when they choose names at random, and names chosen are forced to be soldiers. The ages were 18–45 years old. The French were furious because

Figure 3.5 Narrative orientations by language group in Ontario

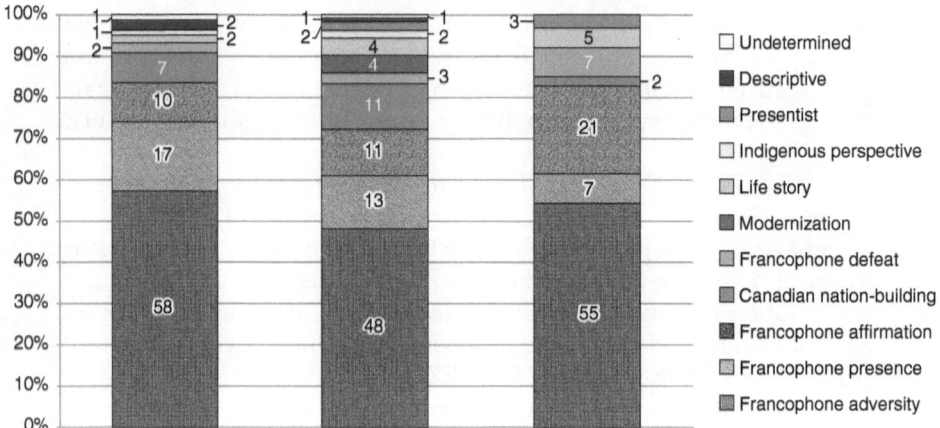

they thought it was for them, the French. The French were angry with the English. Also, they introduced regulation 17. Regulation 17 is when students can only speak, learn French for a time limit, 30 minutes or 1 hour. The French struggled and spoke to remove this rule, and they have won. (0110A02-South)

The *francophone adversity* narrative orientation among non-francophone students is telling. It offers evidence of the impact of francophone culture and education on students' historical consciousness. These students live in an anglo-dominant environment outside the school, yet they can still tell the history of French Canada using some of the symbols and mythistories of this historical community. In doing so, students do not simply remember factual information about the collective past; they also present narratives expressing the doubts and fears of French Canadians. Living at the crossroads of many cultures, students may choose a narrative vision that best represents their own contradictions, torn as they are between multiple social, cultural, and linguistic affiliations. They opt for a nuanced assessment of francophones' past, one that represents their desire to reconcile their cultural heritage with the past and future of French Canada. Instead of telling an enthusiastic and militant narrative, these students write stories that highlight the major challenges to and fears for the future of their linguistic community. The following excerpt, from a Lebanese student, is illustrative of this narrative perspective:

> Oppression continues to this day as francophones live in a region dominated by anglophones. There was also the attempt to secede in Quebec but the movement never got it. To conclude, the history is one of fight for liberty and rights that continues these days. (0212A03-East)

If *francophone adversity* is the dominant orientation, students also draw on *francophone affirmation*. One tenth (11%) of francophones and anglophones (10%) and more than one fifth (21%) of allophones embrace this narrative template. A significant proportion of students belonging to different linguistic groups share a positive vision of the past and are rather optimistic about the future. The following anglophone student makes a very positive assessment of the current situation of francophones despite their long struggle for the survival of their language:

> Francophones are Canadians who speak French. This began when the French from France came to Canada to take territory. The English also came to take territory. This has caused competition between these two countries as a dominant language. The French had to work hard to keep the French language in the country of Canada because the English had the majority. Now the French language is important to know to have a job. Now there is school, sport, extracurricular activity, book, film and other entirely in French in Canada and this is all caused by the work that the French have done to keep the language in the country. (0210A02-East)

A similar view is expressed by the following student, originally from Hungary, who acknowledges the determination and resilience of French Canadians and the bilingual nature of Canada today:

> Driven by a desire for political and religious purity the English majority tries to eradicate the French language in different ways (Regulation 17). After failing on the legal side as well (deportation of the Acadians) the English seems to relax their grip on the French communities. Today, Canada is an independent country, it should be noted that this country is considered to be bilingual and multi-cultural. The resilience of the French ethnic group has allowed various ethnic groups to migrate together and in equality. (0112A17-East)

Interestingly, few students (between 2% and 7%) in any of the three linguistic groups have a negative vision, which suggests that Ontario participants do not view their community in defeatist terms. Overall, when we add up all the stories of *francophone experience* (francophone affirmation, francophone defeat, francophone adversity, francophone presence), we get tremendously high responses: 74% for francophones, 87% for anglophones, and 90% for allophones. This indicates that narratives of French Canada are exportable beyond traditional French-speaking circles and can be appropriated without much difficulty by allophone and anglophone students, sometimes with even more enthusiasm.

The *Canadian nation-building* orientation is appealing to 11% of francophones, 7% of anglophones, and 2% of allophones. It may seem strange to see francophone students using this narrative orientation more frequently than anglophones. As we will see in the next chapter on identity, most students in this group identify strongly as Canadian, which explains their positive relationship to the Canadian grand narrative. For these students, Canadian and Franco-Ontarian identities are complementary, and this leads them to tell stories of the Canadian experience in which the historical contribution of francophones constitutes an integral part. In the following narrative, this student from Eastern Ontario begins with the discoveries of Jacques Cartier and the French explorations and then takes up the classic themes of the Canadian nation-building pattern – Confederation, the colonization of Western Canada, the building of the transcontinental railway, and immigration – but without losing sight of the fact that the purpose is to explain the presence of francophones in Canada:

> Jacques Cartier discovered a land that later became Canada. Samuel de Champlain also came, and started populating Canada. In the beginning, they settled more in Eastern Canada, Newfoundland, Quebec, etc ... After the people of France learned that they had found a new land, family was sent to New France what he called Canada before. They sent themselves to be able to populate the lands. Canada was declared a country in 1867. View that Canada was a slum where slavery was not really used. Many African-Americans came to Canada. They still did not treat equal to whites but it was better than in the US. Many people from around the world like, from Ukraine, China, and Jews came to Canada because their lifestyle would be better than their home countries. Also many came for gold research and for the construction of the railway. Many francophones who lived in Quebec, New Brunswick etc. ... We start to travel to the west hoping to find something. They discovered that in western Canada, in Saskatchewan, Manitoba they had a lot of grassland so they had to pass the word of

people from the east. So many people started to settle across Canada. This is how francophones are everywhere in Canada. (0110A09-East)

Quebec: The Transmission of a Common Historical Memory

The Quebec sample is characterized by greater cultural homogeneity due to the presence of regions with large French-speaking majorities, such as Saguenay, Central Quebec, and Quebec City. Nearly nine tenths (86%) of Quebec students have French as their mother tongue, more than one tenth (13%) have a mother tongue other than English or French, and barely 1% have English as a mother tongue.

The five students in this last small group prefer three types of narrative: *modernization*, *francophone adversity*, and *francophone presence* (see figure 3.6). Given the sample size, we can only speculate. It may be that stories of *modernization* and *francophone presence* constitute a particular narrative posture that makes it possible for these students to set aside questions of identity that particularly affect the francophone majority in Quebec, with whom they are not always in agreement. In the *modernization* vision, socio-economic transformations take precedence over French Canadian historical experiences and allow the narrator to avoid certain contentious issues pertaining to the national question in Quebec. The *francophone presence* narrative places the historical experience of francophones at the heart of the storyline, but without a particular positive or negative perspective on the development of the nation.

Finally, the stories of *francophone adversity* may express, as in Ontario, a form of conformism in terms of adopting the dominant narrative shared by the greatest number of people in Quebec. In predominantly French-language schools, this may well be the *de facto* choice, as there may be no counter-narrative available to them. This interpretation of the past is thus self-evident and becomes a vision the student has internalized.

Sometimes an independent narrative emerges with its own themes. The following English-speaking student from Gatineau attaches great importance to Irish immigration, possibly in relation to the strong presence of Irish Canadians in the Ottawa region dating back to the nineteenth century:

> What I consider most important in history is the Irish potato crisis. This forced the inhabitants to come to settle in Quebec. Irish culture is very present in Quebec culture, so Ireland and its culture are linked to francophone history. Also, many Quebeckers have Irish origins in Quebec today.

Figure 3.6 Narrative orientations by language group in Quebec

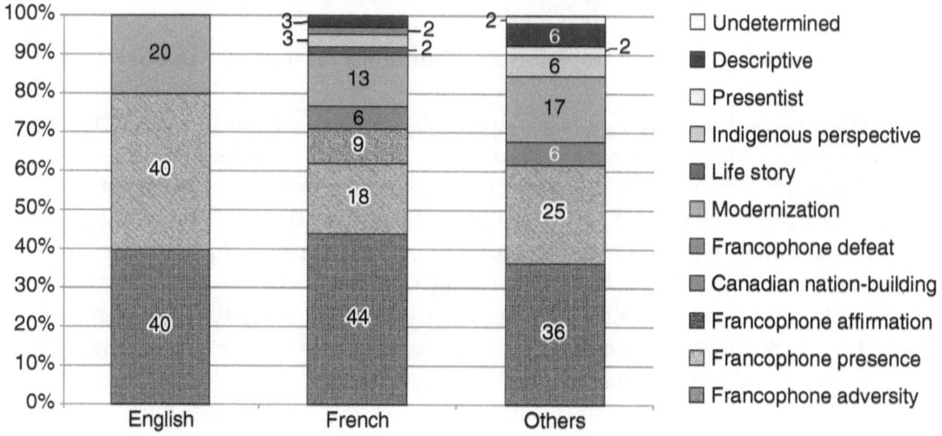

Category	English	French	Others
Undetermined		2	2
Descriptive	3	2	6
Presentist	3		6
Indigenous perspective	20	13	17
Life story		6	
Modernization		9	6
Francophone defeat	40	18	25
Canadian nation-building			
Francophone affirmation	40	44	36
Francophone presence			
Francophone adversity			

The reason why I find it important is because of the feelings that this feels for me. When the teacher taught on this topic, I found it sad that thousands of people died of malnutrition had to come by boat or is they were piled up and where hygienic needs were not respected. (0105A11-Gatineau)

When comparing the Ontario and Quebec results, we find that Quebec francophones share many trends with their Ontario peers. Francophone Québécois prefer to tell stories of *francophone adversity* (44%), followed by *francophone presence* (18%), *francophone affirmation* (9%), and finally *francophone defeat* (6%). These percentages are comparable to those found among Ontario's francophones. The lower number of francophones in Ontario who tell stories of *francophone experience* can be explained in two ways. First, the *Canadian nation-building* orientation is significantly stronger in Ontario and marginal among Quebec students, regardless of language. Second, the *modernization* orientation is practically non-existent in Ontario narratives. Only 4% of francophones in that province use this narrative compared to 13% of francophone students in Quebec. As for anglophones and allophones attending Franco-Ontarian schools, this story is completely ignored. The interest in stories of *modernization* in Quebec is visibly an effect of the school program. School history in Ontario possibly plays a similar role with regard to the use of the *Canadian nation-building* orientation among Ontario students.

In this excerpt, a francophone student from Quebec City describes the difficult conditions that led to the birth of the French colony:

> Gradually settlers began to set up francophone colonies. With the years, after famine crises, lack of jobs, and many difficult situations in Europe, many francophones are settling down to improve their living conditions. Canada, also called New France at the time, changed from being a trading colony to a settlement. Filles du Roi, contracted men and soldiers of the carignan salières regiment settled and began to populate the territory. (0105A19-Gatineau)

As noted in figure 3.6, narratives from Quebec's allophone students are more fragmented that those of Ontario allophone students. No dominant orientation seems to prevail in this group. As with Quebec francophones, stories of adversity attract some interest, but only with 36% of allophone participants. This orientation is followed by *francophone presence* (25%), *modernization* (17%), *Indigenous perspective* (6%), and *francophone defeat* (6%). The optimistic *francophone affirmation* narrative orientation attracts no allophone students.

We see from these results that allophone students in Ontario are more supportive of French Canadian history than their peers in Quebec. It could well be that the Franco-Ontarian identity project is conceived essentially within the Canadian framework and does not conflict with the mixed ethnocultural backgrounds and identities of allophones. In Quebec, the identity project is based on a certain political tension between Quebec and Canada. This situation can lead allophones to approach French Canadian or Quebec history with some apprehension; it may also help explain the fragmentation of narratives among non–French-speaking participants. Paul Zanazanian, from McGill University, came to a similar conclusion in his study of anglophones in Quebec, arguing that the current grand narratives of Quebec history do not encourage stories of cultural integration among the two linguistic groups.[7] In this circumstance, some allophones prefer to offer narratives of *modernization* or *Indigenous perspective*, which shift the focus to issues of social history, race relations, and colonialism, as stated by the following student from Montreal:

> In –33000 BC arrived the Amerindians. The Amerindians traded, their religion was called animism and they lived in longhouses that contained several families (5 and more). Then, later, thanks to Christopher Columbus (1492) and Jacques Cartier (1503) who discovered America, the Europeans traded with the Amerindians (rifles, spices, alcohol, etc. against furs). Then, the Europeans wanted to assimilate the Amerindians

in order to be able to take possession of their colony in order to be able to exploit their soil which was rich (mines) and to be able to expand their trade by the river. One of the techniques that the Europeans used for assimilation was to pass blankets to Native Americans. However, not all Native Americans died of the diseases that Europeans brought to them. (GR0516-Montreal)

The Struggle of Francophones

The internal structure and content of narratives can tell us more about the impact of language on students' ideas. Table 3.4 presents key terms that Ontario students associate with French–English relations. Note that terms related to sociolinguistic groups – "English," "anglophone(s)," "French" "francophone(s)" – are cited as often by anglophones as by francophones. The notions of "culture" and "language" are not exclusive to francophone students either. The term "culture" is used predominantly by anglophones (59%), followed by francophones (22%) and allophones (19%). We find a similar pattern for the references to "language," "school," and "right(s)."

When looking more specifically at themes related to Franco-Ontarian struggles, francophone students seem to differentiate themselves. Events such as "Regulation 17" and "Montfort Hospital" are cited more frequently (52% and 47%) by francophones compared to anglophones (32% and 36%) and allophones (16% and 17%). Still, many students in all three language groups use the Regulation 17 crisis to structure a narrative that serves to build their sense of belonging to the francophone community, as found in these narratives written respectively by a francophone, an anglophone, and a francophone student:

- The government wanted to abolish education in French and francophones have struggled to continue teaching in French
- At the beginning, teaching in French was done secretly
- When the authorities went to the schools to stop teaching in French, the teachers had to fight to show that they wanted to preserve the rights of francophones (0111A03-North)

An example of this is when Regulation 17 was established for all francophones. They had no right to learn the French language, to communicate in that language. It was a disaster for French Canadians. The people who made Regulation 17 are anglophones threatened by the French language. Even with this new law, they had teachers who taught in French language because it was very important to them. (210A17-East)

Table 3.4 Key terms used by students by language group in Ontario

Key terms	Anglo frequency	%	Franco frequency	%	Allophone frequency	%
English	130	47	108	39	39	14
Anglophone(s)	31	37	37	45	15	18
Struggling	21	44	24	50	3	6
Culture	35	59	13	22	11	19
Flag	12	29	25	61	4	10
Right(s)	50	43	51	44	14	13
School(s)	70	38	73	40	39	22
Teaching/teach	35	41	35	41	16	18
French	286	42	285	41	109	17
Francophone(s)	143	35	184	45	84	20
I	71	39	56	31	55	30
Hospital/Montfort	37	36	48	47	17	17
Language	110	48	73	32	46	20
We	47	31	92	60	15	9
Regulation 17	35	32	56	52	17	16

> The French were angry with the English. Also, they introduced regulation 17. Regulation 17 is when students can only speak, learn French for a time limit, 30 minutes or 1 hour. The French fought to remove this rule, and they won. (0110A02-South)

More significant differences are found when we examine the use of the first-person singular and first-person plural in text. Anglophones (39%) and allophones (30%) use the "I" form more frequently than francophones (31%). These numbers are extremely important, considering that allophone students make up only 16% of the Ontario sample. It appears that non-francophones prefer to adopt a personal posture when telling the history of French Canada. For this student from Southern Ontario, narrating the history of francophones in Canada is a way for him to inscribe his own personal experience in reference to Ontario and Quebec histories:

> I am not really a great expert in the history of francophones but I know some information about French in Ontario. Someone had explained to me that there was just some francophone schools in Ontario just because it was not really great to speak French here, so that's when Quebec tried to be a country alone without Canada because it wanted nothing from the English there, just French for everyone. (0210A06-South)

In contrast, the references to "we" are far more frequent among francophone students (60%) compared to anglophones (31%) and allophones (9%). The latter group is obviously reluctant to use the first-person plural to tell the history of the French Canadian community. Franco-Ontarian-born students repeatedly refer to predecessors as members of their own identity group. French colonists who were defeated on the Plains of Abraham, French Canadians who migrated to Ontario and Western Canada, and Franco-Ontarians who lost their education rights in the 1910s are all part of their common community of memory. As we will see in chapter 4, a strong sense of national belonging among participants directly affects this use of "we" when telling the history of the nation. The following francophone student from Eastern Ontario provides a clear example:

> At one point, there was a conflict with Britain over the land, which led to the Battle of the Plains of Abraham, led by the General in the Citadel of Quebec and General Wolfe. The French lost and had to turn Canada to Britain, which is why we are led by Queen Elizabeth II today. They took away our rights as French, forcing us to speak and write in English. Some politicians fought for our freedom in the 1800s. We Franco-Ontarians originally came from Quebec. Our flag was officialized around the 1970s. (0110A05-East)

In Quebec, we find comparable results (Table 3.5). Yet the large sample size of francophone students tends to distort the results by language group. References to "anglophone(s)" and "francophone(s)" are common among all Quebec students. As in Ontario, these linguistic terms are inseparable from the cultural reality of students in the province of Quebec, even if they find themselves in a majority situation. That being said, francophone students have a tendency to use these terms in reference to a long, continuous struggle for the French fact. The French still have an uncertain future in Quebec, as indicated by the following student from Montreal:

> Francophones have always had to be strong and proud of who they are to keep their identity even if everything was changing. The Patriots are excellent examples of French pride. They fought for French. And today, English is still gaining the upper hand, not only over the French, but over the whole planet. Francophones have always had to be strong and must continue to be strong with globalization and Americanization. French is less and less present in Quebec and who knows when it will disappear? (GR0427-Montreal)

Non-francophone students present the struggle of the French language differently. While it an important aspect of their narratives,

Table 3.5 Key terms used by students by language group in Quebec

Key terms	Anglo		Franco		Allophone	
	frequency	%	frequency	%	frequency	%
Anglophone(s)	14	10	111	79	16	11
Assimilation	5	6	66	80	12	14
Canada	16	4	338	83	53	13
Canadians	5	5	103	89	7	6
Culture	5	6	74	87	6	7
Right(s)	5	8	45	78	8	14
Francophone(s)	26	20	90	69	14	11
I	8	7	97	90	3	3
Language	4	2	230	93	13	5
We	12	3	327	87	36	10
Quebec	2	4	49	85	6	11
Québécois	5	6	81	91	3	3

the language used in text is more descriptive, as if past realities did not carry the same emotional attachment. Predecessors are not portrayed as strong and proud defenders of their language rights, as stated above. The Conquest is not a defeat but a significant event in the larger transformation in the colony's governance that brought changes to the lives of the French colonists. The following allophone student, originally from South Africa, offers an example of such a descriptive narrative:

> By losing the colony, citizens lost some aspect of life that existed before like the French language and religion [that were found] in all the regions of Canada. Only the province of Quebec is entirely French and another province like New Brunswick is bilingual and some people no longer place importance on religion as in the past. (0105A12-Gatineau)

Perhaps the references to more loaded terms such as "assimilation" help distinguish the ways in which francophones and non-francophones tell narratives of French Canada. Francophone students (80%) are more likely than anglophones (6%) and allophones (14%) to refer to assimilation, and they use it in one particular narrative way – with regard to English Canadians' historical attempts to dominate francophones and take away their language rights. Allophones and anglophones tend to use this term less frequently and also more broadly, including in references to the assimilation of Indigenous peoples by French and English settlers. The following two narrative excerpts, one from a francophone from Quebec City and the other from an allophone student from Montreal, illustrate these differences of interpretation:

> In 1763, the colony officially became British. All the French of the colony returned to France. There is only one trace of French left: Canadians. So because of Canadians, who fought for centuries to not be assimilated by the British and become anglophones. (04A12-Quebec City)
>
> Then, the Europeans wanted to assimilate the Aboriginals in order to be able to take possession of their colony, in order to be able to exploit their soil which was rich (mines) and to be able to expand their trade along the [St-Lawrence] river. (GR0516-Montreal)

Interestingly, the use of first-person plural is very frequent among francophone students (87%) in Quebec but also present among anglophones (7%), who, as we noted, represent a very small group of participants. This is to say that identification with a collective "we" is an important element of students' narratives that goes beyond mother tongue. Allophone students in Quebec have found ways to identify with social groups outside their families and linguistic communities. In doing so, they have strategically placed themselves as members of an imagined community that traces its origins back to colonial times. As might be expected, the same pattern is not evident among Quebec anglophone students, who find it very difficult to align themselves with the perspective of francophones, who often view English Canadians as adversaries responsible for the Conquest of New France. Perhaps the conclusion of the following student's narrative best describes the situation in Quebec:

> At a time when the French language is no longer threatened, Quebecers continue to fight against the English in a jealous way and believe that they should be a sovereign and independent country despite the fact that they are better being a province of Canada. (0205A22-Gatineau)

Conclusion

Results from our study indicate that young women have a more optimistic view of their past: they place the history of francophones in a bigger Canadian picture, and they have greater interest in cultural and social aspects of society. Female students position themselves explicitly as narrators and acknowledge the role of women as social actors. Male students tend to tell stories of the francophone historical experience, emphasizing military and political aspects of the past. They also have a less positive outlook than female students. An important variation, however, must be brought to this portrait. In the Quebec sample, these important gender differences do exist, but the gap is significantly less pronounced, as if there was a greater convergence of stories of the collective past, at least as far as young women and men are concerned. This suggests that gender differences are not universal but are socially constructed and dependent on context.

In terms of language, there are interesting variations between Ontario and Quebec participants. Young francophones in Ontario show less enthusiasm than non-francophones for narratives of the *francophone experience*; they also use more frequently other narrative frameworks such as *Canadian nation-building*. Another difference in the way of telling their history relates to the use of the first-person singular and first-person plural in text. Francophone students are more likely to refer to the collective "we" when talking about predecessors, while non-francophone students prefer to position themselves directly in text as first-person narrators.

In Quebec, the results are different. Francophone students take ownership of the *francophone experience* narrative; non-francophones do so to a lesser degree. The situation of allophone students is interesting, in that many of them tell narratives similar to those of francophone Québécois, indicating interest in or even rapprochement with the collective past of the dominant historical group. Anglophones, by contrast, are reluctant to embrace the historical vision of their French-speaking peers. They choose instead to live in several interpretative realms that do not fall into a single narrative orientation. The limited sample of participants makes it difficult to generalize for this language group. That being said, our results suggest that gender and language seriously affect how young French Canadians engage with the collective past and adopt a narrative voice. The theory of historical consciousness attends to the context of narrative representations and the identity of narrators. It helps explain why students from different gender and linguistic backgrounds tell distinctive stories of the collective past. It also creates opportunities for young people to analyse their own and others' narratives in ways that reveal the convergences and divergences between male and female students, between francophones and anglophones or allophones.

4
Collective Identity

Gender and language are cultural factors that affect how people relate to the past, but collective identification also shapes historical consciousness. Our sense of belonging – or collective identification – has a strong impact on how we see the world and think about ourselves as historical beings. Collective identification can be described as the personal attachment an individual establishes with a group. This identification contributes to the construction of the self, making a person a member of the collectivity to which she or he belongs.[1] Collective identification is a useful concept in research about historical consciousness because it makes it possible to articulate the relation between the individual (the self) and the collective (us) in the construction of historical identity. This concept provides an additional tool for evaluating how young French Canadians identify with certain groups, as well as how this identification process affects their narrative representations of the past. As Rüsen contends, narrative and identity are central elements of historical consciousness. Historical narration orients practical life by situating the self in the context of temporal and collective experiences.

People identify with various groups, ranging from families, to social clubs and religious organizations, to world movements. While such identification often involves political entities such as a sovereign state, it may also include societal groups such as "nations within" a state that seek collective rights and recognition.[2] As these imagined communities are "neither natural nor self-evident," collective identification must be constructed and maintained over time.[3]

Schooling plays an important role in this identity-building process. Indeed, education ministries in Canada have traditionally promoted through their policies and curricula a particular sense of belonging to Canada.[4] This national belonging has been understood as a prerequisite for democratic stability and social cohesion. But the multi-national nature of Canada has led French and English Canadians to devise their own separate nation-building projects. In the province of Ontario, francophones have access to a public French-speaking school system that promotes its own distinct sense of collective identification. As the Canadian and World Studies curriculum for Ontario's francophone schools points out:

> In French-language schools, quality learning takes place in an environment conducive to the construction of Francophone identity. Indeed, to awaken and open up to the Francophonie, to become aware of its challenges, to identify its characteristics, to engage with it with pride and to contribute to the vitality of its institutions is undoubtedly the added-value of Francophone education.[5]

Quebec school history is consistent with this approach. The HEC program has been criticized by some for its lack of attention to collective identity; it does, however, present specific lines of analysis that invite students to study the national culture specific to Quebec society:

- Name movements of thought that are manifest today in Quebec (e.g., Indigeneity, feminism, nationalism)
- Give characteristics of Quebec's cultural identity (e.g., French language, values of freedom and equality)
- Identify the means for disseminating culture (e.g., literature, theatre, music, sculpture)[6]

Surprisingly, few studies have focused on the impact of collective identification on students' historical consciousness despite school history's inherent interest in identity building.[7] This chapter presents students' narrative orientations in relation to their sense of identification. By conducting a cross-analysis of data on students' collective identification with their historical narratives, we determine the role of identity in the functioning of historical consciousness. More specifically, we show that identity orients students' narrative ideas about the collective past through social categorization and comparison. While the process of collective identification is similar among both Ontario and Quebec students, there are nonetheless important differences in students' attachment to the "nation."

Canada: A Country of Variable Identities

In the first chapter, we noted that Quebec students identify primarily as "Québécois" (69%) and then as "Canadians" (20%). In Ontario, the proportion is reversed: 55% "Canadian" and 26% "Franco-Ontarian." To help us understand the impact of identity on historical consciousness, we asked participants to assess their own sense of collective identification with various groups on a spectrum ranging from low identity (1) to high identity (7). How does their sense of belonging affect the ways in which they tell the history of French Canada?

The first finding from our analysis is that Canadian identity is important to students in Ontario. As seen in figure 4.1, the overwhelming majority of participants identify strongly with Canada. In fact, 80% of them indicate a strong sense of belonging (levels 5–6–7) to the country. These figures confirm the results of Patrick Fournier and Mike Medeiros in their comparative study of Quebec and Ontario citizens, which reveals that nearly 90% of young Franco-Ontarians surveyed feel very positive about Canada.[8]

This sense of collective identification among Franco-Ontarian students is strongly linked to the types of narratives they tell. The more participants identify with Canada, the more their stories are geared toward certain narrative orientations, particularly *Canadian nation-building*. In total, 90% of stories of *Canadian nation-building* were produced by Franco-Ontarians, mostly from Eastern Ontario, who identify strongly with Canada. These stories highlight the great moments in the development of the colony following the arrival of Europeans in America. Christopher Columbus, Jacques Cartier, and Samuel de Champlain are the emblematic figures of this colonial period. This episode is followed by the creation of the Canadian federation in 1867, the building of the transcontinental railway, the successive waves of immigrants, and the important role played by Canada during the two world wars. Numerous stories of nation-building also refer to French Canadians and the part they played in developing the country, especially at the time of Confederation but also during domestic and international armed conflicts. Some students also connect the past of Canada to the multicultural nature of the country today.

The following excerpts, one from Northern Ontario and two from Eastern Ontario, offer examples of narratives from students who identify strongly with Canada:

> People from Europe/Great Britain came for fishing. At one point, a sailman explored further the continent. He discovered Canada. Another one wanted to populate the new country. He led the construction of the railway across all of Canada in order to populate the west. The population has grown. There was also the Gold Rush that attracted +++ immigrants to Canada. Growing up a lot and formed various provinces to join Canada. We have been under the command of Great Britain. We fought for our

Figure 4.1 Narrative orientation and identification with Canada for Ontario students

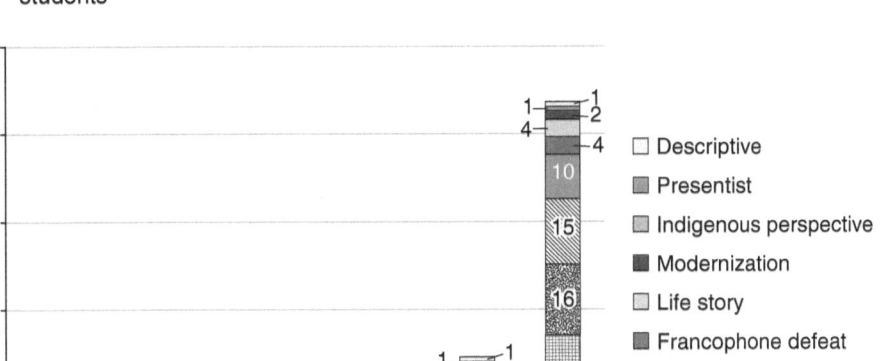

independence. We had to fight for French and French rights. The various groups joined to form modern Canada. We had to accept different cultures to settle the North and the Prairies (West). We have grown a lot thanks to the wheat/cereal market. We continue to welcome many immigrants who make us grow. (0110A16-East)

Voyageurs came from France and discovered Canada. Samuel de Champlain and Christopher Columbus were French-speaking explorers who founded Canada. The French were the first ones to settle the country of Canada. Canada now has many different languages but the most popular are English and French. (0212A02-North)

On July 1, 1867, French, English, and then Aboriginals formed Canada. From that moment, the francophones were part of Canada. They participated along with 700,000 Canadians in the First World War – French Canadians also participated in the Second World War. (0110A03-East)

Interestingly, a strong sense of belonging to Canada does not simply produce narratives of *Canadian nation-building*. Stories of *francophone adversity*, *francophone affirmation*, and *francophone presence* are also influenced by students' collective identification. This may be surprising when we consider that these narratives are not attuned to Canadian nationalism. Instead, they tend to emphasize linguistic conflicts between French and English Canadians in the history of the country and the evolution of French Canadian identity over time. Some of these narratives even discuss the current political debates surrounding the creation of a Franco-Ontarian university:

> Jacques Cartier arrived in Canada, being the first [European] to find the land. There were more English-speaking people than French. And this has caused trouble between the two groups. Because of Regulation 17 Francophones did not have the right to go to school and therefore, students attended school in churches because the English could do nothing inside them. Basically, they had the right to have an education in French there. Today they are trying to have a Franco-Ontarian university. (0211A10-North)
> After the English and French settled their argument, they decided to divide the territory of Canada into two (Canada East and Canada West). This was intended to give French Canadians (later called Quebecers) a place where they could live in peace, but there were also French Canadians who stayed there (Canada West). Several years later, French Canadians became francophones (or Franco-Ontarians) as known nowadays. (0210B04-South)
> To conclude, Quebec is the only predominantly French-speaking province because it is the only territory that the French managed to defend. The French in Canada were mostly at the mercy of the English which explains the proportion of cultures in Canada. (0210A07-South)

That Franco-Ontarian students who identify strongly with Canada produce stories both critical of Canadian nationalism and strongly rooted in French Canadian history may seem contradictory. How can this be possible? In our pilot project with young Ottawa citizens, we postulated that Canadian and Franco-Ontarian identities are not antithetical; rather, they constitute communicating vessels that allow young Franco-Ontarians to define themselves as Canadians while assuming a francophone perspective on Canada's historical experience.[9] Our results confirm this hypothesis. Canadian identity can act as a conduit for students who view themselves as "Canadian" to tell the history of French Canada from the larger perspective of the francophone presence. Canadian identity would thus be a kind of unexpressed variant of French Canadian character, one that better corresponds to students' bilingual and multicultural identities. From this point of view, a strong sense of belonging to Canada does not necessarily imply the construction of a nationalist historical consciousness derived from a narrow vision of the country in which francophones would occupy a secondary place in the great Canadian mosaic. The following narratives express this view:

> Now we can find francophones across Canada, in Ontario, Manitoba, Alberta, etc. We have come a long way to have our freedom of language, but because of these brave and proud francophones, we are stronger and prouder than ever. (0110A16-East)
> During Regulation 17 we did not give up our rights and we fought back to get what we wanted, to speak our language. (0111A12-North)
> Francophones have worked very hard to have their rights and freedoms just like the English. In the end, the French won and the French language became as an official language. There were problems of discrimination against francophones (ex: Montfort hospital) but these people are the reason why French is an official and popular language in Canada. (0211A01-East)

The analysis of key terms in relation to collective identification provides additional evidence. As indicated in Table 4.1, the concepts used frequently (in raw terms and as a comparative percentage between strong and weak identification) by Ontario students who identify strongly with Canada refer to key aspects of Franco-Ontarian history. The relationship between "French" (83%) and "English" (83%), "language" (85%), relations between "Quebec" (88%) and "Ontario" (93%), "Regulation 17" (87%), and the French-language "school(s)" question (89%) are recurring elements in the stories of these participants.

The following Ottawa student sums up quite well the beliefs of many Franco-Ontarians who identify strongly with Canada:

> In my opinion, the history of francophones in Canada is the story of a people who had to struggle constantly to be able to speak their language. (0111A06-East)

For these participants, it is clear that identification with Canada encourages the internalization of events from the collective past into their own consciousness and makes it possible for them to associate with predecessors in the *longue durée* of history. Collective identification thus mobilizes the memory of past events with a conception of historical continuity for the group to which students belong. It reminds young francophones that their predecessors also fought for language rights, often successfully, and that they too can overcome today's challenges. Grounding their identity in the collective past generates this sense of

Table 4.1 Key terms in relation to identification with Canada for Ontario students

Key terms	High identification		Low identification	
	frequency	%	frequency	%
French	416	83	84	17
Canada	317	92	29	8
English	177	83	37	17
Francophone(s)	185	86	30	14
Language	152	85	26	15
Country	129	87	19	13
Quebec	132	88	17	12
We	122	92	11	8
War	113	88	16	12
Ontario	84	93	6	7
School(s)	79	89	10	11
France	78	85	14	15
Regulation 17	73	87	11	13

a common venture among a collective *we*, the people. As indicated in Table 4.1, a total of 122 mentions (92%) of the word "we" were recorded in the stories of students with a strong Canadian identity, compared to only 11 mentions (8%) for students with a low Canadian identity. When considering all Ontario narratives together, 74% of all uses of the first-person plural pronoun come from students with a strong Canadian identity.

For understanding the role of first-person plural in students' narratives, Henri Tajfel and John Turner's social identity theory (SIT) is helpful.[10] SIT explains that part of a person's conception of self comes from the group to which that person belongs – the "ingroup." As a consequence of this identification with the ingroup, the person gradually assigns emotional significance to that identification, and self-esteem comes to be dependent on it. To maintain this self-esteem over time, the person and the group members not only compare their ingroup favourably against other ones but also minimize their perceptions of differences between ingroup members so as to strengthen group cohesion. The use of the first-person plural becomes a rhetorical device for connecting with the collective past and for stabilizing a person's identity in relation to that of other members so that "everything began in the 1600s when *we* French people discovered Canada" (0111A13-East), "*we* have waged wars to keep *our* beautiful language" (0110A16-East), and "still today *we* must fight" to preserve our language (0112A11-East). These terms point to students' historical awareness as contemporary members of a historical group and help set the scene for a meaningful narrative that allows students to tap into the past so as to forge a positive identity connection as young French-speaking citizens. French colonists are no longer bygone strangers, they are part of who *we* are. They remind us of *our* collective responsibility for the future of the French language in America.

Interestingly, the use of first-person plural among Ontario participants with a strong sense of identification is also indicative of a particular picture of the group that is broader than that of the province of Ontario and that dates back to a historic, pan-Canadian vision of French Canada. Indeed, many students speak about "we" in relation to other Canadians, especially when referring to events such as traditional French Canadian national holidays: "We celebrate the St-Jean-Baptiste Day" (0111A04-North). In this context, Québécois are occasionally perceived by Franco-Ontarians as distant, inward-looking, and ethnocentric in their relations with other citizens of the country because they define their national identity in provincial terms, as the following Ottawa student reveals:

> According to Quebec, Quebecers are the only francophones. When they wanted independence, it shocked me a bit. They forgot us! In their passion for a country with a unique culture they forgot that a large part of their culture was outside Quebec, as part of the country they wanted to excommunicate. (0112A13-East)

Quebec students display a much more limited collective identification with Canada than their Ontario peers. As indicated in figure 4.2, only 43% of participants reported a strong sense of belonging to Canada, compared to 80% in Ontario. These results are consistent with the findings presented in chapter 2 on the geographical notion of "country," which indicate that only a minority of participants chose to focus their narrative on Canada. Since Quebec students do not identify strongly with Canada, collective identification has only a limited effect on their narrative orientation. In fact, a sense of belonging to Canada influences students' ideas only to the extent that it is moderate (levels 1–4). And interestingly, it is not the *Canadian nation-building* orientation that offers conclusive results – indeed, no student who identifies very strongly with Canada tells this type of national narrative.

Figure 4.2 Narrative orientation and identification with Canada for Quebec students

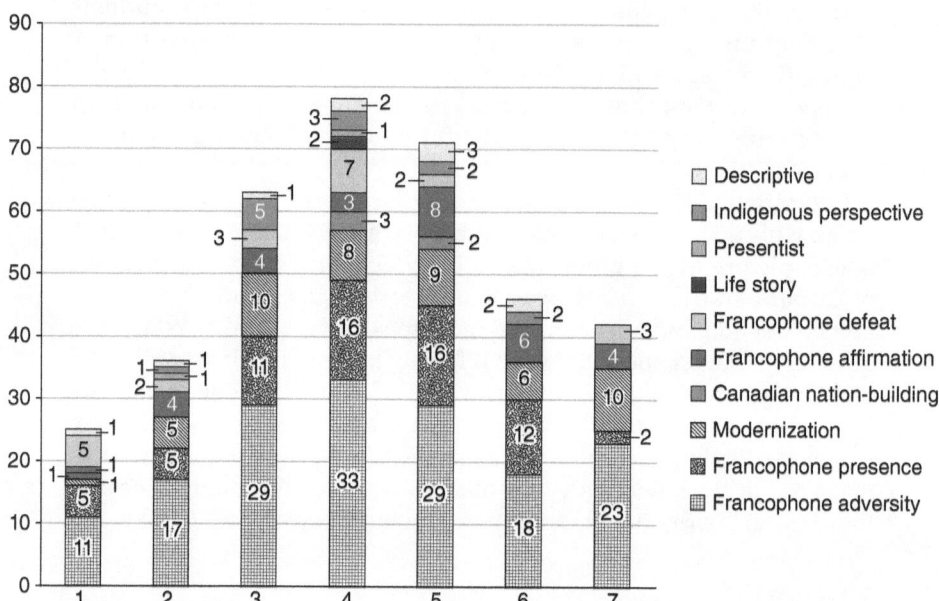

When examining the data more closely, we find that the only narrative orientation affected positively by identification with Canada is that of *modernization*. The number of stories focused on the social and economic development of the country increases as participants identify more favourably with Canada. In total, 67% of stories of *modernization* come from participants who identify moderately or strongly with Canada (levels 4–5–6–7). We believe that stories of *modernization* represent a strategic way for these young Québécois to conceive national history in less nationalist terms. Their narrative vision is focused on the socio-economic development of society, with many references to the fur trade, commerce, and industrialization. Some also address economic crises and the recent recession, as illustrated by the following students:

> We discovered a land (New France), we sent settlers to populate it. But there was a gender problem, there were more men than women, so we sent the Filles du Roy to find husbands, to make children, and allow for an increase of population. (GR0014-Montreal)

Collective Identity 121

Before the arrival of the Europeans, the Aboriginals occupied the lands of North America. One day, several boats docked on the shores of this unknown land. The French landed in Gaspésie while the English settled on the east coast of what will later be the United States. There was the fur colony and then the settlement colony. The fur trade had its reign but was replaced by wood lumber during the blockade of Napoleon. Then, the first phase of industrialization arrived and led to urbanization, then the second phase of industrialization with unionization. We fell into economic crisis and we had to go beat up a couple of Germans (World War II) to restart the economy. Then Quebec became ambitious and wanted to become independent, we tried twice, it did not work. Supposedly, it was due to ethnic votes and money. In any case, it's a big scandal. After that Quebec became more globalized, and now we face another recession. (GR0106-Central Quebec)

An analysis of the key terms in relation to collective identification helps confirm this narrative trend (Table 4.2). The concepts most often cited by Quebec students who identify strongly with Canada deal with relations between the "French" (58%) and the "English" (53%), the colonial period with "New France" (59%), "colony/colonies" (81%), "Filles du Roi" (72%), "Aboriginal/Indigenous" (53%), "francophone(s)" (64%), "language" (52%) and "war(s)" (61%).

In most cases, the colonial period is seen as a vast project of territorial expansion in America, characterized by the fur trade and the *coureurs des bois*, as well as both positive and negative relations with Indigenous peoples. The "Filles du Roi" frequently appear as those who saved the colony from demographic collapse. Then stories shift after the conquest of New France. From then on, the focus is on the impact of the Industrial Revolution, on recessions, and on social struggles. Unlike their Ontario peers, Quebec students rarely refer to Western Canada, Ontario, or Upper Canada in their vision of the country. Their stories take place in New France and later in the province of Quebec:

The king finally decides to turn the fur colony into a colony of settlement and to favour the arrival of settlers, he give the fur monopoly over to the Hundred Associates for + or – the arrival of 4000 inhabitants in 15 years. (04A10-Quebec City)

Thanks to the Filles du Roy, Quebec was able to develop and to have many industries including wood lumber and fur that were sold in France. (0205A12-Gatineau)

There was the crisis of the 1930s. In 1929, the Krash of the New York Stock Exchange caused a global economic crisis. A large number of

Table 4.2 Key terms in relation to identification with Canada for Quebec students

Key terms	High identification		Low identification	
	frequency	%	frequency	%
French	350	58	256	42
Quebec	189	56	146	44
English	187	53	163	47
Canada	171	55	142	45
France	233	60	158	40
We	169	61	108	39
Francophone(s)	145	64	83	36
New France	142	59	99	41
Colony/colonies	118	81	27	19
Aboriginal/Indigenous	71	53	64	47
War(s)	102	61	64	39
Language	103	52	94	48
Country	65	34	34	44
Filles du Roy	46	72	18	28
Commerce	43	69	19	31

workers were unemployed and the unemployment rate was climbing. (0105A17-Gatineau)

Another interesting element particular to this group is the limited impact of identification with Canada in terms of using the collective "we." Unlike Franco-Ontarian students, Quebec participants who identify strongly with Canada do not necessarily use the first-person plural more frequently than others. This suggests that a sense of Canadian belonging does not affect Quebec students' narrative representations in the same way. Their identity connection with Canada does not lead them to tell more nationalist narratives. Most of them do not see the Canadian state as their national "ingroup," so for them, collective identification with Canada is not a determining factor in establishing a strong association with the country's past as a whole.

Franco-Ontarian and Québécois: Cultural or National Identities?

Our investigation did not pay attention solely to Canadian identity. Given the multi-national nature of Canada, we also asked students in each province to express their sense of identity as "Franco-Ontarian" and "Québécois," two conceptual terms that now characterize French

Canadian identity. The purpose was to determine whether young French Canadians have multiple allegiances and, if so, to examine the extent to which those allegiances are complementary in telling the history of French Canada. The results are indicative of a larger phenomenon, that of the attachment of francophones to their provincial or linguistic community.

As seen in figure 4.3, Ontario students do not have a strong sense of belonging to French Ontario. In total, 40% of participants identify strongly as Franco-Ontarian (levels 5–6–7). The majority (60%) express instead a moderate sense of belonging to French Ontario. These findings contrast sharply with those in figure 4.1 on Canadian identity and remind us of a crucial reality: Ontario's francophone community does not have a geographic, historical, and imagined sense of self. In some ways, Franco-Ontarians are like English-speaking Ontarians when it comes to their understanding of the country; they view regional allegiances as secondary to national ones.

For geographer Marie Lefebvre, the break-up of French Canada in the 1960s has led to the creation of "softer identities" outside Quebec, thus suggesting that the strength (or weakness) of post–French Canadian identities is tied to collective geographic roots in communities of memory and destiny.[11] From this point of view, young Franco-Ontarians do not imagine their francophone community in terms of a strong and distinct cultural identity; instead, they consider the Canadian and Franco-Ontarian identities as communicating vessels allowing them to identify with the Canadian state with no negative effect on their Franco-Ontarian sense of self. In fact, many young francophones are not comfortable with the Franco-Ontarian identity to the degree that it is perceived as exclusive, even ethnic; they see it as imperfectly defining their relations with other cultures with which they share practices, both inside the school and outside. From this perspective, Canadian identity is more fluid and inclusive and does not conflict with francophone identity in French-speaking communities in Ontario or elsewhere in the country. As this student from Eastern Ontario sums it up: "Francophones are Canadians who speak French" (02010A02-East).

How does this sense of identification affect students' narratives of the collective past? According to our analysis of narrative orientations (see figure 4.3), Franco-Ontarian identity only has an impact on narrative if it is expressed moderately by students. We see an increase in stories of *francophone experience*, particularly *francophone adversity*, up to a moderate level of collective identification (levels 4–5). This result suggests that Franco-Ontarian identity can contribute, but only to a certain

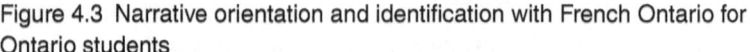

Figure 4.3 Narrative orientation and identification with French Ontario for Ontario students

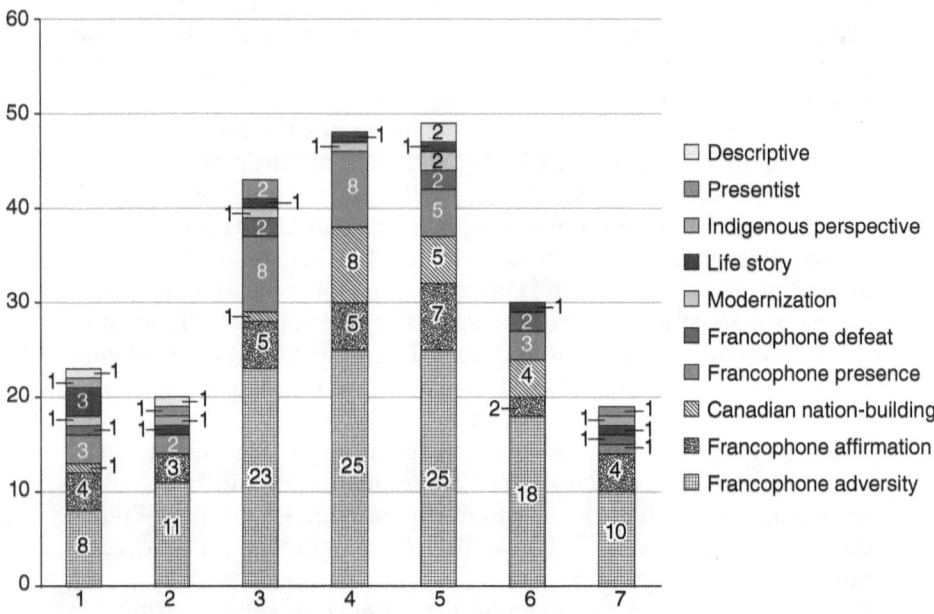

extent, to the production of stories presenting the historical experience of French Canada. Interestingly, identification with French Ontario does not lead to the telling of more radical or militant narratives of the collective past (e.g., *francophone defeat* or *francophone affirmation*). On the contrary, two thirds of these narratives come not from students with a very strong sense of Franco-Ontarian identity, but rather from those with a medium or even low sense of identification (levels 1–4). Thus, those who identify with French Ontario opt for a much more nuanced vision of the past, one that expresses doubts and fears about the future of francophones in Canada. These narratives most likely represent their own experiences as young Franco-Ontarians living in a minority situation.

The following excerpts from students who identify with French Ontario are good examples of the *francophone experience*. While some talk about the historical development of Franco-Ontarian communities and the legacy of predecessors, others take a more affirmative stance and even blame the "Other" for forcing the assimilation of francophones through draconian and even exaggerated measures such as "beating students" who spoke French (0111A04-North). In these students' narratives, we typically find a dualistic structure characterized by ongoing confrontations and conflicts, either between France and Great Britain during the colonial period, or between francophones and anglophones in modern Canada:

> There are francophones everywhere in Canada. Their stories are presented in schools and museums. Even here in Windsor, far from the French majority, the names of French families are still present and go back several generations in French Canadian history. (01112A12-South)
> At one point, there was a conflict with Britain over land control, which led to the Battle of the Plains of Abraham, with the General at the Citadel of Quebec and General Wolfe. The French lost and had to return Canada to Britain, which is why we are led by Queen Elizabeth II today. They took away our rights as French, forcing us to speak and write English. Some politicians fought for their freedom in the 1800s. (1110A05-East)
> Francophones have to fight to be able to keep their language. Thanks to the people of that time that today we are able to have French schools. The English who were in power banned the use of French in schools. So there was regulation 17. Often the students and teachers were beaten by the police who forbade the teaching in French. Today we have the St-Jean-Baptiste Day to celebrate the Francophonie. We also have a flag for us. (0111A04-North)

As with the earlier results on narrative orientation, the analysis of key terms (see Table 4.3) also indicates a limited impact of Franco-Ontarian identity on students' narrative structure. In fact, two key terms have a very positive relationship with the Franco-Ontarian identity: "we" (74%) and "Franco-Ontarian/Canadian" (70%). These two elements are closely related to each other. The use of the first-person plural is indicative of a particular understanding of the past that reinforces students' associations with predecessors in a linguistic community extending from colonial times to the present. Franco-Ontarians who identify as such are more likely to ascribe significance to their own history because it represents the story of their own people and contributes to their confidence or self-esteem as francophones today.

The following narrative excerpts present the views of participants who identify as "Franco-Ontarian." These students explicitly associate themselves with the past of French Canada (and not exclusively French Ontario) and notably with French colonists who later will become

Table 4.3 Key terms in relation to identification to French Ontario for Ontario students

Key terms	High identification		Low identification	
	frequency	%	frequency	%
French	145	53	131	47
Canada	91	53	82	47
Francophone(s)	63	39	68	61
We	57	74	20	26
Quebec	49	64	28	36
Language	49	56	39	44
Country	47	59	33	41
English	45	39	71	61
Franco-(On/Can)	40	70	17	30
Ontario	31	53	27	47
France	31	55	25	45
Regulation 17	30	57	23	43
School(s)	29	54	25	46

"Franco-Ontarians." In text, they use symbols such as the flag and St-Jean-Baptiste Day strategically to express their collective pride:

> We Franco-Ontarians originally came from Quebec. Our flag was officialized around the 1970s. (0110A05-East)
> Franco-Ontarians were at the origin of the French who came to settle in New France. As the population grew in Eastern Canada, we began to colonize Northern Ontario. (0111A21-North)
> St-Jean-Baptiste Day is also celebrated by Franco-Ontarians with performances by francophone artists. This holiday is to celebrate French Canadians. (0111A04-North)

As might be expected, the results for Quebec students are drastically different. Nearly 70% of participants identify strongly with Quebec (see figure 4.4). In many respects, these results correspond to those obtained in chapter 2 on geographical orientation, which reveal that a strong majority of participants evoke the Quebec territory to locate their history. This is not merely a coincidence. As we pointed out earlier, the redefinition of French Canada in the 1960s led to the emergence of various French-speaking identities, which are now associated with provincial entities. In Quebec, the conflation of the province with the nation no doubt lies behind this strong sense of collective identification.[12]

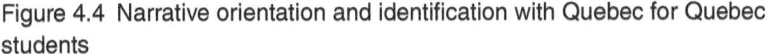

Figure 4.4 Narrative orientation and identification with Quebec for Quebec students

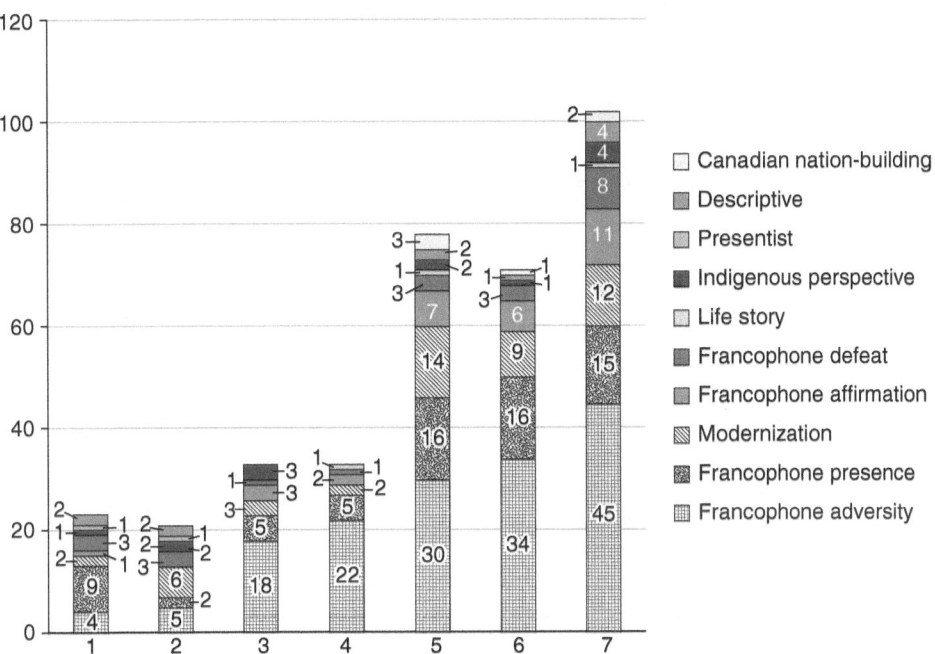

According to our results, a strong sense of belonging to Quebec positively affects certain types of narratives. The more students identify with Quebec, the more their narratives are influenced by the *francophone experience*. In fact, of all narrative orientations, the one with the highest incidence among these students is that of *francophone adversity*, with 69% of stories of adversity written by students with a strong Quebec identification. These results are logical and consistent with the ones of Ontario students.

In either case, a moderate or strong sense of identification with the linguistic or provincial community (Franco-Ontarian or Quebec) favours the telling of stories that share a common vision of the past, a national history characterized by French Canadian adversity over time. The power of the *francophone adversity* orientation lies in its capacity to structure a variety of specific historical narratives of French Canada.

Although the Quebec and Ontario narratives use the same starting point (the European explorations), the former is structured around four constant features specific to Quebec collective memory.

The first feature, shared by both groups, corresponds to the colonization of New France and its territorial expansion across America, its commercial and cultural relations with the Indigenous peoples, and its various settlements, notably along the St. Lawrence River. Samuel de Champlain, Jean Talon, and the "Filles du Roi" are the emblematic figures of this era, which, despite the severe climate and lack of resources, is generally perceived by Québécois as the golden age of New France:

> The history of francophones in this country began when French merchants came to America to trade with First Nations. In the beginning, settlement was slow because the companies (which dealt with the fur trade) wanted to get rich and not fulfil their obligation to populate New France. However, in 1663, various measures were taken by the State to populate the colony and balance the number of men and women (such as the Filles du Roy). Thanks to this increase, the population of New France grew from 3,000 people at the beginning of the French regime to 65,000 in 1760. (04A14-Quebec City)
> In 1604, Samuel de Champlain landed in Quebec City. This is the beginning of francophones on our territory. Until the Quiet Revolution, Catholic values were central to the Quebec way of life. (02015A15-Gatineau)

Then comes a critical period commonly referred to as the Conquest. This is when the British (*les Anglais*) appear in the story. It coincides with the Seven Years' War and the devastating victory by the British in the Battle of the Plains of Abraham (1759), in which both commanding generals, General Wolfe and the Marquis de Montcalm, died in battle. This event is the turning point in the French colonial adventure in America. The Treaty of Paris of 1763 makes official the end of the war and the transfer of New France (Canada) to Great Britain. This also marks the beginning of British domination and assimilation of francophones in the anglo-dominant political space:

> Subsequently, violent battles from French Canadians were successful, but the British took over. The King of France was at war with England and could not save his colony and spend money for it. He therefore signed a peace treaty, giving New France to England. The English first imposed their language and their religion on the French Canadians. (0205A08-Gatineau)
> Having lost the war of the Conquest, New France passed into the hands of the British. Despite the fact that they were now in a British colony, French Canadians were able to retain some aspects of their culture. However,

during the British regime (1760–1867) Great Britain often tried to assimilate French Canadians through various means, but they have always remained attached to their culture. (04A14-Quebec City)

The third narrative feature of Quebec stories is defined by a long period of survival (*la survivance*), during which French Canadians have to fight vigorously for their existence in British North America. The armed rebellions of 1837–38, which were crushed by the British authorities and led to the union of the two colonies of Lower and Upper Canada, are symbolic of this collective struggle for survival. While some students present this period in rather dark tones (with reference to the public hangings of Patriots following the rebellions), others write instead about both negative and positive relations between French and English Canadians, with an emphasis on the social and political development of francophones in Canada:

> The English have always had priority over the French who were a minority, they (English) were much more to speak the English language. They (francophone) experienced injustice. There was the rebellion of the patriots. The English hung them because they could not assimilate them. (0105A08-Gatineau)
>
> The colony called Province of Quebec will be divided in two, Lower Canada and Upper Canada, and French Canadians will settle south in Lower Canada. Later, following the agreement with other provinces of British North America, BNA Act will lead to the creation of the Province of Quebec where the French Canadians will settle and will become Quebecers, where we are currently living. (04B19-Quebec City)

The last narrative feature of *francophone adversity* addresses the contemporary period and offers a mixed appreciation of the historical development of Quebec society. Although important progress has been made, especially during the Quiet Revolution, momentum is lost and the future is highly uncertain. Assimilation still looms in this age of globalization characterized by the dominance of English-language culture. For a few, the current situation in Quebec is the result of collective apathy and a lack of political activism to protect French-language rights:

> In terms of their way of life, their religion and their language, francophones have always had to fight to stay as they always were. They felt different from the rest of the Canadian population and today we still feel the difference. That is why many francophones want to separate from Canada and make Quebec a country. (05B16-North of Montreal)

The English put in place the political system. The French language is disappearing. (05A05-Saguenay)
Even today only a minority of the population is concerned about our language. I'm sure the slogan "I remember" is not appropriate. (GR0631-Montreal)

Collective identification with Quebec orients students' narratives; it also influences students' ability to conceive their stories in the broader Canadian context. For the majority of participants, Canadian and Quebec identities are not compatible. Quebec and Canada are two distinct national groups, each with its own territory, memories, and norms. This social categorization has two main effects on students' historical consciousness. First, they equate the history of French Canadians with the history of the province. "Country" is reduced to the "state of Québec" (*l'État québécois*), a political term that has gained legitimacy in the province since the Quiet Revolution and that has redefined the Quebec government's role in socio-economic affairs.

Second, categorization leads students to another related phenomenon known as "social comparison." Once persons categorize themselves within a group and identify with that group, they tend to compare their own "ingroup" against another group – the "outgroup." In the case of Québécois, the outgroup represents Canadian citizens living outside Quebec, sometimes referred to as "Rest of Canada." The construction of this dichotomous ingroup/outgroup narrative structure minimizes perceptions of ingroup differences and amplifies the differences between groups. Social comparison is obvious in narratives of students who strongly belong to Quebec. They focus on the history of the dominant group – the Québécois. French Canadian communities in Ontario and elsewhere in Canada are completely occluded by students, who do not hesitate to assimilate them with English Canada. In this context, the struggle for cultural survival takes place exclusively in terms of Quebec:

We are not Canadians but Quebecers. We speak French unlike other provinces, which differentiates us from these people. (GR0424-Central Quebec)
Fortunately, the French kept a piece of territory, Quebec. From now on, they are no longer called "French" but "Québécois." (GR0512-Montreal)

Some narrative orientations are positively affected by a strong sense of identification with Quebec; others are not. The less strongly students identify with Quebec, the more likely they are to produce *life experience*

Collective Identity 131

or *descriptive* narratives. In either case, students tell narratives with little emotional attachment to the collective past, which is often presented as a chronological list of simplified historical information. In the following excerpt, this student from Montreal bluntly claims that Quebec history is simply long and boring:

> In short, Quebec history is long and uninteresting and filled with details with which we cannot be too excited. This is my personal interpretation of the history of French Canada. (GR0609-Montreal)

The use of key terms is just as revealing of a certain vision of the past among students who identify strongly with Quebec. As seen in Table 4.4, these participants most frequently refer to "French" (79%), "English" (76%), "Quebec" (76%) or "province" (72%), "language" (80%), "colony" (80%), and "New France" (82%). These concepts, as discussed in the analysis of orientations, highlight the connexions among Quebec's provincial territory, history, culture, and French language in the development of francophones.

Equally interesting, the use of the first-person plural is characteristic of a particular internalization of the past for students' personal orientation. As pointed out earlier in the analysis of Franco-Ontarians' narratives, references to the collective "we" make it possible to understand how each student identifies with certain characteristics or groups in the construction of a meaningful narrative. In total, 290 references (85%) were recorded in the narratives of students who identify strongly with Quebec compared to only 55 references (15%) for those with weak collective identification with Quebec. Clearly, collective identification with Quebec makes students far more likely to feel deeply attached to the past, and the numerous references to "we," "our," and "us" offer additional evidence in text.

Indeed, because of this sense of belonging, students imagine a collective past in which they personally relate to predecessors in such a way that *"we* arrived in America and *we* populated Quebec" (04A11-Quebec City), *"we* resisted" the taking over of New France (0205A07-Gatineau), *"we* have *our* own revenge with the baby boom" (04A10-Quebec), and *"we* could have converted to English language" (04A02-Quebec) but instead *"we* have developed *our* mode to thinking and *our* Quebec identity" (GR0233-Central Quebec). These observations concerning the use of the past in relation to students' identity-building are expressed in the following narrative excerpts. They reveal students' deep commitment to Quebec and their pride that they live in a French-speaking environment in America. While some speak proudly of Quebec as "our

Table 4.4 Key terms in relation to identification with Quebec for Quebec students

Key terms	High identification		Low identification	
	frequency	%	frequency	%
French	526	79	143	21
France	367	81	84	19
Quebec	314	76	97	24
English	306	76	98	24
We	290	85	55	15
Canada	283	78	82	22
Territory	227	79	61	21
New France	221	82	47	18
Francophone(s)	191	72	74	28
Language	181	80	44	20
Colony/colonies	159	80	40	20
War(s)	149	78	41	22
America	121	78	34	22
Country	99	79	27	21
Province	72	72	28	28

country," others express their emotional relationship to French ancestors by referring to them as "our" people:

> When this colony was taken by the English, they wanted to convert us to their culture. We even tried to become a country! We are the only province in Canada with such a unique and developed language. This is our language very different from that of France (different accents and expressions) that makes our country ... Oops we are not yet a country! (0205A07-Gatineau)
>
> We, descendents of French settlers, have the right to say with pride that we are a people that has been able to assert itself and that despite the inconveniences, we will continue our fight towards success. (0105A18-Gatineau)

Conclusion

The analysis of data on collective identification indicates that most participants have a strong attachment to historical communities, whether they define such communities in cultural, linguistic, or national terms. Recent theories of identity-building have drawn attention to the fluidity of social boundaries and community attachments with regard to personal agency, individual autonomy, and present-day affiliation. Citizens are drawn to transcend traditional categories of group identity grounded in memory, history, and national belonging. Our results provide more nuanced conclusions.

Participants in both Ontario and Quebec still feel *strongly* connected to established historical communities. In Ontario, Canadian identity is very strongly felt among students – more strongly than their collective identification with the Franco-Ontarian community. This hybrid national identity finds its roots in bilingualism and the minority culture in which Franco-Ontarians live their daily lives. For some, this identity favours the production of narratives oriented toward *Canadian nation-building*. For others, it stimulates the use of various memory experiences of the collective past to shape narratives of French Canadian adversity. Either way, Canadian identity acts as a gateway for these participants to tell various histories of the nation. As Lefebvre observes, the anglo-dominant environment in which French-speaking minorities operate "thus commands various forms of identification and modality of belonging to the Francophonie."[13]

Quebec students express collective identification differently. A minority of participants identify strongly with Canada, with most preferring to express a strong sense of belonging exclusively to Quebec. For the majority of them, these identities are not compatible. In fact, a strong sense of Canadian identity does not produce militant, nationalist narratives, but rather a vision rooted in economic and social history. We think this narrative orientation is a way for Quebec students to present national history without having to take a political stance in relation to the future of Quebec or Canada. In this sense, Canadian identity fosters the construction of a particular social consciousness that revolves around the processes of settlement, urbanization, industrialization, and unionization of society.

Collective identification with Quebec produces more predictable results. The more students identify as "Québécois," the more their stories are imbued with a distinctive francophone experience, that of *francophone adversity*. Interestingly, this narrative orientation is also common to Franco-Ontarian participants, which suggests that young French Canadians still share, at a certain level of generalization, a common vision of the historical experience of francophones in Canada even though they inhabit and belong to two distinct political entities. In either case, students' collective identification acts as a cultural lens that filters their narrative visions of the collective past. This lens helps them understand what categories and groups they belong to, what distinguishes strangers from community members, and what separates the historical experience of their community ingroup from that of the outgroup. The transmission of such visions of the collective past is accomplished through different public and private tools including, but not limited to, school history. As we will see in the next chapter, history educators are becoming more preoccupied with matters of collective identification, given that the promotion of a common national identity can serve to maintain the power and privilege of certain authoritative narratives, thereby undermining the various collective allegiances of today's citizens, allegiances that do not neatly fit traditional communities and their narrative representations.

5
Narrative Competence

The narrative activity of our study had two interrelated functions: (1) to probe the historical consciousness of young French Canadians, and (2) to engage them in the production of a historical narrative of the nation. As noted in the introduction, inviting students to reconstruct their vision of the collective past in the form of a narrative leads them to mobilize knowledge and experiences from historical culture using a familiar cultural tool that is also commonly used in the discipline of history to create representations of the past. In our view, narratives aim to construct historical meaning (to make sense of the past) based on a temporal vision of change over time that informs us about the relationship young people maintain with history, memory, and the collective past and about how this relationship forges their sense of identity and their vision of their national community.[1] But how might the theory of historical consciousness help young people generate usable narratives beyond the practical needs of collective memory? In this chapter, we address this question from an educational perspective.

Canadian Historical Thinking and the Missing Key Concept

The analysis of students' narratives has highlighted the diversity of interpretations that young people have developed. These narratives have a powerful influence on students' historical and political ideas, even challenging preconceived notions about what it means to be Canadian in a diverse, multi-national country like Canada. But they also point to important blind spots and simplifications that need to be addressed in the context of formal education. School history can play a key role in revealing the nature of historical narratives as well as their impact on community- and identity-building.

In both Ontario and Quebec, the mission of the French-speaking school system is built around certain principles and expectations. One of these relates to competence in historical thinking. Today's programs of study emphasize a particular understanding of how to think critically about the past. This distinctive Canadian model was first developed by Peter Seixas and his colleagues under the Historical Thinking Project, a national project based on influential works by English educational scholars under the auspices of the Schools Council History 13–16 Project (later referred to as the Schools History Project).[2] As Seixas recounts: "The Canadian project consists of six ideas that look very much like the British notion of second order concepts, and we go so far as to call them 'historical thinking concepts.' They are 'second order' in that they are procedural: they are not, to paraphrase Peter Lee, what history is about."[3]

These concepts include primary source evidence, historical significance, continuity and change, cause and consequence, historical perspective, and ethical judgment. Unlike first-order content knowledge (e.g., colonists, commerce, revolution, war, and rights), historical thinking concepts are meta-historical in the sense that they shape the way people engage with the past and *do* history. Historians, for instance, do not study *evidence*; rather, they conduct research, using evidence to support their historical claims. Historical thinking concepts have resulted in a variety of standards among Canada's provincial school systems that specifically address students' historical learning. In Ontario, today's curriculum articulates five historical thinking concepts, and this has left the notion of "ethical judgment" out of the educational picture. In Quebec, the concepts are not addressed individually in the history curriculum; instead they are embedded in broader competencies pertaining to (1) the examination of social phenomena from a historical perspective and (2) the interpretation of social phenomena using the historical method.

Recently, the Canadian model of historical thinking has been criticized for paying too little attention to the interpretive, deconstructionist nature of history, as well as for its insufficient attention to the dynamic relationships among past, present, and future as captured by the notion of historical consciousness, and for ignoring narration as an essential meta-historical concept and ultimately as a competence. As Seixas himself recognizes, the Canadian historical thinking model has "omitted discussion of how these historical thinking concepts ... can contribute to the construction and critique of narrative interpretations."[4] The result, as history educator Catherine Duquette recently pointed out, is that notions of "historical consciousness" and "narration," so essential to culture and to the discipline of history, are largely absent from Canadian history education.[5] This may seem paradoxical in a context of school reform that aims to place greater emphasis on inquiry, multiple perspectives, and thinking skills. How are students supposed to evaluate competing narratives of Canada's past if they have not first learned how narratives are constructed?

For Quebec historian Jean-François Cardin, the current situation is rooted in a certain misunderstanding of "new pedagogies" that place students at the heart of their learning and that dispute the role of narratives in education; such narratives are perceived as harmful to active learning of the history method, and to source analysis in particular.[6] Writing in the US context, Barton and Levstik make a similar argument: "We cringe when the word *narrative* comes up in education settings, for we fear we're about to be assaulted with claims that are simplified, overstated, or unreflective – or all three at once."[7] These criticisms are not entirely misplaced. For decades, the teaching of history in the Western world has been accomplished through the transmission of national narratives – the so-called grand narratives – with all the educational consequences that we know today. Perhaps James Loewen's popular book *Lies That My Teacher Told Me* best encapsulates the views of many.[8] Reintroducing narratives in the history classroom would thus amount to a return to traditional education. As Marc-André Éthier puts it, "if history is to be taught as a science, then schools should respect its disciplinary nature and insist not on reinstating one or more stories, but on the practice of the historical inquiry."[9]

Narration and the History Discipline

We believe that this opposition between "narration" and the "history discipline" is sterile. It creates an imaginary gap between the historian and his or her work, between the historian-narrator and evidence-based representations of the past. In many ways, the controversy over the nature of history as generated by postmodern theorists like Hayden White and Keith Jenkins is largely over. For years now, the act of narration has been studied and recognized as an epistemological foundation of history knowledge; today it represents a proven construction that, as Paul Ricoeur contends, "exposes the discourse of the historian."[10] Historian Alun Munslow sums up quite well the situation that has arisen from the "narrative turn" that now prevails in the field of history: "For [Keith] Jenkins, who was writing then in the early to mid-1990s, history was plainly a textualized discourse that was unavoidably 'positioned.' I endorse this judgement today. It is never possible to empty 'history' of the author-historian and/or his or her theories, attitudes, values, arguments, ideologies and so forth."[11]

For Seixas, the narrative turn has led to a consensus on three propositions about historical narration and how it works. First, narrative representations and the past are conceptually and ontologically different. The historical narrative is a construct that provides the past with a sense of coherence and direction. It does not simply show what actually happened, as Leopold von Ranke once contended. This realistic notion of history – that it is an objective reality "out there" that can be recovered and truthfully represented in the *right story* of the past – has given way to more deconstructionist approaches that reveal the presumptive and contingent nature of historical knowledge. Most historians – at least in the academic world – now accept that their narratives are not direct copies of the past (the *mimesis* in Ricoeur's term) but rather historical representations of a particular linguistic mode or discourse (the *diegesis*). As such, they cannot be cross-referenced with the past itself (for it is gone), only with other representations of it.

Second, there can be more than one historical narrative for any given set of events from the past, centring on different questions, perspectives, ethical choices, and narrative focalizations. Whatever students may think (often naively), there is no such thing as a complete, definitive grand narrative that encompasses all aspects of the past. As Seixas contends, "there are simply too many aspects, too many vantage points, too many scales, and so on, from which the phenomenon can be viewed."[12] In addition, narratives set out to answer particular questions about the past, and these questions are vast besides being informed by contemporary realities. In other words, new events trigger additional questions about the past that were not initially envisioned in earlier narrative works. "The past," as Arthur Chapman puts it, "has a future and the future keeps rewriting the past."[13]

Finally, all narratives can be critiqued for their plausibility. Unlike fictional narratives, historical narratives aim at representing a coherent reality of the past that conveys true, verifiable statements. But since history is a mode of narrative representation, it has no absolutist epistemological meaning in itself, only a sense of correspondence as "plausibility."[14] History is thus a complex activity that demands strategies for explaining argumentation and for justifying narrative arrangements, and these disciplinary strategies differentiate historical narratives from other stories of the past generated by the practices of collective memory.

Thus it becomes possible to envision a model of narrative competence that would inform the development of historical consciousness. Indeed, the need to make sense of and give meaning to the world implies a process whereby individuals transform the past and make its actualization possible through history. As Rüsen argues, "the linguistic form within which historical consciousness realizes its function of [temporal] orientation is that of the narrative."[15] It is through narration that it becomes possible to inscribe the dimensions of time (temporality) in a continuous process and thus to offer a synthetic vision of the human experience, one that allows for the orientation of personal life in time as well as for the formation of identities. But histories are inherently plural and changing in society. There are always conflicting views about the past and the future, and some of these are driven purely by ideological or political agendas.

Narrative competence is about learning to understand why narratives are plural, multifaceted, and never definitive. It also involves coming to appreciate the intellectual tools emerging from the history discipline for evaluating these representations, how they are constructed, and what powers and limitations they have. Without this sort of disciplinary competence, people are like passengers on a ship with no rudder for steering through "the shoals of the competing narratives that vie for [their] allegiance."[16]

Narration, Content, and Expression

In the field of narratology, Gérard Genette's seminal work *Discours du récit* (and his revised translated edition *Narrative Discourse*) represents perhaps the most comprehensive theory of narrative. Using French author Marcel Proust's epic *A la recherche du temps perdu* (*Remembrance of Things Past*), Genette extended the earlier ideas of folklore scholars like Vladimir Propp to identify what he considered the three conceptual pillars of narrative: story, narrative, and narration. For him, "story" and "narrating" could only exist by means of "narrative," which he equated with discourse:

> Story and narrating thus exist for me only by means of the intermediary of the narrative. But reciprocally the narrative (the narrated discourse) can only be such to the extent that it tells a story, without which it would not be narrative (like, let us say, Spinoza's *Ethics*), and to the extent that it is uttered by someone, without which (like, for example, a collection of archaeological documents) it would not in itself be a discourse. As narrative, it lives by its relationship to the story that it recounts, as discourse, it lives by its relationship to the narrating that utters it.[17]

As a literary theorist, Genette concerned himself mainly with narrative in the form of tales and novels, and thus he did not address the particulars of *historical narrative*, which, as we have seen earlier, seriously transforms our understanding of narrative because of its truth, retrospective dimension, which involves studying the past from a posterior vantage point. This retrospective view makes it possible to investigate the past through hindsight, which in turn enables historians to see things both in terms of the bigger picture and in terms of what has since unfolded. Furthermore, we expect historical narratives to have referentially based truth founded in evidence, not based merely on verisimilitude – that is, on the *appearance* of truth.

Munslow has proposed a model that in our view better characterizes narrative competence in history.[18] This model, represented in figure 5.1, considers three elements that are in constant interaction: narration (authorial function), content/story (the past), and expression (mode of representation).

The Content/Story

First, the past has to be organized into story-form. As we noted earlier, the past is not initially structured as a coherent story to be recovered. Historical actors had visions and narratives of their own, but these are contextually situated in the past and were created for purposes of their own time; as such, they do not provide us with the present-day stories we generate *about* this past.[19] The content/story element is where the narrator creates the story-space, which delimits the beginning and the end as well as the orderly arrangement of events to be narrated.

The concept of story-space requires a more detailed understanding of the explanatory strategies for content/story that historians use as way to present a unique narrative interpretation. After all, historical narratives are not simply summaries of established facts. When historians write narratives, they offer constructed *arguments* that are "amenable to scrutiny and debate."[20] These strategies might best be considered in terms of key questions that implicitly drive the work of narrators: How was the story created? What is the orderly arrangement of the discrete elements? How is the argumentation historically plausible? What ethical choices were made? How are these choices culturally bound?

What follows from these questions is a discussion of the role of historical thinking in structuring an argument in story-form. As Rüsen contends, the principle of narrativity leads to a distinct strategy of explanation that "underlies the peculiarity of historical thinking."[21] For him, this mode of thinking is structured around five interrelated principles: orientation in the temporal change of time, historical significance and perspective, rules of empirical research, forms of representation, and temporal direction for present-day purposes. Interestingly,

Figure 5.1 Munslow's act of narration

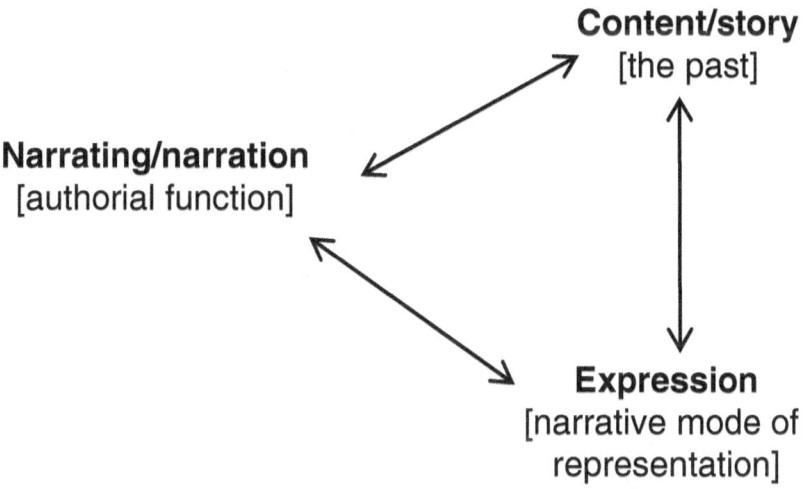

these principles, which more or less correspond to the key concepts of Canadian historical thinking presented earlier, have recently been transposed by Seixas in terms of how they apply to what he calls "narrative plausibility," that is, the disciplinary patterns of narrative construction.[22] Seixas's transposition helps us understand how historical narratives present particular arguments about the past based on key concepts and related dimensions, as well as the logic of the claims made by their authors. Table 5.1 presents historical thinking concepts as adapted by Seixas to the dimensions of narrative plausibility.[23]

- Historical narratives must be well-founded in evidence; they cannot be purely imaginary, nor can they contradict widely accepted truths. But *evidentiary plausibility* does not refer simply to established "facts" like dates and events because narratives are not truthful copies of the past. Evidentiary plausibility refers more broadly to the "body of evidence whose interpretation supports a particular narrative."[24] Sources from the past (relics and records) have to be selected and analysed according to their own particular historical context, the questions that drive the narrative argumentation, and the meanings ascribed to them. Narrators thus make critical judgments with regard to what sources count as evidence. Wineburg and his colleagues at Stanford have developed a set of heuristics for historians to use when dealing with historical evidence: sourcing

Table 5.1 Narrative plausibility in reference to historical thinking concepts

Historical thinking concepts	Dimensions of narrative plausibility
Evidence	Evidentiary plausibility
Continuity and change	Temporal plausibility
Cause and consequence	Causative plausibility
Perspective taking	Empathetic plausibility
Ethical dimension	Normative plausibility

(looking at the source type, subtext, and authorship), contextualization (situating the source in temporal and spatial context), and corroboration (comparing sources with one another for accuracy and reliability). As Seixas reminds us, working with evidence is never merely a technical problem of finding the right facts and then piecing them together like a jigsaw puzzle; rather, it is a "complex web of relationships between past and present, and thus between the historical discipline and everyday life."[25] Historical narratives thus enhance their evidentiary plausibility through the effective use and referencing of sources, so as to justify their relevance and utility.[26]

- Elements of continuity and change are key to narrative. Orderly arrangements of events over time (e.g., beginning, turning point, progress, decline) are fundamental to a coherent story of the past. For Seixas, these might be regrouped under the dimension of *temporal plausibility*, for they serve to establish in Rüsen's words a "temporal experience" of past times – and thus, a means of understanding the past and its specific temporal quality, as well as its translation into an understanding of the present and expectations regarding the future.[27] The challenge for narrators is to avoid naively assuming that continuity prevails over time – instead, continuity and change always coexist in history to various degrees. As Seixas contends, "the puzzle is to figure out how much of each there was, for whom, in any particular period in the past."[28] Recent growth in quantitative and statistical history, demographic history, and social history has altered our understanding of continuity and change and mapped out different pictures of the past and of the lives of societies previously ignored in historiography.
- Historical narratives, as David Thomson observes, "rest (if only implicitly) on a whole series of judgments about the relative importance of some events or people in 'causing' other subsequent developments."[29] Historical narratives thus aim at causal explanation. When establishing causal relationships, the chronological sequence of events is important but not sufficient. It is also

necessary for narrators to establish the immediate causes and the underlying factors (such as the political context and the *mentalités* of the time), as well as the role of historical actors (their agency) in promoting or resisting change. The dimension of *causal plausibility* helps us understand the degree to which the events assembled as causes in the narrative "convincingly determine the events and conditions identified as consequences."[30]

- For historical narratives to be possible, narrators must understand historical actors and the meanings of their actions using the relics and records they left behind. Only when we recognize their perspectives can we appreciate the minds and feelings of people who lived in places and times different from ours. *Empathetical plausibility* makes it possible to understand human experience in its complexity. It is woven into each of the previous dimensions. The analysis of historical evidence, as Seixas contends, requires "contextualizing it in the world views of its time, so perspective-taking is hardly an operation separate from reading sources at all."[31] Empathetical plausibility is also key to continuity and change and to cause and consequence. In order to confront difference over time, narrators must be in a position to evaluate how much has changed and how much has remained the same "in the make-up of the human psyche."[32] In the same way, to understand the role of historical actors and their agency, it is necessary to understand their thinking and care about their perspectives. This requires "imaginative intellectual and emotional participation."[33] Empathetic plausibility is also bound to the last dimension, "normative plausibility."

- Historical narratives, according to Munslow, always have "moral/ethical dimensions."[34] On the one hand, narrators are not neutral agents; they bring their own assumptions to the study of the past. The questions that drive their inquiries, the mechanisms and methods they use to acquire historical knowledge, and how their stories are structured are all informed by ethical considerations. Deconstruction was once regarded by positivist historians as "something to be avoided"; today, deconstructionist historians argue that ethical principles or what might be called *normative plausibility* cannot be avoided and ought to be recognized and explored.[35] As we will see in the next section, questions, methods, concepts, and language are contextually situated tools and practices and thus "bring with them the unavoidable imposition of the present on a past where people lived by ethical standards and mores different from our own."[36] On the other hand, we expect narratives to provide a sense of direction, to guide our actions and shape our moral-ethical consciousness. As Rüsen contends, "the sense-creating procedures of historical consciousness are necessary for moral values and for moral reasoning."[37] As historical beings, we use narratives as a moral compass to explain past actions, consider possible memorial obligations to predecessors, and change or justify ways of acting in the world. The normative plausibility of historical narratives would thus be the result of a careful interpretation of past and present values informing our actions, identities, and relations with predecessors. Presentism – that is, the naive imposition of present-day values and norms on the past – is the antithesis of successful normative plausibility, for it fails to look at the past in its complexity and to grasp its temporal quality, which differentiates it from the present.

The transposition of the Canadian historical thinking concepts onto elements of narrative plausibility provides us with a useful model for discussing the necessary elements for the realization of content/story. It shows that the organization of the past into story-form requires important narrative decisions comprised of the narrator's own ethical and epistemological orientations in investigating aspects of the past and in creating a structured, logical arrangement (the emplotment, or *mise en intrigue*, in Ricoeur's term) of events in a narrative argumentation.

Interestingly, narrative theorists like Gérard Genette, Roland Barthes, Tzvetan Todorov, and Vladimir Propp have argued that the story-arrangement is also governed by distinctive narrative choices, or "laws which govern the narrative matter," in Claude Bremond's words.[38] These laws reflect the logical constraints that any series of events must respect in order to be coherent and intelligible. Propp, for instance, was the first to identify schematic narrative patterns in folk tales based on a series of constantly recurring functions intended to structure their content/stories.[39] In the field of history, scholars like Paul Ricoeur, Louis Mink, Hayden White, and James Wertsch have similarly discussed the intrinsic structure of historical narratives, suggesting, among other things, that schematic templates are powerful cognitive tools that provide distinctive ways of emplotting events for memory and identity purposes.[40]

What follows from this analysis is that historical narratives are representations of the past based on distinctive rules of argumentation and thinking judgments. Students, including the ones we surveyed in our study, may hold narrative misconceptions, thinking that stories either recount subjective personal interpretations of the past that are all equally plausible and valid or, on the contrary, offer true definitive accounts of what happened in the past, so that knowing history amounts to knowing the *right story*. In either case, history is impossible. As Peter Lee and Rosalyn Ashby contend, many stories are told in society and "they may contradict, compete with, or complement one another, but this means that students should be equipped to deal with such relationships, not that any old story will do."[41]

In our study, participants used (perhaps implicitly) different strategies to make their narratives both coherent and plausible to the reader. Causal plausibility is one of the most recurrent dimensions, if not *the* most recurrent, found in their texts. Indeed, many students structured their stories in terms of cause/effect relationships, showing how one significant event led to another. The following is a typical example:

> Then there was the war of the thirteen-colony. This war has resulted in a large increase of English immigrant to Southern New France. This increase did nothing to the French, because the English had their side of country and the French, theirs. (0205A14-Gatineau)

In this excerpt, the student refers to the American War of Independence (the "war of the thirteen-colony"). According to him, this war "has resulted" (the direct cause) in the mass migration of British subjects to the colony of Canada, which he equates with "New France." Interestingly, for this student author, this war had both short- and long-term effects on the Canadian colony. It led to the direct arrival of many (large increase) British subjects in the colony; yet their mass arrival did not cause significant problems for French Canadians "because the English had their side of the country and the French, theirs." Here, the student is referring to the fact that the authorities of the time took measures to redirect the hordes of Loyalists arriving from the thirteen colonies to the English-speaking territories of southern Ontario (Upper Canada) and the Maritimes (Nova Scotia and New Brunswick). Although some Loyalists did settle in the province of Quebec (Lower Canada), they were much fewer in numbers, so they did not significantly affect in the long term the demographic weight of francophones in Canada. In this example, we can appreciate how this Quebec student has used causal plausibility to structure his historical argument about the development of French Canada.

Once learning history is viewed as developing an understanding of how narratives are structured in story-form, with distinctive procedures and principles, it becomes easier to promote narrative competence. But narration requires another key element, the *telling* (the narrative mode of representation), because for every content/story there is always an author-narrator.

The Narrative Expression

We noted earlier than narrative is not "merely a medium of report" designed to show what actually happened; it uses aesthetic principles to turn the past into "the-past-as-history."[42] Following Aristotle's rhetoric, Victor Ferry has recently revealed how narratives in the history discipline are dependent on both "extratechnical" evidence from the dimensions of narrative plausibility and rhetorical "technical" evidence generated by the narrator.[43] For Ferry, the discursive nature of narrative makes it impossible to separate the two sets of proofs even if historians tend to ignore how the narrative act "goes all the way through the process" of their historical investigation.[44] As he observes, the persuasive power of historical narrative is partly based on "processes that are part of the very structure of the text."[45]

We discussed in the previous section how historical narratives rely on various kinds of plausibility – most notably evidentiary plausibility – for their value and credibility in the domain of history. But how does technical evidence – that is, the rhetorical act of narrating – make historical narratives more plausible? To answer this question, we have to look at three interrelated elements of narration as a mode of representation: the historian as narrator, voice, and focalization.[46]

First, historians use narratives as a way to present their arguments. Their role is not to rescue stories from the past but to offer representations of it – reference to the past, explanation of the past, and meaning of the past. These representations are neither fixed nor universal; rather, they reveal the historian's own argument and positionality – his or her historical perspective, emotions, and beliefs. "Before you study the history," as E.H. Carr famously put it, "study the historian ... and b]efore you study the historian, study his historical and social environment." It is thus for Carr in this twofold light that "the student of history must learn to regard him."[47] Talking more broadly about narratology, Barthes asks us to always consider this question when approaching narratives: Who is speaking? Answers to this question help reveal the *diegetic universe* that historians create when arranging their narratives. This universe represents the spatio-temporal environment in which the story unfolds.[48] In our study, for example, some students imagined a diegetic universe confined solely to the historical realities of the province of Quebec, while others focused on Canada or North America as a whole. In the same way, many students told political narratives of European colonialism, while a small number, mostly in Quebec, established a socio-economic context. Variations in the narrative diegetic universe occur for different reasons: the perspective of the narrator (his/her point of view), the purpose of the narrative (the goal set by the narrator), the relationship between the subject and the narrator (how he/she relates to and engages with sources), and the context in which the narrative is produced (the historical culture in which the narrator lives).

Narrators can increase the plausibility of their narratives by generating arguments within a diegetic universe that better reveals their own subjectivity. Unlike fictional stories, historical narratives must be framed in ways that comply with the canons of historical argumentation. As Chapman observes, histories are written by narrators (hence subjective) but are written in ways that are open to scrutiny by an interpersonal audience (the narratee[s]). The plausibility of their narrative argument is thus linked "to the degree to which the patterns of explanation (and of sense-making) are made explicit and acceptable to the audience."[49] For Gerald Prince, narrations are always characterized by the type of narratee to whom they are addressed even if there is no explicit mention of this in text. "In all narrations," as Princes contends, "a dialogue is established between the narrator(s), the narratee(s), and the characters."[50] This dialogue develops as a function of the distance between the entities and the purpose of their relationship. In historical narratives, the narrator/narratee relation, developed through dialogue, metaphors, symbolic situations, and referencing systems, plays a central role because the narratee is more than a passive spectator – he or she contributes to the overall plausibility of the narrative through evaluative judgments about the quality of the argumentation (accuracy of the information presented, logic and coherence of the argument, methods employed, sources used, etc.).

In our study, for instance, participants were explicitly instructed to write a personal narrative for research purposes. As a result, students created narrative representations knowing that (1) the narratee was not their history teacher but an external reader (the researcher), and (2) the purpose was not to let others evaluate their understanding of formal curriculum objectives but rather to set down their own personal visions of the past. As we have shown in previous chapters, this approach made it possible to discover how our participants envisioned this narrative dialogue between the narrator and the narratee in text, as well to determine what diegetic context and sources of information they used for structuring their arguments. Because the participants implicitly knew that their performance was not tied to some prescribed learning outcome, we were able to identify some of the forces outside the school system, such as mythistories, that act to historicize the views of these young citizens.

Looking at the historian as narrator leads us to consider the twin concepts of voice and focalization. "Voice," as Munslow contends, "is concerned with the audibility of the historian-author who 'tells the story.'"[51] The narrator has a particular voice that is usually made clear through narrative choices. This voice can be personal and explicit, with references to the "I" form in text, but it can also be external or implied without direct reference to the narrator, as is often the case in history textbooks – thus leading to students' naive illusion that there is no narrator. Focalization refers to the focal choices of the narrator with regard to organizing and presenting the diegetic universe. It is defined in terms of the point of view from which the story is being told: Is it the narrator, the characters, or the historical agents? If the voice deals with "who speaks" in the story, focalization is concerned with "who sees" within the diegetic universe.[52] The narrator thus has power over both the voice and the focalization of the narrative discourse. Following the work of Genette, at least four types of voice and focalization can be found in historical narratives:

- The first-person narrator: the author tells the story in the first-person, recounting his/her own views in the content/story (the homodiegetic narrator). Here, the focalization can be internal to the diegetic universe, as in an autobiography or family history.
- The first-person actor: the author gives a direct voice to historical actor(s), who is/are observer(s) or member(s) of the events being narrated. As with the first position, the narrator becomes homodiegetic to the story and the internal focalization is on historical actors (e.g., first-person account from witness).
- The external narrator to the diegetic universe: the author tells the story without direct involvement in the content/story. Such a position is heterodiegetic to the universe, with an external focalization, meaning that the narrator does not know or follow the thoughts of historical actors in the content/story (the narrator is like an external observer).
- The omniscient narrator: as with position 3, the author tells the story without a direct role in the content/story. Such a position is heterodiegetic to the universe but with zero focalization, meaning that the narrator can explore the thoughts of actors and, at the same time, explain and analyse the situation, knowing more than the historical actors themselves due to his retrospective view on events (this is the typical history narrator).

These four positions are obviously not incompatible, and historians often resort to more than one type of voice and/or focalization in narrative. Indeed, the forms that historians use in their writing often reveal their distinctive purpose and their own identity as narrators. A work by French historian Arlette Farge, *La vie fragile. Violence, pouvoirs et solidarités à Paris au XVIIIe siècle* (Fragile Life: Violence, Powers, and Solidarity in Eighteenth-Century Paris), offers an interesting illustration. As Furry explains in a detailed analysis of her writing, the power of Farge's narrative resides in her skill at using different voices and rhetorical devices that enhance both the disturbing human aspects of eighteenth-century public violence and the plausibility of her argumentation. The following excerpt is telling:

> "Carnage," "frightful butchery," "aftermath of battle," "besieged city" ... locals are amazed by the magnitude and the injustice of the accident that took place during the fireworks which have just ended: everyone is a little disappointed, the most beautiful part of the show was consumed by the flames, before having the time to explode in stylistic light figures. The crowd is about to leave the square and hit the boulevards where further illuminations are awaiting people. The easiest way is to take Rue Royale, which is what the crowd does. Walking peacefully but in the opposite direction, those who remained at the entrance of the boulevards seek to reach the square. In order to do so, they take or intend to take the Rue Royale as well. At the same time, carriages held behind the colonnade brutally make their way through. A ruthless pushing and shoving ensues; the two columns of people, ready for the show, meet in a frightful "press." A "river of people" is now divided by the carriages into "extremely tight crowds that roll in different directions along the street, several men and women so throbbed, already too weak to sustain such violent shocks had the misfortune of meeting under their feet ditches and stones." The confusion soon becomes general, and panic reaches this human tide ... Crowded to the extreme, without any recourse, others die standing against each other: "The blood came out through their mouth, nose, and ears, and they only fell to the ground when the crowd could no longer support them," indicates one of the police reports.[53]

Right from the beginning, Farge uses eyewitness testimony: "carnage," "frightful butchery," and "aftermath of battle." The tone is clear, the words are striking. Their purpose is to place the reader in the historical context using first-hand observations. Farge then opts for two other strategies. First, she closes the distance between the narrator and the story-space, adopting a simultaneous relationship with the narrated events so as to transmit emotions and judgments peculiar to the historical agents themselves. The following account is revealing: "The crowd is about to leave the square and hit the boulevards where further illuminations are awaiting people. The easiest way is to take Rue Royale, which is what the crowd does." Through this process, Farge presents a story that borrows directly from the agents. By indicating that the easiest way, taking Rue Royale, is the one followed by the crowd, Farge writes her argument in synchronicity with the events; her own judgment on the itinerary is that of the people described in the scene. Then Farge changes her tone and opts for a more external position by adopting a traditional posture as the omniscient narrator. The last part of the narrative excerpt is typical. A quote from a witness, who is recounting the violent scene, is purposely placed in quotation marks and accompanied by the following statement: "indicates one of the police reports." With this citation process, Farge takes a step back, relying openly on a source she purposely quotes in a classic, scholarly way. The following excerpt, quoting a primary source, offers an additional example of this classic posture: "Regularly solicited by the Crown to contemplate its sacred, religious, political and authoritarian scene, huge crowds in thick columns, come for the day to contemplate, according to precise itineraries and rites, a monarchy that cannot exist without being seen."[54]

Throughout the book, Farge uses various rhetorical strategies to engage the reader. The use of the first-person plural "we," for instance, allows the narrator/narratee to connect with the past and envision eighteenth-century French society in the *longue durée* of human history, as in the following excerpt: "we do not purposely go to an execution, but we accomplish through this existential gesture, of living common events with others on the very places where social reality is invented, created."[55] In this example, the use of "we" is not exclusively in reference to past agents – or in reference the narrator and the agents. It implicitly associates the narratee with the event, with this "existential gesture," as if all human beings were somehow participating in common ritual actions. Through her writing, Farge offers the reader a narration that is rich in meaning and lessons. The narrator's story changes according to her objectives. The book, which is a history of the relationship between the French people, the Crown, and social violence, allows the narratee to understand a collective reality comprised of a multitude of social manifestations, including riots, "carnage," and "frightful butchery." Opening here and there various windows onto tragic events of the French past, Farge invites the reader to imagine life in eighteenth-century Paris. The author accomplishes this performance through the intimate relationship she has forged with the sources she strategically uses in her narration. Farge, who was strongly influenced by the writing of Michel Foucault, is fully aware of the role and impact that the narrator can have on the reader. As she puts it: "For me, it's not fiction. I am convinced that words, the place of words, the syntax, the wording, the expression, the writing process, makes it possible for a story to present sensitive, unrevealed movements, opinions, crowds, and feelings. Words can do that."[56]

Of course, our participants engaged in significantly less elaborate acts of narration than are described here. On the one hand, the students did not have unrestricted time and access to the resources and archival materials that would allow them to establish a close relationship with the past, as Farge was able to do in her work. But as we argued in the introduction, this was not the purpose of our study of history, memory, and historical consciousness. On the other hand, none of the participants in either province had received any formal education in historical narrative writing as part of their schooling. As we pointed out earlier, this aspect of history education is not part of current programs of study in Quebec and Ontario, even when students are expected to know what narratives are.

The results are consequential. The students' narratives are highly simplified, selective stories of the collective past with linear patterns of historical development and limited focalization as well as limited voices to reflect the diversity of experiences that characterize Canada's past. That being said, many students – consciously or not – use various technical and extratechnical evidence to tell the history of French Canada. Some offer narratives in synchronicity with the narrated events, recounting the past as an unfolding: "When [Columbus] arrived on the soil of this beautiful land, he realized that they were not the first ones" (04A20-Saguenay); or through a homodiegetic narrator: "When I was in elementary school on every 25th of September we went outside and sang 'Our Place' by the Franco-Ontarian flag" (0111A02-East). Others choose rhetorical methods to give direct voice to witnesses, or they purposely blend narrative voices through the use of the collective "we": "Since the arrival of the French in Canada we had to fight for equality" [0111A112 North]). A few even assume the classic posture of the historian, with explicit quotes or references to sources: "I'm sure the motto 'I remember' is not appropriate" (GR0631-Quebec City).

Through these processes, the students have produced, within the limits of our activity, narratives that are coherent, instructive, and rich in meaning. Other studies have suggested that narrative is a powerful tool for knowledge comprehension and communication. It facilitates an understanding of chronology, temporality, and causation. Narrative also boosts personal agency, for it places students in the position of narrators who can make their own representations of the past. But without any formal training, disposition, and strategy for constructing historical narratives, young people lack the intellectual tools to generate more plausible narratives of the collective past, and as result, they continue to rely heavily on established authorial perspectives or schematic narrative frameworks supplied by the historical culture.

Our recent study with pre-service teachers offers useful lessons.[57] Facing the same narrative task as the one presented in this study, these young history teachers were able to produce highly complex and informative narratives of the collective past despite limited time and resources at their disposal. Of course, these history majors present a unique case, given that they have far more extensive knowledge of history and experience with the discipline than our high school participants. But it is precisely because they had pursued graduate studies in history that they were able to develop more sophisticated narrative ideas and forms of historical consciousness. As such, they constitute an interesting model of knowledge progression for learners. Our history teachers' performances make it possible to imagine a form of learning progression based on research – one that is intended not to turn students into "mini-historians" but rather to improve their narrative competence over time. Programs of study designed around competency frameworks encourage both students and teachers to work toward achieving the same performance objectives, in much the same way that minor hockey or soccer players learn from their coaches to play the game using professional performance as a model for skills development.[58]

Conclusion

Historical thinking is no longer exclusively the concern of scholars; over the past twenty years, it has been well integrated into history education programs across Canada and in many other jurisdictions around the world. A growing number of educators now accept that the history discipline can offer young people a way of thinking critically about the past and the present, as well as a solid counterbalance to collective memory.

However, it is evident from our study that the current disciplinary approach has not helped students develop the intellectual tools required for narrative competence. As history educator Robert Martineau points out, "rarely are the resources of 'narrative thinking' considered to reflect on situations or realities of the past, to generate representations based on historical sources, and to offer plausible interpretations expressed in the form of a narrative."[59] As we have argued, narration is central to human activity. It is also an effective educational means for probing the historical consciousness of young people so that they can understand how the different forces of historical culture, both formal and informal, affect their visions of society and their sense of identification with past and contemporary communities.

In this chapter we have argued that schools could improve students' ability to construct historical narratives that are (1) coherent and purposeful for orienting life in time, (2) historically plausible, and (3) expressed through rhetorical technical evidence. Using works in history and narratology, we demonstrated how narrative competence is structured in terms of extratechnical evidence (the content/story) and technical evidence (mode of expression). Historical thinking, we argued, can structure the arrangement of the story-form so as to help generate evidence-based arguments. Moreover, a historical narrative strengthens its plausibility through the act of narration. The narrator's choice and voice along with focalization and sense of audience contribute to turning the past into history; this furthers its overall narrative plausibility. Throughout this process, narrators must make important epistemological and ontological decisions, for "the past as history" is always a matter of memory, narrative identity, and representation. As Munslow concludes, "at its most basic the logic of history lies in the historian making content/story, narrational and expression decisions through the continuous loop of reciprocity and aesthetic over-determination between the past and the mode of expression selected for the history. The choice made between alternative and perhaps competing modes of representation is a fundamental decision made by all historians."[60]

Unfortunately, in the current Canadian school context students rarely get the opportunity to reflect on their own representations of the collective past beyond the attainment of formal curricular objectives. Thus, they do not acquire the necessary skills to criticize their narrative understanding of the past so as to eventually develop a more reflective historical consciousness. We believe this educational undertaking is crucial for twenty-first-century democracy, considering that young people will have to deal with a plurality of narratives in their personal and social lives, which are characterized by a growing fluidity of identities and conflicting memories. As Seixas also concludes: "Students will grapple with multiple narratives, and if there is not one grand narrative that they memorize uncritically, they should still understand the necessity of the quest for larger stories in order to make sense of their lives, and the importance of the search for good ones."[61] A narrative strategy like the one used in our study offers a promising approach for engaging students on a rarely travelled yet valuable lifelong learning path: the production and evaluation of historical narratives that orient their lives over time.

Conclusion

This study has probed the historical consciousness of young citizens in the provinces of Quebec and Ontario. Unlike traditional investigations of students' acquisition of historical knowledge, our research has been able to map out their narrative representations of the collective past. In light of our inquiry, it appears that, far from being historically disconnected and ignorant as often claimed, our participants have constructed thought-provoking historical narratives that reveal the impact of both formal and informal education on their historical consciousness. For the first time in recent Canadian education, a large-scale study has compared the visions of students from different regions and backgrounds. Our results bring to light diverse representations of the collective past but also the permanence of a shared memory of French Canada in the narrative structures of our participants. Using additional variables such as geographic region, gender, language, and sense of collective identification, our study has revealed the impact of historical culture, language, and identity on students' narrative representations of the collective past, present, and envisioned future.

Young French Canadians and History: The Practical Function of Narrative Frameworks

Participants in both provinces still hold important memories of and historical perspectives on French Canada. These are characterized by the fragility of their minority condition in the face of the English-speaking majority, which in turn singularizes the historical trajectory of their community over time. The two groups share a common history that begins with the discovery (or *re*discovery, for some) of America by French explorers and the early years of colonial rule. This shared history between Quebec and Ontario students culminates in the Conquest of New France, which Quebec students view as a defining event. After that key moment, we observe a divergence of narrative representations among participants.

The stories provided by young Québécois unfold almost exclusively within the diegetic universe of the province of Quebec, while those of young Franco-Ontarians are expressed in the context of Canada or French Ontario. It is also interesting that young Québécois and Franco-Ontarians do not highlight common historical moments in the same way. For the former, New France was a golden age that was brutally ended by the British Conquest during the Seven Years' War. For the latter, New France marks the beginning of a French-speaking community in America that has endured to this day. Franco-Ontarian students spend less time recounting this period and mention far fewer events, characters, and historical facts about New France; instead, their narratives tend to stress the development of French Canada *after* the Conquest. In other words, the British takeover of 1759–60 is not the pivotal traumatic element in their narratives – that honour goes to more recent struggles for French-language rights, especially the infamous Regulation 17 of 1912.

Saying this is not to say that Québécois and Franco-Ontarians no longer share aspects of a common historical culture. When we examine more specifically the internal structure of students' narratives, we find that the *French Canadian experience* framework is dominant for both groups. This template, as we revealed, includes four constants: the French filiation, the cult of difference, the importance of struggle, and the sense of fragility. This suggests that, through this big-picture framework of French Canada, students in the two provinces craft narratives that correspond to their own regional affiliations and identifications. Indeed, Quebec and Ontario students plot different events in their narratives that play more or less the same functions in terms of collective experience: the British Conquest of 1759–60 and the Rebellion of the Patriots of 1837–38 for the Québécois, and Regulation 17 of 1912 and the recent battle for Montfort Hospital for the Franco-Ontarians.

Our study supports Wertsch's findings in his narrative work with Eastern Europeans. Schematic frameworks provide students with powerful interpretative tools that heavily influence their narrative representations of the collective past. The fact that our participants live in different provinces and study under different school regimes does not prevent them from telling a history of French Canada shaped by common narrative visions. Rather, students' representations are informed by a "stock of historical information" or mythistories that are already emplotted in general, schematic ways in the collective memory of their linguistic group. Jacques Cartier, Samuel de Champlain, Étienne Brûlé, the Conquest, and Regulation 17 are more than names and events on a timeline; they are embedded in certain schematic pictures in the historical memory of French Canadians. So when the name "Champlain" is pronounced, a particular semantic network is activated in the minds of young francophones, and this leads them to create a picture of the past that already possesses a certain story-shape. The mythistories available to them in collective memory make it possible for Quebec and Franco-Ontarian participants to envision the past of their community in very similar configurations. The fact that students from immigrant backgrounds, with limited experience of Canada, also subscribe to this pattern suggests that powerful forces of historical culture, notably schooling, are helping shape their French Canadian historical consciousness much as it does for native Canadians. Interestingly, studies conducted in the United States show similar narrative patterns among young Americans. The "quest for freedom" schematic template provides the foundational narrative structure for making sense of national history in terms of progress and freedom.[1] As Bruce VanSledright sums it up, "the story of freedom and progress that animates the U.S. history textbooks and is oft repeated in history classrooms is, without much doubt, a schematic narrative template, functioning as a powerful cultural tool complete with identity markers. To know it, believe it to be true, and be able to repeat it with conviction function as declarations of a speaker's Americanness. Without it, one remains a cultural outsider."[2]

In our study, one additional reason why the *French Canadian experience* framework is so frequently used by students in both provinces is its salience; it conveniently explains their present-day experiences as French Canadian citizens. Over the course of time, francophones have faced important challenges to their cultural survival and have often been the direct victims of British/English Canadian oppression. But they are a resilient people, and time and again they have found imaginative ways to fight discrimination and (re)gain the collective rights and freedoms that are necessary for their group survival and societal flourishing. Even today, with additional powers at their disposal, their linguistic minority situation in Canada – and North America more broadly – reminds them that nothing can be taken for granted. They must continue to maintain cultural vigilance in the face of globalization. As one Franco-Ontarian student puts it, "it is more difficult to pass on this language and culture to future generations because the world around us is predominantly anglophone" (0211B04-East).

The Limits of Schematic Narrative Frameworks

Narrative frameworks are convenient heuristics for making sense of past and present realities, but they also have their drawbacks. Their ubiquity renders them almost invisible to community members. As narrative frameworks are not "readily available to consciousness," they can be used unreflectively when narrating the past, serving as an intuitive matrix for emplotting memories into story-form.[3] Many students in our study framed their narratives in ways that were consistent with mythistories carried from generation to generation. Did students know these existed? To what extent did their narratives reflect their own personalized history as opposed to collective memories? It is hard to answer these questions, for we did not have the opportunity to conduct post-test interviews with the participants. What we can say at this point is that cultural membership and a sense of collective identification seriously affected how they privileged certain frameworks. Indeed, we found that the students who displayed the strongest sense of belonging to their community (whether it was Quebec/Ontario or Canada) were the same ones who provided the most militant narratives (e.g., nearly all narratives of *Canadian nation-building* were produced by students who identify strongly with Canada). This suggests that collective identification can act as a lens that polarizes students' narrative ideas and reinforce mythistories entrenched in collective memory.

Another pitfall of narrative frameworks is that they tend to evade historical uncertainty and complexity. Schematic templates are structured in such overarching, generalized ways that once a schema is selected for shaping a story (e.g., a history of national progress), it becomes difficult for the narrator, particularly for a novice, to bring additional perspectives and counter-evidence into their structure of argumentation, or what Denis Shemilt calls their polythetic narrative framework – a form of narrative knowledge that (1) takes into account additional voices and (2) admits alternative perspectives.[4] So it is no surprise that most students in our study wrote stories that occluded entire periods and perspectives that did not fit their narrative orientation: Indigenous views on colonialism, historical perspectives on immigrants, life experiences of women and oppressed minorities, and so forth. In many ways, their representations of the past were oversimplified linear stories operating in a binary mode: selected temporal events followed by long temporal spaces. This "monothetic event-space" structure amounts to a selection of changes separated by historical periods of quiescence "in which nothing happens."[5] Historical narratives aim for coherence and intelligibility. They work with connections, colligatory concepts, and patterns expressed over time and space. Reducing the complexity of the past to a selective set of "events-spaces" inevitably leads students to make significant omissions, distortions, or generalizations that do not accurately represent past and contemporary realities.

In many ways, students' ideas originate in collective memory and run against modern Canadian historiography as if these two sets of historical representations operated in silos. For Létourneau, the current situation is partly the result of poor knowledge transfer from the academic world to the practical world of cultural life. Historians, he argues, have been incapable of (or indifferent to) offering students and more broadly the general public new, original syntheses of the historical experiences of the nation that would counter collective memory.[6] Because their works are typically located within a scholarly dialogue among a community of learned specialists, most historians are "uncomfortable with the kinds of simplistic syntheses" they feel obliged to make when reaching out to students and the public.[7] In other words, scholarly publications by historians do not seem to inform the practical lives of Canadians, at least not in the same powerful ways that collective memory does. The outcome is predictable: the void has been filled with popular histories "for dummies" that reinforce grand narratives along the lines of collective memory.[8] As Éric Bédard puts it in his popular *Histoire du Québec pour les nuls* (Quebec History for Dummies), "I am trying here [in this book] to synthesize the most important facts in Quebec's history. At least those retained in the collective memory."[9]

The power of these national histories resides in their ability to convey a straightforward, usable narrative through vernacular rhetorical strategies that ring true to many. Like Wineburg and his colleagues, we believe that the histories students glean from this cultural, practical life curriculum may be "far more powerful in shaping their ideas about the past than the mountains of textbooks that continue to occupy historians' and history educators' attention."[10] Despite alarming comments about the death of French Canada, our results indicate far more continuity with the collective past than critics suggest. Engaging this cultural form of knowledge in the context of formal education offers schools a unique opportunity to challenge and enrich students' narrative ideas – not simply reinforce them.

The Need for Narrative Competence

The results of our study raise the question of schooling in the formation of historical consciousness. What place should a narrative approach like ours occupy in history education? How can schools foster the construction of a more reflective historical consciousness and the development of more complex narratives, founded in evidence and open to multiple voices and perspectives? Students learn history through narratives supplied to them both inside and outside the school system. So when asked to produce a history of the collective past, they employ a cultural tool already familiar to them. From a didactic point of view, the use of narrative is strategic in that it does not require the mastery of a new historical thinking tool. But few actually know how historical narratives are constructed with a particular narrative grammar, mode of expression, and rules of argumentation. In many ways, students are like junior car drivers on the cultural highway without a driver's manual.

Indeed, historical narratives, as Rüsen contends, are the result of a "specific manner of reasoning and arguing theoretically and methodologically in the process of making sense of the experience of time."[11] Students see only the end result of this process in the form of grand narratives, which rarely expose the constructed, discursive nature of narrative writing or alternative perspectives that might call into question the tenets of the nation's past. In fact, most of them have not developed an understanding of narrative as a *form of historical knowledge*. "If young people are to get a useful history education in this cultural moment," as Seixas argues, "they must not only be exposed to a good historical drama but also be allowed to see the ropes and pulleys behind the curtains."[12] Grand narratives offer the promise of intelligibility and simplicity. But such narratives come with important historical blind spots. The past is more complex and diverse than students' understandings suggest.

Our study does not claim that these oversimplifications are representative of all Canadian students or that their narrative views are irreversible. But students clearly need additional intellectual tools if they are to understand how narrative representations are constructed. They need to learn the specific manner of reasoning and arguing, to use Rüsen's words, so as to better understand how narratives are emplotted through a selective reconstruction of historical realities. As Barton rightly observes, the scholarly evaluation of historical narratives revolves precisely around "the extent to which this selectivity is justified."[13] All narratives are inherently selective, and some are more plausible than others. In the end, students must realize that their representations of the past – and the ones they consume – have serious limitations and, as such, may not provide the most suitable historical narrations for the complex world in which they live. Focusing on the "protection of our own culture," as some students put it, may be a noble objective for French Canadian identity, but this focalization is unable to provide a comprehensive narrative of the multifaceted experiences of French Canadians. As we have argued, French Canada can be interpreted through various frames of reference (social history, postcolonialism, Indigenous perspectives, etc.). Limiting national history to the collective memory of the dominant francophone group marginalizes other equally significant experiences, and this, in the end, undermines social inclusion and participatory democracy. Young citizens – immigrants in particular – are more likely to integrate into society and engage in the democratic process if they feel that their own experiences are fairly represented.[14]

In the circumstances, what can be done in Canadian history education? While there is no simple solution to this question, our study of historical consciousness suggests three important ways in which we could better mobilize young people's historical representations for the purpose of life orientation.

1. First, studies suggest that students are more likely to revise their (mis)conceptions when they have access to relevant evidence from their own experiences. Indeed, students do not acquire new knowledge as if it were being imprinted on some sort of mental hard drive; they learn additional information based on what they already know – or think they know.[15] Our research suggests that educators should adopt a constructivist view of history learning and teach in reference to students' own narrative ideas of the collective past. As we have shown, language, gender, and identity seriously affect how students engage with the past and create narrative representations of it. Educators should thus use this personal connection to explore students' identity, prior knowledge, and historical beliefs – in other words, what they accept, ignore, or (dis)miss in their understandings of the past. If we want students to progress in their historical thinking, we need to develop progression models and related learning strategies that allow educators to see where individual students stand with regard to their (mis)conceptions about the past and about the nature of history so that we can gradually transform these conceptions into more powerful and usable ones.[16] "A correct understanding of the epistemological underpinnings of history," as Jeffery Nokes and Susan De La Paz note, is a prerequisite for argumentative historical narrative.[17] Indeed, as VanSledright and his colleagues have discovered, students' epistemic beliefs greatly shape how they think about history and its knowledge claims.[18] For instance, those who look for hard factual evidence and who trust narratives to reveal a true representation of the past (naive objectivism) have a hard time accepting that history is based on disciplinary criteria and evaluative principles for crafting historical interpretations. As a matter of fact, these naive beliefs generate one of the greatest challenges for engaging students in thinking historically. Cultivating narrative competence thus requires

that we understand what learners *believe* about historical knowledge. The historical narratives students employ, if they are to be truly useful for orienting their lives in modern, complex societies, must be coherent and helpful, as well as historically rigorous, well-founded in evidence, and informed by alternative perspectives; in other words, narrative representations must be polythetic in nature.[19]

Indeed, our study suggests that formal history learning may not be the most relevant source for structuring narrative representations of the collective past. Schooling as an institution is part of a larger learning environment embedded in historical culture. Once educators become familiar with the structure of and influences on the simplified narratives students acquire and bring to class, they will be better equipped to engage these representations and call them into question through supplementary historical sources and counter-narratives. For instance, students might discover that French and English Canadians were/are not dichotomous, monolithic groups fixed in time, and that some English Canadians have been sympathetic to French Canadians and supportive of French-speakers' rights in Canada. They might also realize that Indigenous peoples did not exist just in colonial times; they are still here, and they continue to live and shape Canadian society today and are demanding the same kinds of collective rights and recognition as French Canadians themselves.

2. Second, history educators should teach students about the constructed nature of historical narratives. In many ways, students learn history through narratives (e.g., lectures, textbooks, movies, and oral stories). Yet these are rarely problematized and deconstructed in any disciplined way. If we want students to think historically and to develop more critical approaches to the collective past, educators should explain the structure, the grammar, the mode of expression, and the purpose of historical narratives in society.[20] Stories may well be a primary mode of thought, but they are not the past, and hence they set limits on what we consider significant enough to tell and remember. As Peter Lee and Rosalyn Ashby contend, history is always "more important than any particular story it tells."[21] History as a discipline has its own procedures, concepts, and rules of argumentation, all of which are designed to make critical claims about the past. Many narratives are told in society that may contradict, compete with, or complement one another, and this means that students should be equipped with the intellectual tools to confront the constructed nature of these representations of the past.

In this book, we have argued that historical narration is structured in terms of extratechnical evidence (the content/story) and technical evidence (mode of expression), which, taken together, strengthen the plausibility of narratives. Argumentative historical writing is a complex and difficult activity that is still poorly integrated into Canadian history education. In fact, narrative writing is still seen as a literacy skill (taught in language arts), not a feature of history learning. Equally problematic, when narrative is used in schools, it is often presented naively, in contrast to argumentation (the typical five-paragraph essay), as if narration was exclusively a literary genre and not a form of historical knowledge production. As Kadriye Ercikan and Peter Seixas note, one clear difference between North American and European models of cognition "can be seen in respect to the 'narrative competence' in historical thinking."[22] Cognition models influenced by German writings on historical consciousness make the relationship between historical thinking and narrative more explicit and teachable.[23] International research suggests that students who engage progressively and frequently in historical narrative writing are more likely to (1) develop personal engagements with the past and with predecessors, (2) generate pictures of the past that are coherent and intelligible, and (3) acquire historical thinking and literacy skills.[24] Unfortunately, little has been done in Canada to research the narrative competence of various stakeholders (historians, museum curators, history teachers, etc.) in reference to novices.

So far, studies have focused exclusively on young people's narrative works without consideration of the larger writing process in the domain of history. Narrative competence should include expertise in "writing like a historian." In this regard, the discipline of history can help identify some of the ways in which historians produce narrative representations. Likewise, more needs to be done to develop ways to assess students' narrative writing. Our study provides an example of what is possible in classrooms – how narration can be utilized as a means to assess prior knowledge and as a tool for evaluating performance. Narrative writing could also be used in conjunction with other strategies such as interviews, scenarios, and debates to further students' engagement, appropriation, and knowledge transfer.

When history is understood and taught as a form of knowledge that contributes to the construction of narrative competence, it becomes possible to develop strategies that will help students create more valid representations of the past that will, in turn, shape their historical consciousness. This does not mean that students will become "mini-historians," as some critics have claimed, but it does mean they will gradually learn how narrative interpretations are created and used in society. We believe, like Shemilt, that "unless and until people are able to locate present knowledge, questions, and concerns within narrative frameworks that link past with past and past with present in ways that are valid and meaningful, coherent and flexible," their uses of the past will perpetuate traditional types of historical consciousness that poorly fit the demands of twenty-first-century Canadian society.[25]

3. Finally, school history should not force students to develop any particular national identification through stories of collective memory; rather, it should teach them to identify with various historical experiences. Traditionally, school history has focused on nationalism as a way to promote ethnocultural integration and social cohesion. This nation-building approach has long been particularly obvious to French Canadians in a minority situation. French Canadian collective memory is alive and present in various forms in the minds of young citizens, who do not hesitate make use of persistent mythistories when structuring their representations of the past. Furthermore, in a global, multi-national country such as Canada, school history can no longer pretend to promote exclusive national belonging. As found in this study, national identification seriously affects the ways in which students relate to the past – in particular, to distinctive cultural experiences.[26] Evidence from research conducted in divided multicultural settings such as Northern Ireland suggests that our participants are hardly alone. "Although students in Northern Ireland hope to move beyond sectarian views of the past," Barton and McCully note, "they find it difficult to do so" precisely because deep identity attachments combined with dichotomous, monolithic views of group relations make national history a hotly contested terrain.[27]

So history education should not ignore the positive relationship between history and identity, but it *should* avoid nationalist simplifications. This means, as Barton argues, that schools and programs of study should more carefully "consider the choices they make in selecting some experiences and perspectives as representative of any particular group," for students will draw selectively from these when constructing their narrative identification with the collective past.[28] Schools should also offer and expand more accurate and balanced individual and group experiences. Expanding historical experiences might involve countering stereotypical portrayals of groups, as presented in textbooks and students' narratives, by showing how members of such groups never acted in a single collective pursuit but instead endorsed multiple viewpoints (e.g., some English Canadians supported French-language rights in Ontario; some French Canadian leaders cooperated with British authorities to promote federalism; some women played decisive roles in various periods of Canadian history; some white settlers sought to protect Indigenous rights). It might also entail presenting group histories beyond the usual national framework of Canada. French Canadian history, for instance, was heavily influenced by French and British as well as Indigenous historical experiences (e.g., the French and American revolutions, the British parliamentary system, free trade agreements, immigration patterns, *métissage*, Indigenous treaties and ways of knowing). Students' historical narratives could thus be redefined in reference to alternative big pictures of the past of North America, Europe, Asia, and the world. Multiple contextualization is a key principle for educating students to live in a complex world.[29]

Final Thoughts

Canada is a complex country divided by province, language, history, and national allegiance. It is one of the few states in the world that contains all of these recognized forms of diversity and that has vast experience in dealing with them peacefully. We understand that in such a multi-national state – one in which historical groups claim their own self-government rights and cherish narrations that predate the Canadian federation – we cannot expect collective memory to be neutral on issues of identity and belonging, for these are vital to the survival of historical culture.[30] Collective memory makes it possible to "identify a familiar from a stranger [and] separate their group experience from that of others."[31] Yet simplified representations of the nation breed exclusion and mutual ignorance; they poorly equip citizens with the visions and tools for dealing with twenty-first-century diversity. To be truly usable, students' national narratives must be more complex and open to different voices and perspectives. If they are to play a more productive role in this process, history educators need to be more conscious of and proactive in providing students with what we call engagement in narrative competence.

Any sound approach to helping students develop this competence must provide them not only with a preferred narrative to orient their practical lives (which is traditionally the role of collective memory), but also with the scholastic opportunities and intellectual tools for making sense of multiple narratives of the nation – that is, the *de*construction and *re*construction skills of narrative competence. Students must come to understand and appreciate that there are diverse and possibly contradictory narratives of the collective past that coexist within society without undermining social cohesion and democratic stability. Indeed, what has historically defined Canadians is not their shared collective memory, which never existed, but their historical commitment to distinctly *Canadian* accommodations and deliberations as these touch on the past and future of the country. That deliberative process is only possible – and viable – if citizens have the dispositions, abilities and tools to understand one another and build a democratic society founded on mutual respect and accommodation of differing narrative representations of the nation.[32] If history education is to play a meaningful role in shaping the historical consciousness of young French Canadians, it must find ways to orient them in these global times.

Notes

Introduction

1 Bruner, "Narrative and Paradigmatic Modes of Thought."
2 Létourneau, *Je me souviens?*
3 Wineburg et al., "Forrest Gump," 176.
4 Conrad et al., *Canadians and Their Pasts*.
5 Rüsen, *History*, 1.
6 Barton and Levstik, *Teaching History for the Common Good*, 1.
7 As political theorist Benjamin Barber puts it, a political community, most particularly a democratic one, is not a natural form of association. It is "an extraordinary and rare contrivance of cultivated imagination." Public education, and history education in particular, play for Barber an essential role in educating citizens "for excellence – by which term I mean the knowledge and competence to govern in common their own lives." In Barber, *An Aristocracy of Everyone*, 5.
8 Anderson, *Imagined Communities*, 6.
9 Ampuja, *Theorizing Globalization*, 282.
10 See for instance Blum, *National Identity and Globalization*.
11 Sharma, "Globalisation as we know it is over."
12 Ignatieff, *Blood and Belonging*, 14. See also his *Rights Revolution*.
13 Keating and McGarry, "Introduction," 4.
14 The founding nations of Canada is a rather loose and still contested concept for defining the original peoples who created the country as we know it today. Originally, the term referred to the two European ethno-linguistic groups (French, English) who colonized the land and established the Dominion of Canada in 1867, and who were later recognized by the Royal Commission on Bilingualism and Biculturalism as a way to define the Canadian identity. In recent years, the Indigenous peoples in Canada (First Nations, Métis, and Inuit), who were historically excluded and

marginalized for colonial and racialized reasons, have been included in the definition. See Russell, *Canada's Odyssey*.
15 Kymlicka, *Finding Our Way*.
16 Taylor, *Reconciling the Solitudes*; Meisel, Rocher, and Silver, *Si je me souviens / As I Recall*.
17 Bouvier et al., eds. *L'histoire nationale à l'école québécoise*; Laville, "Quelques avenues nouvelles des guerres d'histoire scolaires dans le monde"; Lévesque, "History and Social Studies in Québec"; Osborne, "Teaching History in Schools."
18 Cited in Létourneau, "La renationalisation de l'histoire québécoise," 5 (translation).
19 Bédard, "Une action légitime, nécessaire et urgente" (translation).
20 Beauchemin and Fahmy-Eid, *The Sense of History*.
21 Ibid., 2.
22 Ibid., 21.
23 Laville, "Un cours d'histoire pour notre époque" (translation).
24 Martineau, *Fondements et pratiques de l'enseignement de l'histoire à l' école*.
25 Lévesque, "On Historical Literacy."
26 Cardin, "De la supposée 'dénationalisation' des programmes d'histoire" (translation).
27 Éthier, "Contre la Coalition pour l'histoire" (translation).
28 Moisan, "Exploration d'une approche critique."
29 Beauchemin and Fahmy-Eid, *The Sense of History*, 42.
30 Farmer, Chambon, and Labrie, "Urbanité et immigration"; Yves Frenette, "Immigration et francophonie Canadienne."
31 Heller, *Crosswords*; Heller, "Quel(s) français et pour qui?"
32 Gérin-Lajoie, "La problématique identitaire," 177 (translation).
33 Thériault, "De l'école de la nation aux écoles communautaires." See also Gilbert, "La refondation de la communauté franco-ontarienne par l'école"; and Gilbert and Lefebvre, "Le sort de la culture dans la francophonie canadienne."
34 Gilbert, "La refondation de la communauté franco-ontarienne par l'école," 222 (translation).
35 Granatstein, *Who Killed Canadian History?*; Sandwell, "We Were Allowed to Disagree."
36 Stanley, "Why I Killed Canadian History," 102.
37 Anderson, "The Stories Nations Tell," 6. See also Marker, "Teaching History from an Indigenous Perspective"; Donald, "Forts, Colonial Frontier Logics, and Aboriginal-Canadian Relations"; Seixas, "Indigenous Historical Consciousness"; Stanley, "John A. Macdonald."
38 See Saint-Hilaire and Beaulieu, "Trou de mémoire"; Rioux, "Suicide assisté"; Rioux, "Une génération d'amnésiques"; Rioux, "La fin de

l'histoire"; Chouinard, "Enseignement de l'histoire"; Martin and Ouellet, "L'assimilation des francophones."
39 Cuban, "The Lure of Curricular Reform."
40 See Epstein and Peck, eds. *Teaching and Learning Difficult Histories.*
41 Nora, "Between Memory and History."
42 Halbwachs, *On Collective Memory*, 38.
43 Létourneau, "Remembering Our Past."
44 Stanley, "Whose Public?," 34.
45 Gadamer, *Le Problème de la conscience historique.*
46 See Tutiaux-Guillon and Nourrisson, eds., *Identités, mémoires, conscience historique;* Seixas, ed. *Theorizing Historical Consciousness;* and Rüsen, *History.*
47 Zanazanian, "History Teaching and Narrative Tools."
48 Seixas, "A Model of Historical Thinking."
49 Rüsen, *History*, 132.
50 Seixas, "A Model of Historical Thinking," 3.
51 Rüsen, *History*, 2.
52 Ibid., 116.
53 Ricoeur, *Temps et récit*, vol. 1, 85 (translation).
54 Rüsen, *History*, 5
55 Seixas, "A History/Memory Matrix."
56 Seixas, "A History/Memory Matrix for History Education."
57 Lee, "'Walking Backwards into Tomorrow,'" 2.
58 The recent requirement for "knowledge mobilization" by various granting agencies in Canada is an attempt to increase the use of scholarly knowledge among stakeholders and the public. The future will tell us whether these initiatives have increased history transfer, informed public debates, and influenced social behaviours.
59 Ahonen, "The Lure of Grand Narratives," 43.
60 Cherval, "L'histoire des disciplines scolaires."
61 Lévesque, "Going beyond 'Narratives' vs 'Competencies.'"
62 Tosh, *The Pursuit of History*, 206.
63 Wineburg, *Historical Thinking and Other Unnatural Acts.*
64 Rüsen, *History*, 1.
65 Conrad et al., *Canadians and Their Pasts*, 5.
66 Parkes, "The Practical Legacy of Hayden White."
67 Carr, "History as Orientation."
68 On the approach and tools of historical inquiry in education, see VanSledright, *The Challenge of Rethinking History Education;* Levstik and Barton, *Doing History;* and Counsell, Burn, and Chapman, eds. *MasterClass in History Education.*
69 Rüsen, *History*, 12.

70 As we have argued elsewhere, Rüsen's typology should not be viewed as a simple, linear progression in the development of historical consciousness. Learners have inconsistent behaviours when researching, narrating, and thinking historically. Indeed, it is completely understandable that individuals make sense of the past as an uninformed mixing of different levels and forms of competence. In the same way, there is no clear guarantee that progression from "traditional" to "genetic" will take place in prescribed locksteps and ultimately lead to a societal consensus on community-building or societal projects. See Lévesque, "Removing the 'Past.'"
71 Rüsen, *History*, 15.
72 Philippe Perrenoud, "Curriculum: le formel, le réel, le caché," in *La pédagogie: une encyclopédie pour aujourd'hui*, ed. Jean Houssaye (Paris: ESF, 1993), 61–76. (translation)
73 Perrenoud, "Curriculum," 61 (translation).
74 Létourneau and Moisan, "Mémoire et récit de l'aventure historique du Québec"; Létourneau and Caritey, "L'histoire du Québec"; Robichaud, "L'histoire de l'Acadie"; Lévesque, Croteau, and Gani, "La conscience historique de jeunes franco-ontariens d'Ottawa"; Zanazanian, "Historical Consciousness and Being Québécois."
75 One important study conducted in 2000 provides an interesting comparative analysis of historical consciousness among French Canadians of Ontario and Quebec. However, this study relied on the questionnaire of the large-scale European study *Youth and History* and, as such, does not account for the narrative visions of students. See Charland, *Les élèves, l'histoire et la citoyenneté*.
76 Bouchard, *Genèse des nations et cultures du Nouveau Monde*, 50.
77 On the possible role of identity in students' historical ideas, see Charland, Éthier, and Cardin, "Premier portrait de deux perspectives différentes"; and Lévesque, Létourneau, and Gani, "'A giant with clay feet.'"
78 Kölbl and Konrad, "Historical Consciousness in Germany: Concept, Implementation, Assessment," 20.
79 In terms of demographic data, the total for each population (385 for Quebec, 250 for Ontario) sometimes varies due to the fact that some students did not answer all the demographic questions in our questionnaire.
80 Note that the total number of participants is based on the number of students who completed the questionnaire and the consent form. Those who completed only the questionnaire or who failed to return the consent form were discarded from the study.
81 Wertsch, "Collective Memory and Narrative Templates," 140.
82 Propp, *Morphology of the Folktale*.
83 Wertsch, "Texts of Memory and Texts of History."

1. Narrative Orientations

1 This section comes from a text written by Anne Gilbert from the University of Ottawa and was later adapted for this book chapter.
2 The exception to this principle was, of course, the Acadians in the Maritimes, who are the descendants of French settlers who established themselves in various communities in "Acadie" (Acadia). The colony of Acadia was part of New France but was ceded to Great Britain in 1713. In the 1750s, growing tensions between France and Great Britain led to the deportation of Acadians who refused to pledge an unconditional oath of allegiance to the British Crown. The Treaty of Paris (1763) brought a definitive end to the French colonial presence in the Maritimes and in all of New France. Today, Acadians continue to express their own distinctive cultural identity. They live primarily in New Brunswick, Nova Scotia, Prince Edward Island, and Quebec, with a relatively important diaspora.
3 Martel, *French Canada*, 2.
4 See Bock, *Quand la nation débordait les frontières*.
5 For the purpose of this study we use Ontario (Ontarian) and French Ontario (Franco-Ontarian) interchangeably in the text, unless specified otherwise. While we recognize that the two are not conceptually the same, we have decided to do so because all our participants from this province are from French-speaking Ontario and thus represent our Ontario sample population.
6 See the numerous studies about Québec nationalism: Roy, *Histoire des idéologies au Québec*; Monière, *Pour comprendre le nationalisme au Québec et ailleurs*; Sarra-Bournet, ed. *Les nationalismes au Québec*; and Balthazar, *Nouveau bilan du nationalisme québécois*.
7 Royal Commission on Bilingualism and Biculturalism as quoted in Pelletier, "Institutional Arrangements of a New Canadian Partnership," 301.
8 Bouchard, *Genèse des nations et cultures du Nouveau Monde*.
9 Léger, Nantel, and Duhamel, *Le Code Québec*, 93.
10 Martel, *French Canada*, 26.
11 Thériault, *Critique de l'américanité*.
12 Thériault, "Playing with Words," 187.
13 Létourneau, *Passer à l'avenir*, 148.
14 Ibid., 149.
15 Ibid., 81.
16 As quoted in Barber and Sylvestre, "Ontario Schools Question."
17 In 2019 the Ontario government finally reversed its initial decision and approved the funding of the Franco-Ontarian university with support from the Canadian government.
18 This is the point of view of at least some authors. See Choquette, *Langue et religion*; Grisé, "Ontarois"; and Dionne, "1910."

19 Dorais, "Gaétan Gervais."
20 Arseneault, Bock, and Gervais, *L'Ontario français*. This is not the first book to offer a historical summary of French Ontario and to be addressed to students. The historian Robert Choquette had written a similar book twenty-five years earlier. See Choquette, *L'Ontario français historique*. The same year, Gaétan Vallières and colleagues produced a collection of 157 texts with the aim of presenting an account of the historical, social, and political evolution of francophone Ontario. See Vallières, Grimard, and Équipe DOPELFO, eds., *L'Ontario français par les documents*. Finally, the historian Serge Dupuis wrote for the Regroupement étudiant franco-ontarien (REFO) a synthesis in the same vein as those written by Choquette and Gervais. See Dupuis, *400 ans de vie politique en Ontario français*.
21 Sylvestre, "Franco-Ontarians."
22 See Gilbert, "La diversité de l'espace franco-ontarien."
23 EQAO's provincial tests assess student literacy (reading and writing) at three points in their kindergarten to grade twelve education. The Ontario Secondary School Literacy Test measures whether French-speaking and English-speaking students are meeting the minimum standard for literacy across all subjects up to the end of grade nine. Given the dual nature of the Ontario school system, francophone and anglophone students complete the assessment in their own language of instruction.
24 Gilbert and Langlois, eds., *Territoires francophones*.
25 Office des Affaires francophones, *Les francophones de l'Ontario*.
26 Wertsch, "Collective Memory and Narrative Templates."
27 The Durham Report was produced by Lord Durham, a British political reformer, after the failed armed rebellions of 1837–38 in Lower and Upper Canada. His final report was controversial. It called for the granting of responsible government to the Canadian colony, but it also led to the forced union of the two colonies of Canada. According to Durham, this would eventually assimilate the French Canadians, whom he considered a marginalized people with no literature and no history, and hence no future.

2. History, Territory, and the Nation

1 Nora, ed. *Realms of Memory*.
2 Francis, *National Dreams*, 152.
3 Marker, "Teaching History from an Indigenous Perspective," 102.
4 Conrad et al., *Canadians and Their Pasts*, 107.
5 In the original French texts, students used various terms to refer to the Indigenous peoples in Canada (Aboriginals, First Nations, Indians, etc.), some of which had no direct English translation (e.g., Amérindiens). For matters of consistency and clarity, we have decided to use the

most common and frequently used term from students' narratives (Aboriginals), a term also employed by the Truth and Reconciliation Commission of Canada. To distinguish students' ideas from our own argument, we ourselves have employed the more historically sensitive English term "Indigenous peoples."

6 On Étienne Brûlé, see Saint-Pierre, "Étienne Brûlé, premier franco-ontarien."
7 Lamarre, *Le devenir de la nation québécoise*; Courtois, ed., *La Conquête*.
8 There are various works on Regulation 17. See Choquette, *Langue et Religion*; Bock and Charbonneau, *Le siècle du Règlement 17*; and Cecillon, *Prayers, Petitions, and Protests*.
9 Anctil, "*Fais ce que dois.*"
10 Bock, *Quand la nation débordait les frontiers*.
11 See Gratton, *Montfort,*; and Gratton, *Gisèle Lalonde*. See also Lalonde, *Jusqu'au bout!*
12 Guigues Elementary School played a significant role in the development of a Franco-Ontarian identity and collective memory. Built by the Ottawa Roman Catholic Separate School Board, this Ottawa school was as the centre of the controversy over the implementation of Regulation 17. Two schoolteachers in particular, Béatrice and Diane Desloges, refused to implement the provisions of Regulation 17, thus defying the ministerial decree. Both were suspended by the Ontario Ministry of Education for their actions but continued to teach classes clandestinely with the support of local parents and francophone associations until the situation was resolved years later.
13 Fischer, *Champlain's Dream*.

3. Gender and Language

1 Note that female students are also more likely to choose the *francophone defeat* orientation (5% vs 1%), but given the small sample size (7 vs 1), this result is not conclusive.
2 Létourneau, *Je me souviens?*, 158.
3 Truth and Reconciliation Commission of Canada, *Honouring the Truth*, 239.
4 Latané, "The Psychology of Social Impact."
5 Clark, "A Nice Little Wife." See also Brunet, "Des histoires du passé."
6 Martel, *French Canada*, 4
7 Zanazanian, "History Teaching and Narrative Tools."

4. Collective Identity

1 Taylor, *Sources of the Self*.
2 Kymlicka, *Finding Our Way*.
3 Barton and Levstik, *Teaching History for the Common Good*, 48.

4 Osborne, "'Our History Syllabus Has Us Gasping'"; Bouvier et al., eds. *L'histoire nationale à l'école québécoise*.
5 Ministère de l'Éducation de l'Ontario, *Le curriculum de l'Ontario, 9e et 10e année*, 3.
6 Ministère de l'éducation et de l'enseignement supérieur, "Progression des apprentissages au secondaire."
7 These few exceptions include Lévesque, Létourneau, and Gani, "'A Giant with Clay Feet'"; Carretero, Asension, and Rodríguez-Moneo, *History Education and the Construction of National Identities*; Peck, "It's not like [I'm] Chinese and Canadian"; and Barton and McCully, "History, Identity, and the School Curriculum."
8 Fournier and Medeiros, "Unis par la langue?"
9 Lévesque, Croteau, and Gani, "La conscience historique de jeunes franco-ontariens d'Ottawa,"
10 Turner and Tajfel, "The Social Identity Theory of Intergroup Behaviour."
11 Lefebvre, *Entre racines et mouvement*, 124.
12 See Girard, *Résumé des résultats de sondages*. For more recent data, see Léger, Nantel, and Duhamel, *Le Code Québec*.
13 Lefebvre, "Entre racines et mouvement," 118 (translation).

5. Narrative Competence

1 Rüsen, *History*, 193.
2 See Lévesque and Clark, "Historical Thinking."
3 Seixas, "A Model of Historical Thinking," 5.
4 Seixas, "Teaching Rival Histories," 262.
5 Duquette, "Relating Historical Consciousness to Historical Thinking."
6 Cardin, "La place du récit dans l'apprentissage de l'histoire."
7 Barton and Levstik, *Teaching History for the Common Good*, 129.
8 Lowen, *Lies My Teacher Told Me*.
9 Éthier, "Contre la pensée narrative téléologique."
10 Paul Ricoeur as cited in Cardin, "La place du récit dans l'apprentissage de l'histoire," 3
11 Munslow, *Narrative and History*, 3.
12 Seixas, "Teaching Rival Histories," 258.
13 Chapman, *Developing Students' Understanding*, 4.
14 See Körber, *Historical Consciousness*.
15 Rüsen, *History*, 26.
16 Sam Wineburg, "Making Historical Sense," 311.
17 Genette, *Narrative Discourse*, 29.
18 Munslow, *Narrative and History*, 27.

19 For a discussion of how human experience is structured in story form, see Carr, *Time, Narrative, and History*; and Bruner, "Narrative and Paradigmatic Modes of Thought."
20 Chapman, *Developing Students' Understanding*, 5.
21 Rüsen, *History*, 60.
22 Seixas, "Teaching Rival Histories," 263.
23 In Seixas's model, the concept of historical significance has not been transposed onto a dimension of narrative plausibility, as significance is a matter of how particular events or people fit within the narrative. These achieve significance by virtue of their selection and arrangement in the story space. As Seixas contends, "to introduce 'significance' as a dimension of plausibility for the larger narratives themselves might introduce confusion about the earlier definition of historical significance." See Seixas, "Teaching Rival Histories," 267.
24 Seixas, "Teaching Rival Histories," 260.
25 Seixas, "A Model of Historical Thinking," 7.
26 Recently, Wineburg's original heuristics have been challenged for their lack of consideration of other types of evidence in narratives, including artefacts, movies, the Internet, and social media posts. See Marcus et al., *Teaching History with Film*; Gerwin, "What Lies Beyond the Bubble?"; Breakstone et al., "Why We Need a New Approach to Teaching Digital Literacy"; and Goulding, *Historical Thinking Online*.
27 Rüsen, *History*, 26.
28 Ibid., 8.
29 Thomson, *Aims of History*, 57.
30 Seixas, "Teaching Rival Histories," 262.
31 Seixas, "A Model of Historical Thinking," 9.
32 Ibid., 10.
33 Barton and Levstik, *Teaching History for the Common Good*, 207.
34 Munslow, *Narrative and History*, 40.
35 Ibid., 144.
36 Seixas, "A Model of Historical Thinking," 10.
37 Rüsen, *History*, 25.
38 Bremond, "The Logic of Narrative Possibilities," 62.
39 Propp, *Morphology of the Folktale*, 21–4.
40 Wertsch, "Collective Memory and Narrative Templates."
41 Lee and Ashby, "Progression in Historical Understanding," 200.
42 Munslow, *Narrative and History*, 28.
43 Ferry, "Le paradoxe de la preuve en histoire."
44 Munslow, *Narrative and History*, 24.
45 Ferry, "Le paradoxe de la preuve en histoire," 128 (translation).

46 In his work, Munslow adds the elements of time, order, duration, frequency, and agency to the discussion. While these are all important, we believe that many of these elements belong to the previous section on narrative plausibility and would require more space for discussion than possibly available in this chapter.
47 Carr, *What is History?*, 54.
48 See Prince, *A Dictionary of Narratology*.
49 Körber, *Historical Consciousness*, 18.
50 Prince, "Introduction to the Study of the Narratee," 101.
51 Munslow, *Narrative and History*, 24.
52 Ibid., 48.
53 Arlette Farge in Ferry, "Le paradoxe de la preuve en histoire," 124 (translation).
54 Ibid., 123.
55 Ibid., 127.
56 Ibid., 130.
57 Lévesque, Croteau, and Gani, "La conscience historique de jeunes franco-ontariens d'Ottawa."
58 See Gaffield, "Towards the Coach in the History Classroom."
59 Martineau, *Fondements et pratiques*, 178–9.
60 Munslow, *Narrative and History*, 78.
61 Seixas, "Teaching Rival Histories," 264.

Conclusion

1 Barton and Levstik, *Teaching History for the Common Good*, 167; Wertsch and O'Connor, "Multivoicedness in Historical Representations."
2 VanSledright, "Narratives of Nation-State,", 123.
3 Wertsch, "Collective Memory and Narrative Templates," 124.
4 Shemilt, "The caliph's coin."
5 Ibid., 90.
6 Létourneau, "Remembering Our Past."
7 Sandwell, "On Historians and Their Audiences," 84.
8 See Bédard, *Histoire du Québec pour les nuls*; and Ferguson, *Canadian History for Dummies*. For an analysis of the impact of such popular books on education in Quebec, see Létourneau, *La renationalisation de l'histoire québécoise*.
9 Bédard, *Histoire du Québec pour les nuls*, 2.
10 Wineburg et al, "Forrest Gump," 176.
11 Rüsen, *History*, 18.
12 Seixas, "Preface," viii.
13 Barton, "Narrative Simplifications," 200.

14 Epstein and Peck, eds. *Teaching and Learning Difficult Histories*; Zanazanian, "History Teaching and Narrative Tools"; McAndrew and Milot, eds. *L'École et la diversité*; Peck, "'It's not like [I'm] Chinese and Canadian.'"
15 See Donovan and Bransford, eds. *How Students Learn*.
16 Lee and Shemilt, "A Scaffold, Not a Cage."
17 Nokes and De La Paz, "Writing and Argumentation in History Education," 560.
18 VanSledright and Reddy, "Changing Epistemic Beliefs?"; Maggioni, Alexander, and VanSledright, "At a Crossroads?"
19 See our suggested didactical approach to narrative competence in Lévesque, "Why Tell Stories?."
20 See Topolski, "Historical Narrative"; Straub, *Narration, Identity, and Historical Consciousness*; Chapman, "Understanding Historical Knowing"; and Lévesque, "Why Tell Stories?"
21 Lee and Ashby, "Progression in Historical nderstanding," 200.
22 Ercikan and Seixas, eds. *New Directions in Assessing Historical Thinking*, 3.
23 Körber and Meyer-Hamme, "Historical Thinking, Competencies, and their Measurements."
24 VanSledright and Brophy, "Storytelling, Imagination, and Fanciful Elaboration"; Voss and Wiley, "A Case Study"; Shemilt, "The Caliph's Coin"; Barton, "Narrative Simplifications"; Levstik, "Narrative as a Primary Act of Mind?"; Howson and Shemilt, "Frameworks of Knowledge"; Carretero, Asensio, and Rodríguez-Moneo, eds., *History Education*; Duquette, "Relating Historical Consciousness to Historical Thinking"; Monika Waldis et al., "Material-Based and Open-Ended Writing Tasks"; Rogers, "Frameworks for Big History"; Lantheaume and Létourneau, eds., *Le récit du commun*; and Gibson, *Constructing Students' Historical Reference Frameworks*.
25 Shemilt, "The Caliph's Coin," 99.
26 For a more detailed discussion of the impact of social identity theory on French Canadian students' historical narratives, see Lévesque, Létourneau, and Gani, "'A Giant with Clay Feet.'"
27 Barton and McCully. "Trying to 'See Things Differently,'" 400.
28 Barton, "School History as a Resource for Constructing Identities," 102.
29 Létourneau, "Teaching National History to Young People Today."
30 On the nature of multi-national Canada and the national claims of French Canadians, see Caron and Laforest, "Canada and Multinational Federalism"; Gagnon, ed., *Le fédéralisme canadien contemporain*; Resnick, *The European Roots of Canadian Identity*; Kymlicka, *Finding Our Way*; McRoberts, *Misconceiving Canada*.
31 Conrad et al., *Canadians and Their Pasts*, 103.
32 Sears, "Possibilities and Problems."

Bibliography

Ahonen, Sirkka. "The Lure of Grand Narratives: A Dilemma for History Teachers." In *International Perspectives on Teaching Rival Histories*, edited by Henrik Åström Elmersjö, Anna Clark, and Monika Vinterek, 41–62. London: Palgrave Macmillan, 2017.

Ampuja, Marco. *Theorizing Globalization: A Critique of the Mediatization of Social Theory*. Leiden: Brill, 2012.

Anctil, Pierre. *"Fais ce que dois", 60 éditoriaux pour comprendre Le Devoir sous Henri Bourassa (1910–1932)*. Sillery: Septentrion, 2010.

Anderson, Benedict. *Imagined Communities: Reflections on the Origin and Spread of Nationalism*. New York: Verso, 1991.

Anderson, Stephanie. "The Stories Nations Tell: Sites of Pedagogy, Historical Consciousness, and National Narratives." *Canadian Journal of Education* 40, no. 1 (2017): 1–38.

Arseneault, Suzanne, Michel Bock, and Gaétan Gervais. *L'Ontario français: des Pays-d'en-Haut à nos jours*. Ottawa: CFORP, 2004.

Balthazar, Louis. *Nouveau bilan du nationalisme québécois*. Montreal : VLB, 2013.

Barber, Benjamin. *An Aristocracy of Everyone: The Politics of Education and the Future of America*. New York: Ballantine, 1992.

Barber, Marilyn, and Paul-François Sylvestre, "Ontario Schools Question." *The Canadian Encyclopedia*, 2016. http://www.thecanadianencyclopedia.ca/en/article/ontario-schools-question

Barton, Keith. "Narrative Simplifications in Elementary Students' Historical Thinking." In *Researching History Education: Theory, Method, and Context*, edited by L. Levstik and K. Barton, 51–83. New York: Routledge, 2008.

– "School History as a Resource for Constructing Identities." In *History Education and the Construction of National Identities*, edited by Mario Carretero, Mikel Asensio, and Maria Rodrigues-Moneo, 93–107. Charlotte: Information Age, 2012.

Barton, Keith, and Linda Levstik. *Teaching History for the Common Good*. Mahwah: Lawrence Erlbaum Associates, 2004.

Barton, Keith, and Alan McCully. "History, Identity, and the School Curriculum in Northern Ireland: An Empirical Study of Secondary Students' Ideas and Perspectives." *Journal of Curriculum Studies* 37, no. 1 (2005): 85–116.

– "Trying to 'See Things Differently': Northern Ireland Students' Struggle to Understand Alternative Historical Perspectives." *Theory and Research in Social Education* 40, no. 4 (2012): 371–408.

Beauchemin, Jacques, and Nadia Fahmy-Eid. *The Sense of History: Towards a Rethinking of the History and Citizenship Education Program in Secondary III and IV*. Final report. Quebec: Government of Quebec, 2014.

Bédard, Éric "Une action légitime, nécessaire et urgente." *Le Devoir*, 9 March 2013. http://www.ledevoir.com/societe/education/372820/une-action-legitime-necessaire-et-urgente

– *Histoire du Québec pour les nuls*. Quebec: Éditions First, 2012.

Blum, Douglas W. *National Identity and Globalization: Youth, State, and Society in Post-Soviet Eurasia*. Cambridge: Cambridge University Press, 2007.

Bock, Michel. *Quand la nation débordait les frontières. Les minorités françaises dans la pensée de Lionel Groulx*. Montreal: Éditions Hurtubise HMH, Les Cahiers du Québec no 142, collection « Histoire », 2004.

Bock, Michel, and François Charbonneau. *Le siècle du Règlement 17. Regards sur une crise scolaire et nationale*. Sudbury: Éditions Prise de parole, 2015.

Bouchard, Gérard. *Genèse des nations et cultures du Nouveau Monde: Essai d'histoire comparé*. Montreal: Boréal, 2000.

Bouvier, Félix, Michel Allard, Paul Aubin, and Marie-Claude Larouche, eds. *L'histoire nationale à l'école québécoise: Regard sur deux siècles d'enseignement*. Sillery: Septentrion, 2012.

Breakstone, Joel, and al. "Why We Need a New Approach to Teaching Digital Literacy." *Phi Delta Kappan* 99, no. 6 (2018): 27–32.

Bremond, Claude. "The Logic of Narrative Possibilities." In *Narratology: An Introduction*, edited by Susana Onega and Jose Angel Garcia Landa, 61–75. New York: Routledge, 2014.

Bruner, Jerome. "Narrative and Paradigmatic Modes of Thought." In *Learning and Teaching the Ways of Knowing*, edited by E. Eisner, 97–115. Chicago: University of Chicago Press, 1985.

Brunet, Marie-Hélène. "Des histoires du passé: le féminisme dans les manuels d'histoire et d'éducation à la citoyenneté selon des élèves Québécois de quatrième secondaire." *McGill Journal of Education* 52, no. 2 (2017): 409–32.

Cardin, Jean-François. "De la supposée 'dénationalisation' des programmes d'histoire. *Le Devoir*, 11 March 2013. http://www.ledevoir.com/societe/education/372963/contre-la-coalition-pour-l-histoire

- "La place du récit dans l'apprentissage de l'histoire." *A l'école de clio: Histoire et didactique de l'histoire* 1 (2015). https://ecoleclio.hypotheses.org/275
- Caron, Jean-François, and Guy Laforest. "Canada and Multinational Federalism: From the Spirit of 1982 to Stephen Harper's Open Federalism." *Nationalism and Ethnic Politics* 15 (2009): 27–55.
- Carr, David. "History as Orientation: Rüsen on Historical Culture and Narration." *History and Theory* 45 (2006): 229–43.
- – *Time, Narrative, and History*. Bloomington: Indiana University Press, 1986.
- Carr, E.H. *What Is History?* New York: A.A. Knopf, 1962.
- Carretero, Mario, Mikel Asensio, and Maria Rodríguez-Moneo, eds. *History Education and the Construction of National Identities*. Charlotte: Information Age, 2012.
- Cecillon, Jack D. *Prayers, Petitions, and Protests: The Catholic Church and the Ontario Schools Crisis in the Windsor Border Region, 1910–1928*. Montreal and Kingston: McGill–Queen's University Press, 2013.
- Chapman, Arthur. *Developing Students' Understanding of Historical Interpretations*. Oxford: Edxecel/Pearson, 2016.
- – "Understanding Historical Knowing: Evidence and Accounts." In *The Future of the Past: Why History Education Matters*, edited by L. Perikleous and D. Shemilt, 170–214. Nicosia: AHDR, 2011.
- Charland, Jean-Pierre. *Les élèves, l'histoire et la citoyenneté: Enquête auprès d'élèves des régions de Montréal et de Toronto*. Quebec: Presses de l'Université Laval, 2003.
- Charland, Jean-Pierre, Marc-André Éthier, and Jean-François Cardin. "Premier portrait de deux perspectives différentes sur l'histoire du Québec enseignée dans les classes d'histoire et leur rapport avec les identités nationales: recherche sur la conscience historique des adolescents canadiens français et amérindiens." In *Histoire, musées et éducation à la citoyenneté*, edited by Jean-François Cardin, Marc-André Éthier, and Anik Meunier, 183–212. Quebec: Les Éditions Multimondes, 2010.
- Cherval, André. "L'histoire des disciplines scolaires. Réflexions sur un domaine de recherche." *Histoire de l'éducation* 38 (1988): 59–119.
- Choquette, Robert. *Langue et religion. Histoire des conflits anglo-français en Ontario*. Ottawa: Éditions de l'Université d'Ottawa, 1977.
- – *L'Ontario français historique*. Montreal: Éditions Études vivantes, Collection L'Ontario français, 1980.
- Chouinard, Marie-Andrée. "Enseignement de l'histoire – Ignorance collective." *Le Devoir*, 5 October 2011.
- Clark, Penney. "'A Nice Little Wife to Make Things Pleasant:' Portrayals of Women in Canadian History Textbooks Approved in British Columbia." *McGill Journal of Education* 40, no 2 (2005): 241–65.

Conrad, Margaret, et al. *Canadians and Their Pasts*. Toronto: University of Toronto Press, 2013.

Counsell, Christine, Katherine Burn, and Arthur Chapman, eds. *MasterClass in History Education: Transforming Teaching and Learning*. London: Bloomsbury, 2016.

Courtois, Charles-Philippe, ed. *La Conquête, Une anthologie, choix de textes et introduction par Charles-Philippe Courtois*. Montreal: Typo, 2009.

Cuban, Larry. "The Lure of Curricular Reform and Its Pitiful History." *Phi Delta Kappan* 75, no. 2 (1993): 182–5.

Dionne, René. "1910, Une première prise de parole collective en Ontario français." *Cahiers Charlevoix 1. Études franco-ontariennes*. Sudbury: Société Charlevoix et Éditions Prise de parole (1995): 15–124.

Donald, Dwayne. "Forts, Colonial Frontier Logics, and Aboriginal–Canadian Relations: Imagining Decolonizing Educational Philosophies in Canadian Contexts." In *Decolonizing Philosophies of Education*, edited by Ali Abdi, 91–111. Rotterdam: Sense, 2012.

Donovan, Suzanne, and John Bransford, eds. *How Students Learn: History in the Classroom*. Washington: National Academies Press, 2005.

Dorais, François-Olivier. "Gaétan Gervais: témoin et agent d'une mutation référentielle en Ontario français." *Mens, Revue d'histoire intellectuelle et culturelle* 13, no. 2 (2013): 59–99.

Dupuis, Serge. *400 ans de vie politique en Ontario français*. Une initiative du RÉFO dans le cadre du 400e anniversaire de la présence française, avec l'appui de Patrimoine canadien (2014). http://www.refo.ca/resources/DocumentTexte_400web.pdf

Duquette, Catherine. "Relating Historical Consciousness to Historical Thinking through Assessment." In *New Directions in Assessing Historical Thinking*, edited by K. Ercikan and P. Seixas, 51–63. New York: Routledge, 2015.

Epstein, Terrie, and Carla Peck, eds. *Teaching and Learning Difficult Histories in International Contexts: A Critical Sociocultural Approach*. New York: Routledge, 2018.

Ercikan, Kadriye, and Peter Seixas, eds. *New Directions in Assessing Historical Thinking*. New York: Routledge, 2015.

Éthier, Marc-André. "Contre la Coalition pour l'histoire." *Le Devoir*, 11 March 2013. http://www.ledevoir.com/societe/education/372961/contre-la-coalition-pour-l-histoire

– "Contre la pensée narrative téléologique." *Le Devoir*, 27 February 2014. https://www.ledevoir.com/opinion/idees/401205/lar

Farmer, Diane, Adrienne Chambon, and Normand Labrie. "Urbanité et immigration: étude de la dynamique communautaire franco-torontoise et des rapports d'inclusion et d'exclusion." *Francophonies d'Amérique* 16 (2003): 97–106.

Ferguson, Will. *Canadian History for Dummies*. Toronto: Wiley, 2005.
Ferry, Victor. "Le paradoxe de la preuve en histoire. Une approche rhétorique de l'écriture d'Arlette Farge." *Mots. Les langages du politique*, no. 95 (March 2011): 114–37.
Fischer, David Hackett. *Champlain's Dream: The European Founding of North America*. New York: Simon and Schuster, 2008.
Fournier, Patrick, and Mike Medeiros. "Unis par la langue?: Les opinions et les valeurs des Franco-Québécois et des Franco-Ontariens." *Revue d'études canadiennes* 48, no. 2 (2014): 198–223.
Francis, Daniel. *National Dreams: Myth, Memory, and Canadian History*. Vancouver: Arsenal Pulp Press, 1997.
Frenette, Yves. "Immigration et francophonie canadienne." In *Franco-Amérique, Vision et visages de la Franco-Amérique*, edited by Dean Louder and Éric Waddell, 345–56. Sillery: Septentrion, 2008.
Gadamer, Hans-Georg. *Le Problème de la conscience historique*. Paris: Éditions du Seuil, 1963.
Gaffield, Chad. "Towards the Coach in the History Classroom," *Canadian Issues / Thèmes canadiens* (October–November 2001): 12–14.
Gagnon, Alain-G., ed. *Le fédéralisme canadien contemporain. Fondements, traditions, institutions*. Montreal: Les Presses de l'Université de Montréal, 2006.
Genette, Gérard. *Narrative Discourse: An Essay in Method*. Ithaca: Cornell University Press, 1980.
Gérin-Lajoie, Diane. "La problématique identitaire et l'école de langue française en Ontario." *Francophonies d'Amérique*, no. 18 (2004): 171–9.
Gerwin, David. "What Lies beyond the Bubble? Trying Out One of the Stanford History Education Group's New History Assessments." *The Social Studies* 105 (2014): 266–73.
Gibson, Lindsay. *Constructing students' Historical Reference Frameworks in Canadian History Using Visual Source-Based Timelines*. Paper presented at the annual meeting of the American Education Research Conference, San Antonio, April 2017.
Gilbert, Anne. "La diversité de l'espace franco-ontarien: un défi au développement." In *La gouvernance linguistique: le Canada en perspective*, edited by Jean-Pierre Wallot, 57–75. Ottawa: Les Presses de l'Université d'Ottawa, coll. Amérique française, 2005.
– "La refondation de la communauté franco-ontarienne par l'école : constats et enjeux." In *La rénovation de l'héritage démocratique, Entre fondation et refondation*, edited by Anne Trépanier, 220–42. Ottawa: Les Presses de l'Université d'Ottawa, 2008.
Gilbert, Anne, and André Langlois, eds. *Territoires francophones. Études géographiques sur la vitalité des communautés francophones du Canada*. Sillery: Septentrion, 2010.

Gilbert, Anne, and Mariève Lefebvre. "Le sort de la culture dans la francophonie canadienne: le discours du milieu associatif en contexte." *Recherches sociographiques* 51, no. 3 (2010): 365–87.

Girard, Magali. *Résumé des résultats de sondages portant sur la perception des Québécois relativement aux accommodements raisonnables, à l'immigration, aux communautés culturelles et à l'identité canadienne-française*. Mémoire présenté à la Commission de consultation sur les pratiques d'accommodement reliées aux différences culturelles, March 2008.

Goulding, James. *Historical Thinking Online*. PhD diss., University of Sydney, Australia, 2018.

Granatstein, Jack. *Who Killed Canadian History?* Toronto: HarperCollins, 1998.

Gratton, Michel. *Gisèle Lalonde, Grande dame de l'Ontario français*. Ottawa: Centre franco-ontarien de ressources pédagogiques, 2003.

– *Montfort, la lutte d'un peuple, Ottawa*. Ottawa: Centre franco-ontarien de ressources pédagogiques, 2003.

Grisé, Yolande. "Ontarois: une prise de parole." *Revue du Nouvel-Ontario*, no. 4 (1982): 81–8.

Halbwachs, Maurice. *On Collective Memory*, translated by Lewis Coser. Chicago: University of Chicago Press, 1992.

Heller, Monica. *Crosswords: Language, Ethnicity, and Education in French Ontario*. Berlin: Mouton de Gruyter, 1994.

– "Quel(s) français et pour qui? Discours et pratiques identitaires en milieu scolaire franco-ontarien." In *L'enjeu de la langue en Ontario français*, edited by Normand Labrie and Gilles Forlot, 129–165. Sudbury: Éditions Prise de Parole, 1999.

Howson, Jonathan, and Denis Shemilt. "Frameworks of Knowledge: Dilemmas and Debates." In *Debates in History Teaching*, edited by Ian Davies, 73–83. Abingdon: Routledge, 2011.

Ignatieff, Michael. *Blood and Belonging: Journey into the New Nationalism*. New York: Farrar, Straus and Giroux, 1994.

– *Rights Revolution*. Toronto: Anansi Press, 2000.

Keating, Michael, and John McGarry. "Introduction." In *Minority Nationalism and the Changing International Order*, edited by M. Keating and J. McGarry, 1–18. New York: Oxford University Press, 2001.

Kölbl, Carlos, and Lisa Konrad. "Historical Consciousness in Germany: Concepts, Implementation, Assessment." In *New Directions in Assessing Historical Consciousness*, edited by Kadriye Ercikan and Peter Seixas, 17–28. New York: Routledge, 2015.

Körber, Andreas. *Historical Consciousness, Historical Competencies – and Beyond? Some Conceptual Development within German History Didactics*, 2015, 56 S. – URN: urn:nbn:de:0111-pedocs-108118. https://www.pedocs.de/volltexte/2015/10811/pdf/Koerber_2015_Development_German_History_Didactics.pdf

Körber, Andreas, and Johannes Meyer-Hamme. "Historical Thinking, Competencies, and Their Measurements: Challenges and Approaches." In *New Directions in Assessing Historical Thinking*, edited by K. Ercikan and P. Seixas, 89–101. New York: Routledge, 2015.

Kymlicka, Will. *Finding Our Way: Rethinking Ethnocultural Relations in Canada*. Toronto: Oxford University Press, 1998.

Lalonde, Gisèle. *Jusqu'au bout!* Ottawa: Le Nordir, 2003.

Lamarre, Jean. *Le devenir de la nation québécoise selon Maurice Séguin, Guy Frégault et Michel Brunet 1944–1969*. Québec: Les éditions du Septentrion, 1993.

Lantheaume, Françoise, and Jocelyn Létourneau, eds. *Le récit du commun: L'histoire nationale racontée par les élèves*. Lyon: Presses universitaires de Lyon, 2016.

Latané, Bibb. "The Psychology of Social Impact." *American Psychologist* 36, no. 4 (1981): 343–356.

Laville, Christian. "Un cours d'histoire pour notre époque." *Le Devoir*, 2 May 2006. http://www.ledevoir.com/non-classe/108098/un-cours-d-histoire-pour-notre-epoque

– "Quelques avenues nouvelles des guerres d'histoire scolaires dans le monde." *Canadian Diversity / Diversité canadienne* 7, no. 1 (2009): 18–24.

Lee, Peter. "'Walking Backwards into Tomorrow': Historical Consciousness and Understanding History." Paper presented at Annual Meeting of American Educational Research Association, New Orleans, 2002.

Lee, Peter, and Rosalyn Ashby. "Progression in Historical Understanding among Students Ages 7–14." In *Knowing, Teaching, and Learning History: National and International Perspectives*, edited by P. Stearns, P. Seixas, and S. Wineburg, 199–222. New York: NYU Press, 2000.

Lee, Peter, and Denis Shemilt. "A Scaffold, Not a Cage: Progression and Progression Models in History." *Teaching History* 113 (2013): 13–23.

Lefebvre, Marie. "Entre racines et mouvement. L'identité dans la francophonie canadienne." In *Territoires francophones. Études géographiques sur la vitalité des communautés francophones du Canada*, edited by A. Gilbert, 108–26. Sillery: Septentrion, 2010.

Léger, Jean-Marc, Jacques Nantel, and Pierre Duhamel. *Le Code Québec: les sept différences qui font de nous un peuple unique au monde*. Montreal: Éditions de l'Homme, 2016.

Létourneau, Jocelyn. *Je me souviens? Le passé du Québec dans la conscience de sa jeunesse*. Quebec: Fides, 2014.

– *Passer à l'avenir: histoire, mémoire, identité dans le Québec d'aujourd'hui*. Quebec: Boréal, 2000.

– "Remembering Our Past: An Examination of the Historical Memory of Young Québécois." In *To the Past: History Education, Public Memory and Citizenship Education*, edited by Ruth Sandwell, 70–87. Toronto: University of Toronto Press, 2006.

- *La renationalisation de l'histoire québécoise: Récit d'une OPH (Opération Publique d'Histoire) de son initiation à sa consécration*, Louvain-La-Neuve, Belgium, Érasme College, 2014. http://www.tonhistoireduquebec.ulaval.ca/wp-content/uploads/2015/01/La-renationalisation-de-l'histoire-québécoise.-Récit-d'une-OPH-Opération-publique-d'histoire-de-son-initiation-à-sa-consécration.pdf
- "Teaching National History to Young People Today." In *Palgrave Handbook of Research in Historical Culture and Education*, edited by Mario Carretero, Stefan Berger, and Maria Grever, 227–42. London: Palgrave Macmillan, 2017.

Létourneau, Jocelyn, and Christophe Caritey. "L'histoire du Québec racontée par les élèves de 4e et 5e secondaire: L'impact apparent du cours d'histoire nationale dans la structuration d'une mémoire historique collective chez les jeunes Québécois." *Revue d'histoire de l'Amérique française* 62, no. 1 (2008): 69–93.

Létourneau, Jocelyn, and Sabrina Moisan. "Mémoire et récit de l'aventure historique du Québec chez les jeunes Québécois d'héritage canadien-français: coup de sonde, amorce d'analyse des résultats, questionnements." *Canadian Historical Review* 84, no. 2 (2004): 325–56.

Lévesque, Stéphane. "Going beyond 'Narratives' vs 'Competencies': A Model for Understanding History Education." *Public History Weekly* 4 (2016). DOI: dx.doi.org/10.1515/phw-2016-5918

- "History and Social Studies in Québec: An Historical Perspective." In *Challenges and Prospects for Canadian Social Studies*, edited by Alan Sears and Ian Wright, 55–72. Vancouver: Pacific Educational Press, 2004.
- "On Historical Literacy: Learning to Think Like Historians." *Canadian Issues* (Summer 2011): 42–6.
- "Removing the 'Past': Debates over Official Sites of Memory," *Public History Weekly* 6 (2018). DOI: dx.doi.org/10.1515/phw-2018-12570
- "Why Tell Stories? On the Importance of Teaching Narrative Thinking." *Canadian Issues* (Fall 2014): 5–11.

Lévesque, Stéphane, and Penney Clark. "Historical Thinking: Definitions and Educational Applications." In *Wiley International Handbook of History Teaching and Learning*, edited by Scott Alan Metzger and Lauren McArthur Harris, 119–48. Hoboken: Wiley-Blackwell, 2018.

Lévesque, Stéphane, Jean-Philippe Croteau, and Raphaël Gani. "La conscience historique de jeunes franco-ontariens d'Ottawa : histoire et sentiment d'appartenance." *Historical Studies in Education / Revue d'histoire de l'éducation* 27, no. 2 (2015): 21–47.

Lévesque, Stéphane, Jocelyn Létourneau, and Raphaël Gani. "'A Giant with Clay Feet': Québec Students and their Historical Consciousness of the Nation." *International Journal of Historical Learning, Teaching, and Research* 11, no 2 (2013): 159–75.

Levstik, Linda. "Narrative as a Primary Act of Mind?" In *Researching History Education: Theory, Method, and Context*, edited by Linda Levstik and Keith Barton, 1–9. New York: Routledge, 2008.

Levstik, Linda, and Keith Barton. *Doing History: Investigating with Children in Elementary and Middle Schools*, 4th ed. New York: Routledge, 2011.

Lowen, James. *Lies My Teacher Told Me: Everything Your American History Textbook Got Wrong*. New York: Touchtone, 1995.

Maggioni, Liliana, Patricia Alexander, and Bruce VanSledright. "At a Crossroads? The Development of Epistemological Beliefs and Historical Thinking." *European Journal of School Psychology* 2, nos. 1–2 (2004): 169–97.

Marker, Michael. "Teaching History from an Indigenous Perspective." In *New Possibilities for the Past: Shaping History Education in Canada*, edited by Penney Clark, 98–112. Vancouver: UBC Press, 2011.

Marcus, Alan S., et al. *Teaching History with Film: Strategies for Secondary Social Studies*. New York: Routledge, 2010.

Martel, Marcel. *French Canada: An Account of Its Creation and Break-Up, 1850–1967*. Canadian Ethnic Group Series, no. 24 (1998).

Martin, Laurence, and Valérie Ouellet. "L'assimilation des francophones en Ontario n'est pas enseignée dans toutes les écoles." *Radio-Canada*, édition Ottawa-Gatineau, 4 May 2016.

Martineau, Robert. *Fondements et pratiques de l'enseignement de l'histoire à l'école: Traité de didactique*. Quebec: Presses de l'Université du Québec, 2010.

McAndrew, Marie, and Micheline Milot, eds. *L'École et la diversité: perspectives comparés*. Quebec: Presses de l'Université Laval, 2010.

McRoberts, Kenneth. *Misconceiving Canada: The Struggle for National Unity*. Toronto: Oxford University Press, 1997.

Meisel, John, Guy Rocher, and Arthur Silver, *Si je me souviens / As I Recall*. Montreal: IRPP, 1999.

Ministère de l'éducation et de l'enseignement supérieur. "Progression des apprentissages au secondaire: histoire et éducation à la citoyenneté 3e secondaire." Quebec: Government of Quebec, 2011. http://www1.education.gouv.qc.ca/progressionSecondaire/domaine_univers_social/histoire2/index.asp?page=cultureHistoire

Ministère de l'Éducation de l'Ontario. *Le curriculum de l'Ontario, 9e et 10e année: études canadiennes et mondiales*. Toronto: Queen's Printer, 2013.

Moisan, Sabrina. "Exploration d'une approche critique de la mémoire collective pour une formation historique renouvelée en classe d'histoire nationale au Québec." *Enjeux de l'univers social* 12, no. 3 (2016): 4–9.

Monière, Denis. *Pour comprendre le nationalisme au Québec et ailleurs*. Montreal: Presses de l'Université de Montréal, 2001.

Munslow, Alun. *Narrative and History*. London: Palgrave Macmillan, 2007.

Nokes, Jeffery, and Susan De La Paz, "Writing and Argumentation in History Education." In *Wiley International Handbook of History Teaching and Learning*, edited by Scott Alan Metzger and Lauren McArthur Harris, 551–78. Hoboken: Wiley-Blackwell, 2018.

Nora, Pierre. "Between Memory and History: Les Lieux de Mémoire." *Représentations* 26 (1989): 7–24.

Nora, Pierre, ed. *Realms of Memory: The Construction of the French Past*, translated by Arthur Goldhammer. New York: Columbia University Press, 1996.

Office des Affaires francophones. *Les francophones de l'Ontario. Données du recensement de 2011 selon la Définition inclusive de francophone*. (DIF). Toronto: Government of Ontario, 2011. https://www.ontario.ca/fr/page/profil-de-la-population-francophone-de-lontario-2016.

Osborne, Ken. "'Our History Syllabus Has Us Gasping': History in Canadian Schools: Past, Present, and Future." *Canadian Historical Review* 81, no. 3 (2000): 108–37.

– "Teaching History in Schools: A Canadian Debate." *Journal of Curriculum Studies* 35 (2003): 585–626.

Parkes, Robert. "The Practical Legacy of Hayden White." *Public History Weekly* 6 (2018): 17. DOI: dx.doi.org/10.1515/phw-2018-11994

Peck, Carla. "'It's not like [I'm] Chinese and Canadian. I am in between': Ethnicity and Students' Conceptions of Historical Significance." *Theory and Research in Social Education* 38, no. 4 (2010): 574–617.

Pelletier, Réjean. "Institutional Arrangements of a New Canadian Partnership." In *Beyond the Impasse: Toward Reconciliation*, edited by Roger Gibbins and Guy Laforest, 301–32. Montreal: IRPP, 1998.

Perrenoud, Philippe. "Curriculum: le formel, le réel, le caché." In *La pédagogie: une encyclopédie pour aujourd'hui*, edited by Jean Houssaye, 61–76. Paris: ESF, 1993.

Prince, Gerald. *A Dictionary of Narratology*. Lincoln: University of Nebraska Press, 2003.

– "Introduction to the Study of the Narratee." In *The Narrative Reader*, edited by Martin McQuillan, 99–103. New York: Routledge, 2000.Propp, Vladimir. *Morphology of the Folktale*, 2nd ed., translated by Louis Wagner. Austin: University of Texas Press, 1968.

Resnick, Philip. *The European Roots of Canadian Identity*. Peterborough: Broadview Press, 2005.

Ricoeur, Paul. *Temps et récit*, vol. 1. Paris: Éditions du Seuil, 1983.

Rioux, Christian. "La fin de l'histoire." *Le Devoir*, 30 June 2006.

– "Une génération d'amnésiques." *Le Devoir*, 25 May 2006.

– "Suicide assisté." *Le Devoir*, 5 May 2006.

Robichaud, Marc. "L'histoire de l'Acadie telle que racontée par les jeunes francophones du Nouveau-Brunswick: construction et de construction d'un récit historique." *Acadiensis* 40, no. 2 (Summer–Fall 2011): 33–69.

Rogers, Rick. "Frameworks for Big History: Teaching History at Its Lower Resolutions." In *Master Class in History Education: Transforming Teaching and Learning*, edited by Christine Counsell, Katharine Burn, and Arthur Chapman, 59–76. London: Bloomsbury Academic, 2016.

Roy, Fernande. *Histoire des idéologies au Québec au XIXe et au XXe siècles*. Montreal: Boréal, 1993.

Rüsen, Jörn. *History: Narration, Interpretation, Orientation*. New York: Berghahn Books, 2005.

Russell, Peter. *Canada's Odyssey: A Country Based on Incomplete Conquests*. Toronto: University of Toronto Press, 2017.

Saint-Hilaire, Mélanie, and Nicole Beaulieu. "Trou de mémoire: l'histoire des Québécoises d'hier à aujourd'hui." *Gazette des femmes*, 1 January 2000.

Saint-Pierre, Stéphanie. "Étienne Brûlé, premier franco-ontarien." *Encyclopédie du patrimoine culturel de l'Amérique française* (2007). http://www.ameriquefrancaise.org/fr/article-179/Étienne_Brûlé_premier_Franco-Ontarien.html#.WOW3hhjpPnU

Sandwell, Ruth. "On Historians and Their Audiences: An Argument for Teaching (and Not Just Writing) History." In *Becoming a History Teacher: Sustaining Practices in Historical Thinking and Knowing*, edited by R. Sandwell and A. Von Heyking, 77–90. Toronto: University of Toronto Press, 2014.

– "We Were Allowed to Disagree, Because We Couldn't Agree on Anything: Seventeen Voices in Canadian Debates over History Education." In *History Wars and the Classroom: Global Perspectives*, edited Tony Taylor and Robert Guyver, 51–76. Charlotte: Information Age, 2012.

Sarra-Bournet, Michel, ed. *Les nationalismes au Québec, du XIXe siècle au XXIe siècle*. Quebec: Presses de l'Université Laval, 2001.

Sears, Alan. "Possibilities and Problems: Citizenship Education in a Multinational State: The Case of Canada," In *Globalization, the Nation-State, and the Citizen: Dilemmas and Directions for Civics and Citizenship Education*, edited by A. Reid, J. Gill, and A. Sears, 191–205. New York: Routledge, 2010.

Seixas, Peter. "A History/Memory Matrix for History Education." *Public History Weekly* 4 (2015). DOI: dx.doi.org/10.1515/phw-2016-5370

– "Indigenous Historical Consciousness: An Oxymoron or a Dialogue?" In *History Education and the Construction of National Identities*, edited by M. Carretero, M. Ascensio, and M. Rodríguez-Moneo, 125–38. Charlotte: Information Age, 2012.

– "A Model of Historical Thinking." *Educational Philosophy and Theory* (2015). DOI: 10.1080/00131857.2015.1101363

- "Preface." In Stéphane Lévesque, *Thinking Historically: Educating Students for the 21st Century*, vii–x. Toronto: University of Toronto Press, 2008.
- "Teaching Rival Histories: In Search of Narrative Plausibility." In *International Perspectives on Teaching Rival Histories*, edited by Henrik Åström Elmersjö, Anna Clark, and Monika Vinterek, 253–68. London: Palgrave Macmillan, 2017.

Seixas, Peter, ed. *Theorizing Historical Consciousness*. Toronto: University of Toronto Press, 2004.

Sharma, Ruchir. "Globalisation as we know it is over – and Brexit is the biggest sign yet." *The Guardian*, 28 July 2016. https://www.theguardian.com/commentisfree/2016/jul/28/era-globalisation-brexit-eu-britain-economic-frustration

Shemilt, Denis. "The Caliph's Coin: The Currency of Narrative Frameworks in History Teaching." In *Knowing, Teaching, and Learning History: National and International Perspectives*, edited by P. Stearns, P. Seixas, and S. Wineburg, 83–101. New York: NYU Press, 2000.

Stanley, Tim. "John A. Macdonald and the Invention of White Supremacy in Canada." *Canadian Issues* (Fall 2014): 29–32.
- "Whose Public? Whose Memory? Racisms, Grand Narratives, and Canadian History." In *To the Past: History Education, Public Memory, and Citizenship in Canada*, edited by Ruth Sandwell (Toronto: University of Toronto Press, 2006).
- "Why I Killed Canadian History: Towards an Anti-Racist History in Canada." *Social History / Histoire sociale* 33, no. 65 (2000): 79–103.

Straub, Jürgen. *Narration, Identity, and Historical Consciousness*. New York: Berghahn Books, 2005.

Sylvestre, Paul-François. "Franco-Ontarians." *The Canadian Encyclopedia*, 2016. http://thecanadianencyclopedia.ca/en/article/franco-ontarians

Taylor, Charles. *Reconciling the Solitudes: Essays on Canadian Federalism and Nationalism*. Montreal and Kingston: McGill–Queen's University Press, 1993.
- *Sources of the Self: The Making of Modern Identity*. New York: Cambridge University Press, 1989.

Thériault, Joseph-Yvon. *Critique de l'américanité. Mémoire et démocratie au Québec*. Montreal: Québec-Amérique, 2002.
- "De l'école de la nation aux écoles communautaires ou de l'école d'en haut à l'école d'en bas." In *Faire société: société civile et espaces francophones*, 192–209. Sudbury: Prise de parole, 2007.
- "Playing with Words, Playing with Identities." In *Playing with Politics: The Handing Down of Culture, Smaller Societies, and Globalization*, edited by J.P. Baillargeon, 184–91. Toronto: Grubstreet Books, 2002.

Thomson, David. *Aims of History*. London: Thames and Hudson, 1969.

Topolski, Jerzy. "Historical Narrative: Towards a Coherent Structure." *History and Theory* 26 (1987): 75–86.
Tosh, John. *The Pursuit of History*, 4th ed. New York: Pearson Education, 2006.
Truth and Reconciliation Commission of Canada. *Honouring the Truth, Reconciling for the Future: Summary of the Final Report of the Truth and Reconciliation Commission of Canada*. Ottawa: Library and Archives Canada, 2015.
Turner, John, and Henri Tajfel. "The Social Identity Theory of Intergroup Behaviour." In *Key Readings in Social Psychology*, edited by J.T. Jost and J. Sidanius, 276–93. New York: Psychology Press, 2004.
Tutiaux-Guillon, Nicole, and Didier Nourrisson, eds. *Identités, mémoires, conscience historique*. Saint-Étienne: Presses de l'Université de Saint-Étienne, 2003.
Vallières, Gaétan, Jacques Grimard, and Équipe DOPELFO, eds. *L'Ontario français par les documents*. Saint-Laurent: Éditions Études Vivantes, 1980.
VanSledright, Bruce. *The Challenge of Rethinking History Education: On Practices, Theories, and Policy*. New York: Routledge, 2011.
– "Narratives of Nation-State, Historical Knowledge, and School History Education." *Review of Research in Education* 32 (2008): 109–46.
VanSledright, Bruce, and Jerry Brophy, "Storytelling, Imagination, and Fanciful Elaboration in Children's Historical Reconstructions." *American Educational Research Journal* 29 (1992): 837–59.
VanSledright, Bruce, and Kimberly Reddy. "Changing Epistemic Beliefs? An Exploratory Study of Cognition among Prospective History Teachers." *Tempo e Argumento* 6 (2014): 28–68.
Voss, James, and Jennifer Wiley. "A Case Study of Developing Historical Understanding via Instruction: The Importance of Integrating Text Components and Constructing Arguments." In *Knowing, Teaching, and Learning History: National and International Perspectives*, edited by P. Stearns, P. Seixas, and S. Wineburg, 375–89. New York: NYU Press, 2000.
Waldis, Monika et al. "Material-Based and Open-Ended Writing Tasks for Assessing Narrative Competence among Students." In *New Directions in Assessing Historical Thinking*, edited by K. Ercikan and P. Seixas, 117–31. New York: Routledge, 2015.
Wertsch, James. "Collective Memory and Narrative Templates." *Social Research: An International Quarterly* 75, no. 1 (Spring 2008): 133–56.
– "Texts of Memory and Texts of History." *L2 Journal* 4, no. 1 (2012): 9–20.
Wertsch, James, and Kevin O'Connor. "Multivoicedness in Historical Representations: American College Students' Accounts of the Origins of the United States." *Journal of Narrative and Life History* 4, no. 4 (1994): 295–309.

Wineburg, Sam. "Making Historical Sense." In *Knowing, Teaching, and Learning History: National and International Perspectives*, edited by Peter Stearns, Peter Seixas, and Sam Wineburg, 306–25. New York: NYU Press, 2000.
– *Historical Thinking and Other Unnatural Acts: Charting the Future of Teaching the Past*. Philadelphia: Temple University Press, 2001.
Wineburg, Sam, Susan Mosborg, Dan Porat, and Ariel Duncan. "Forrest Gump and the Future of Teaching the Past." *Phi Delta Kappan* 89, no. 3 (2007): 168–77.
Zanazanian, Paul. "Historical Consciousness and Being Québécois: Exploring Young English-Speaking Students' Interactions with Quebec's Master Historical Narrative." *Canadian Ethnic Studies* 47, no. 2 (2015):113–35.
– "History Teaching and Narrative Tools: Towards Integrating English-Speaking Youth into Quebec's Social Fabric." *Minorités linguistiques et Société* 7 (2016): 78–9.

Index

Aboriginal peoples, 45, 70–2, 80–1, 110, 115, 168n37, 172n5; and fur trade, 51–9, 90, 98, 121; and ways of knowing, 90–4. *See also* First Nations; Indigenous peoples
Ahonen, Sirkka, 16
allophone, 99, 101–2, 104–11
America, 23, 34–5, 42–6, 57–8, 62–80, 97–8, 105, 114–19, 121, 128–32, 145; discovery of, 45–6, 71–2, 86, 155–7; North America, 27–9, 31, 35, 38, 62–75, 97, 121, 129, 146, 157–63, 165
Anderson, Benedict, 5
anti-racism, 11
appropriation, x, 13, 36, 163
assessment, 4, 28, 53, 100–1, 172n23
assimilation, 9–11, 68, 75; French, 11, 27, 37–9, 42–9, 84–90, 106–9, 125–9

Barthes, Roland, 144, 146
Barton, Keith, 5, 137, 160–4, 169n68, 174n7
Beauchemin, Jacques, 7
Bédard, Éric, 7, 159
belonging, 10–17, 24, 33, 75, 101–8, 167n12; national, 66, 81, 93–6, 108, 112–16, 119–23, 127, 131–3, 158, 164–5

Bill 101, 41, 47, 57, 78
Bock, Michel, 38, 172n20, 173n8
Bouchard, Gérard, 21, 34
Bourassa, Henri, 32, 76
Bremond, Claude, 144
Brûlé, Étienne, 38, 65, 73, 157, 173n6

Carr, David, 18, 175n19
Carr, E.H., 146
Cartier, Jacques, 32, 45–7, 65, 72–5, 80, 86, 92, 114–16, 157; discovery of Canada, 12–13, 58, 102–5
Catholicism, 9, 32–3, 38, 44, 76, 97, 128, 173n12
causation, 142–3, 145, 152; causative plausibility, 142
Champlain, Samuel de, 57, 65–7, 102, 114–15, 157; and Quebec, 43–6, 67, 73, 88, 128; and Upper Canada, 38, 72–4, 80
Chapman, Arthur, xiii, 138, 147, 169n68
Charland, Jean-Pierre, 170n75, 170n77
Clark, Penney, 94
classroom, 20, 24, 37, 137, 157, 163
colonialism, 70, 82, 105, 167–8n14, 171n2; colonial history, 12, 32, 46, 64, 56, 75, 90–1, 114, 121, 125, 128,

155, 162; colonial narratives, 5, 10–11, 31, 35, 58, 65, 74, 98, 110, 146
Columbus, Christopher, 46, 51, 57–8, 63, 70, 72, 86, 105, 114–15, 151
community, x, 5–9, 14–15, 21, 31, 45, 53, 76–8, 93, 102, 127, 132–3, 135, 155–9, 167n7; building of, 5, 10, 17, 38–9, 59, 170n70; francophone, 10, 33, 39, 47–8, 84–5, 87, 96–7, 99, 106, 123, 125; historical, 27, 46, 55, 100–1; imagined, 5, 32, 65, 110; of memory, 19, 108; national, 7, 27, 29, 49, 135
competence/competencies, 8, 18, 20–1, 30, 136, 167n7, 170n70; narrative, 14, 16, 30, 135–54, 159–65, 177n19
complexity, xi, 20, 143–4, 158–9
conquest, 36, 43, 46–8, 63, 71, 75–6, 89, 94, 109, 128, 155–7; of New France, 32, 59, 74, 110, 121
country/countries: Canada, 10, 27–8, 53, 61–2, 63–6, 81–2, 92–3, 99, 101–2, 113–16, 119–22, 165, 167–8n14; as concept, 24, 29, 31–2, 41, 50–1, 54, 59–60, 62, 72, 97–8, 118, 120–1, 122, 123, 126, 128–32; foreign, 12, 68; and Quebec, 44, 47, 49, 61–2, 64–6, 82, 94, 107–8, 110, 119, 129–32, 145; multi-national, 26, 30, 62, 112, 122, 135, 164, 165–6, 177n30
Croteau, Jean-Philippe, x, xi, 21
Cuban, Larry, 11
curriculum, 3–4, 7–8, 11, 20, 24, 70, 83, 90, 113, 136, 147, 159; learned, 11; "real-life," 3, 4, 16, 20

De La Paz, Susan, 161
Desloges sisters (Béatrice and Diane), 77, 79, 94–5, 173n12
dialogue, 36, 147, 159; national, 38
Duquette, Catherine, xiii, 136

empathy, 91; empathetic plausibility, 142–3
England, 6, 51, 73–6, 97–9, 128
Ercikan, Kadriye, 163
Éthier, Marc-André, 8, 137, 170n77
evaluation, 11, 154, 160
evidence, ix, xiii, 11, 26, 34, 100, 117, 131, 146, 158, 162–92, 164; evidentiary plausibility, 141–2, 146; and narrative, 8, 14–15, 136–7, 140–3, 151, 153, 160–2, 175n26

Fahmy-Eid, Nadia, 7
Farge, Arlette, 149–51
Ferry, Victor, 146
Filles du Roi, 26, 51–2, 57, 71–3, 80–1, 94–6, 105, 120–2, 128
First Nations, 71, 90–1, 128, 167–8n14, 172–3n5. *See also* Aboriginal peoples; Indigenous peoples
focalization, 138, 146–8, 151, 153
France, 32, 49, 51, 65, 71–5, 78, 90, 94, 97–8, 101–2, 110, 115, 118, 121–2, 125–8, 132, 171n2; and empire, 46, 66–7; and king, 57, 121, 128
Francophonie, 6, 39, 48, 51, 65, 86, 96, 113, 125, 133

gender, 4, 29, 52, 83–111, 120, 155, 161
Genette, Gérard, 139, 144, 148
Gervais, Gaétan, 38–9, 172n20
Gilbert, Anne, xiii, 9–10, 21, 53, 78, 171n1
globalization, 5–6, 9–10, 108, 129, 157
Granatstein, Jack, 10
Great Britain, 51, 54–5, 73–5, 90, 108, 114, 125–9, 171n2

Halbwachs, Maurice, 12
heritage, 7, 65, 81, 97, 100
historical consciousness, x, 3, 13–15, 18–22, 26, 29–31, 45, 59, 78, 82–3,

100, 111–14, 116, 130, 135–9, 144, 151–4, 157
historical knowing. *See under* knowledge/knowing
historical research, xiii, 11–12, 21, 24, 113, 135, 155, 159–66
historical thinking, ix–xi, 8, 13, 16, 18, 20–1, 30, 60, 135–7, 140–4, 152–3
historical understanding, xiii, 4–5, 18, 20–1
history wars, 6–7, 10

identification, 4, 7, 11, 21, 24, 28–9, 51, 110, 112–34, 153, 155–6, 158, 164
identity, x–xi, 3–5, 9, 10, 14–15, 21, 24, 27–31, 34, 38–9, 47–8, 52, 57, 61, 78, 89, 95, 99, 102–3, 105, 108, 112–34, 135, 144, 155, 157, 161, 164–5; Canadian, 9, 114, 116, 118, 122–3, 133; ethnocultural, 22–3; Franco-Ontarian, 64–5, 105, 122–5, 173n12; French Canadian, 9, 116, 123, 160; narrative, 93, 111, 149, 153; national, 8, 52, 119, 133–4; Quebec, 50, 96, 131; regional, 81
Ignatieff, Michael, 6, 167n12
ignorance, ix, 11, 45, 52, 155, 165
imagination, 5, 167n7
Indigenous peoples, 5–6, 38, 60–2, 68, 70, 72, 74–5, 80–2, 98–100, 109, 158, 164, 167–8n14, 172–3n5; perspective, 28, 41–2, 52, 54, 56, 58, 85–90, 100, 104–6, 115, 120–2, 124, 127–8, 161; ways of knowing, 11, 91, 165. *See also* Aboriginal peoples; First Nations
intelligibility, 8, 13, 158, 160
interpretation, xi, 13–16, 19, 40, 43, 103, 110, 131, 144, 153, 161; narrative, 11, 135–6, 140–1, 163

Jenkins, Keith, 137

knowledge/knowing, ix, 7–8, 11, 15–20, 61, 87, 135–9, 151–2, 158–63; historical knowing, ix–xi, 3–5, 13, 18, 20, 24–5, 89, 91, 138, 143, 144–5, 147, 148, 155, 160–3, 165

Latané, Bibb, 92–3
Laville, Christian, 8
Lee, Peter, 14, 136, 145, 162
Létourneau, Jocelyn, ix–xii, xiv, 3, 12, 21, 35–6, 61, 88, 159, 170n77, 174n7
Lévesque, Stéphane, x–xi, 8, 21, 49, 170n70, 174n7, 177n19
Levstik, Linda, 5, 137, 169n68
life story, 28, 41–2, 54, 56, 85–9, 100, 104, 115, 120, 124, 127

Martel, Marcel, 31, 34–5, 81, 97
Martineau, Robert, 153
McCully, Alan, 164, 174n7
memory, xi, 3–4, 11–20, 31, 35–6, 48, 65–6, 80–2, 90, 103, 108, 117, 133, 144, 151, 152–3, 173n12; collective, 7, 12, 13, 18, 31, 36, 38, 59, 61, 71, 73, 77, 81–2, 128, 135, 138, 152, 157–61, 164–5; and community, 4, 25, 123; personal, 12–13; public, 15–17, 20; and sites, 11, 29, 62
mentalités, 143
mimesis, 138
modernization, 28, 41–2, 51, 54, 56–8, 85–90, 100, 103–5, 115, 120, 124, 127; of the state, 33, 52
Munslow, Alun, 137, 140–1, 143, 147–8, 153, 176n46
mythistories, x–xii, 12–14, 20, 60, 100, 147, 156–8, 164

narration, 3–4, 7, 12–13, 18, 21, 31, 87, 112, 136–54, 160, 162–3,

165; narratee, 147, 150, 176n46; narrator, 14, 18, 24, 25–6, 28–9, 91, 93, 103, 110–11, 137, 140–54, 158
narrative: historical, 4–5, 18, 21, 23, 30, 52, 81, 83, 97, 113, 127, 135, 138–54, 155, 158, 160–5; framework, 29–30, 40, 50–1, 59, 111, 152, 155, 158, 163; orientation, 25, 27, 29, 31–60, 66, 83–91, 95, 99–100, 102, 104–5, 111, 113, 114–15, 119–20, 123–7, 130, 133, 158; vision, 4, 8, 21, 25, 27–8, 51, 84, 87, 100, 120, 133, 156, 170n75; voice, 92, 111, 146–8, 153
nation, x–xi, 3–12, 31–6, 44, 49–52, 60, 61–4, 81–2, 93–5, 102–5, 108, 135, 158–9; nation-building, 27, 50–1, 95, 104–5, 158; nationalist, x, 5–8, 10, 12–13, 33–7, 43, 58, 68–70, 87, 116, 120, 122; and state, 6, 26–30, 33–6, 59, 62, 66, 112, 122–3, 128, 164–6
New France, 19, 43, 46, 51–2, 55, 57–9, 65, 71–5, 78, 81, 90, 92, 94, 97–8, 102, 105, 126–8, 131–2, 145, 156, 171n2; colony of, 32, 47, 58, 75; conquest of, 31–2, 59, 74–5, 110, 120–2
Nokes, Jeffery, 161
Nora, Pierre, 12
normative plausibility, 142–4

Others, 5, 60, 68, 165

Parkes, Robert, 18
Perrenoud, Philippe, 20, 170n72
plausibility, 138, 141–54
polythetic, 19, 25, 40, 158, 162
positionality, 18, 59, 146
postcolonialism, 28, 161
postmodern, 137
practical life, 20, 112, 159

presentism, 144; presentist perspective, 28, 41, 52, 54, 56, 86, 88–9, 100, 104, 115, 120, 124, 127
Prince, Gerald, 147, 171n2
Propp, Vladimir, 25, 71, 139, 144

racism, 10, 28, 91
rebellion, 27, 33, 35, 41, 43–4, 50, 63, 97, 129, 156, 172n27
recurrent constants, 25, 71
regulation 17, 37, 43, 55, 81, 94–5, 99–101, 116–18, 125–6, 173n8, 173n12; and crisis, 48, 59, 65, 76–9; and Montfort, 48, 53, 59, 77–9, 106–7, 156–7
resistance, 35, 41, 48, 76, 79, 84, 94
revolution, 25, 33–5, 44, 49, 73–4, 77, 97–8, 136, 165; Industrial Revolution, 121; Quiet Revolution, 41, 81, 96, 128–30
Ricoeur, Paul, 13, 137–8, 144
Royal Commission on Bilingualism and Biculturalism, 33–4, 167–8n14
Rüsen, Jörn, 3, 5, 13–14, 16, 18–19, 112, 138, 140, 142, 144, 160, 170n70

Sandwell, Ruth, 10
schema, 25, 40, 60, 144, 152, 156–8
Seixas, Peter, xiii, 13–16, 136, 138, 141–3, 154, 160, 163, 175n23
Shemilt, Denis, 158, 163
social identity theory (SIT), 118, 177n26
sources, xi, 16, 141–3, 147, 150–1, 153, 162
sovereignty, 19, 27, 32, 34, 36, 44, 49, 63, 70, 93, 110, 112
Stanley, Timothy, 10, 13
story, 8, 10, 26–8, 40–2, 46–7, 49, 53–64, 56, 59, 64–5, 71, 83, 85–6, 87–90, 99, 100, 104, 115, 117, 120, 124–5, 127–8, 148–50, 175n19,

175n23; and coherence, 4, 20, 24, 138, 140, 142, 144–6, 151, 153, 162–4; and narrator, 14, 25–6, 28, 93, 103, 137–40, 145–51, 158; story-form, 4–5, 140–5, 153, 157–8; telling, 5, 18, 21, 28, 52, 69–70, 88, 100, 107–8, 111, 123–4, 145, 149
survey, 4, 36, 114, 144
survivance, 36, 74, 129

Tajfel, Henri, 118
temporal plausibility, 142–3
temporality, 19, 139, 152
textbook, 7, 24, 94, 148, 157, 159, 162, 164
Thériault, Joseph-Yvon, 9, 25
tradition, 4–6, 33, 35, 38–9, 61, 85, 94, 102, 112, 132, 137, 150, 155; and narrative, 19–20, 134, 164–5, 170n70; and nation, 5, 6, 12, 56–8, 68, 70, 119
Truth and Reconciliation Commission (TRC), 91, 172–3n5
typology, 19, 170n70

United Kingdom, 12, 26
United States, 4, 12, 26, 32, 61, 68, 73–4, 121, 157

VanSledright, Bruce, 157, 161, 169n68

Wertsch, James, 25, 144, 156
White, Hayden, 18, 137, 144
Wineburg, Sam, 4, 16, 141, 159, 175n26

Zanazanian, Paul, xiii, 13, 105

www.ingramcontent.com/pod-product-compliance
Lightning Source LLC
Chambersburg PA
CBHW030319080526
44584CB00012B/630